D0930100

PSYCHOLOGY PRACTITIONER GUIDEBOOKS

EDITORS

Arnold P. Goldstein, Syracuse University
Leonard Krasner, Stanford University & SUNY at Stony Brook
Sol L. Garfield, Washington University in St. Louis

BEHAVIORAL MEDICINE

Pergamon Titles of Related Interest

Related Journals
(Free sample copies available upon request)

BEHAVIORAL MEDICINE

Concepts and Procedures

ELDON TUNKS
ANTHONY BELLISSIMO
McMaster University

PERGAMON PRESS
Member of Maxwell Macmillan Pergamon Publishing Corporation
New York • Oxford • Beijing • Frankfurt
São Paulo • Sydney • Tokyo • Toronto

Pergamon Press Offices:

U.S.A.	Pergamon Press, Inc., Maxwell House, Fairview Park, Elmsford, New York 10523, U.S.A.
U.K.	Pergamon Press plc, Headington Hill Hall, Oxford OX3 0BW, England
PEOPLE'S REPUBLIC OF CHINA	Pergamon Press, 0909 China World Tower, No. 1 Jian Guo Men Wai Avenue, Beijing 100004, People's Republic of China
FEDERAL REPUBLIC OF GERMANY	Pergamon Press GmbH, Hammerweg 6, D-6242 Kronberg, Federal Republic of Germany
BRAZIL	Pergamon Editora Ltda, Rua Eça de Queiros, 346, CEP 04011, Paraiso, São Paulo, Brazil
AUSTRALIA	Pergamon Press Australia Pty Ltd., P.O. Box 544, Potts Point, NSW 2011, Australia
JAPAN	Pergamon Press, 8th Floor, Matsuoka Central Building, 1-7-1 Nishishinjuku, Shinjuku-ku, Tokyo 160, Japan
CANADA	Pergamon Press Canada Ltd., Suite 271, 253 College Street, Toronto, Ontario M5T 1R5, Canada

Library of Congress Cataloging in Publication Data

Tunks, Eldon.
    Behavioral medicine : concepts and procedures / by Eldon Tunks & Anthony Bellissimo.
       p. cm. -- (Psychology practitioner guidebooks)
    Includes bibliographical references.
    Includes index.
    ISBN 0-08-036832-8 : — ISBN 0-08-036831-X (pbk.) :
    1. Medicine and psychology.   2. Health behavior.   3. Clinical health psychology   I. Bellissimo, Anthony.   II. Title.
III. Series.
    [DNLM: 1. Behavioral Medicine. 2. Primary Health Care. WB 100 T926b]
    R726.5T86   1990
    616'.0019–dc20
    DNLM/DLC
    for Library of Congress   90-7292
                                                     CIP

Printing: 1 2 3 4 5 6 7 8 9   Year: 1 2 3 4 5 6 7 8 9

Printed in the United States of America

 The paper used in this publication meets the minimum requirements of American National Standard for Information Sciences—Permanence of Paper for Printed Library Materials, ANSI Z39.48-1984

Dedication

To Odette, Daphne, Marcel, and Liliana, through whose giving I am able to give.

E.T.

To Vittoria, Alexandra, Julia, and Barbara, who in their own way helped me meet the challenge of working on this book.

A.B.

Contents

Contents

Preface

This book focuses on problems encountered frequently in primary care and addresses the issue of how to improve that care. The conceptual framework of the book is to explain "what" clinicians *do* to address these problems, and "how" they can effectively deal with them. The impetus for writing the book came from our daily clinical work within the interdisciplinary field of behavioral medicine. We recognize that behavioral medicine and the associated cognitive-behavioral therapies do not constitute a simple therapeutic method, but rather amount to a collection of methods that stress the patient's active role in self-awareness, changing beliefs, and the carrying out of prescribed activities as a vehicle to new learning. The content of this book reflects our commitment to the identification of some common principles that can be applied to the treatment of most patients using behavioral medicine approaches.

We would like to highlight two themes. The first is the belief that good patient care is a shared responsibility between the patient and the clinician. The second is that effective treatment must focus on specific actions directed at specific problems and that the whole process must be guided by specific objectives or goals.

We believe that the clinician will benefit from an economical approach that directs the focus toward information needed for intervention. This streamlined approach to patient care should not lead to a lack of awareness of the complexity of human problems. The treatment guidelines are only meaningful if there is a realization that illness is a blow to body integrity as well as to overall well-being. Illness creates alterations in the patient's sense of self, disturbs emotional and cognitive balance, creates distortions in the social systems, and sets up a variety of illness-related roles and functions involving the patient, the family, and the health-care institutions.

We recognize the reality of the typical clinical situation, in which the individual patient usually seeks help and is prepared to receive help at that level. It is typically in the office that the clinician and the patient work toward defining the actual contract for assessment and intervention. With the help of the patient, the clinician derives information about the individual's life experiences and uses this in assessment and treatment. This book provides the clinician with guidelines for using such information most effectively.

In summary, this book is written for the mature clinician, the new clinician, and the student. For the health professional who, because of the demands of clinical practice, needs a clinical manual that addresses the major problems seen in practice, the book provides reliable information about the etiology of common disorders and their treatment. It offers practical knowledge, with adequate discussion of the biological, psychological, and social factors involved in these problems. For the student or the teacher, who must acquire additional detailed information, annotated references for further reading are given in the Selected Reading section. Thus, the book will be an invaluable study manual.

We believe that because of its particular organization, the book addresses clinical problems in a unique way by helping the clinician to quickly locate practical guidelines for treatment. It will help the reader to develop the flexible application of skills and understanding needed to become an experienced clinician. The first two chapters discuss some of the fundamentals of clinical practice. Clinicians who have a grasp of this basic knowledge may choose to go directly to chapters dealing with the treatment of a specific problem.

The production of this book has emerged over a number of years of clinical work. We would like to acknowledge the help of both our patients and our colleagues. We thank Debbie Kuzmenko, who helped put part of the book on the word processor through several revisions, and Jerry Frank, Alicia Jones, and their staff for the continuing support and editorial assistance.

Part I
Fundamentals of Clinical Practice

Authors' Comments on the Theoretical Framework

Both research and clinical practice indicate that a large percentage of the general adult population experiences distressing psychological symptoms. A minority suffers overt psychiatric disorders whereas a larger number experiences significant symptoms such as insomnia, pain, tension, irritability, or fatigue. The latter, rather than the former, presents the more difficult clinical problems because they seem to "fall between two stools." Send them to an internist and they get the verdict that their condition is psychosomatic. Send them to a mental health clinic and they are told that treatment of their medical disorders should precede treatment of their psychological problems, and therefore they should see an internist.

As a partial measure, physicians often resort to prescribing tranquilizers or antidepressants, or they try to deal primarily in terms of the physical symptoms. The extensive development of medical and psychological knowledge over the past few decades has brought new opportunities for the clinician to address the issues of physical and psychological distress.

In the 1970s there was increasing dissatisfaction with the older and unwieldly concepts of "psychosomatic disorder" that had grown largely out of psychodynamic theory and practice. The psychodynamic-based psychosomatic models were esoteric and did not translate well into short-term clinical solutions. Treatment based on such models was practicable only by a few therapists with a minority of patients who were sophisticated enough to be suitable. The approaches did not lend themselves easily to assessment and measurement of outcome in a medico-cultural milieu increasingly sensitive to cost efficiency. A new rationale arose, drawing largely from behavioral psychology, from

3

studies of biofeedback, cognition, and concepts about the "sick role." There were new developments in the field of pain studies that allowed for alternate psychological models. There was the demonstrated efficacy of focused behavioral approaches, the palatability to psychologically unsophisticated patients of approaches that were less psychodynamic, and the simpler rationale that made behavioral concepts appeal to nonpsychologists and psychologists alike. Techniques of measurement that were built in to the behavioral approaches were an incentive for research in the field. The fact that these techniques addressed health problems of major public and economic concern, and not just neuroses, assured behavioral medicine a greater health-care prominence.

Behavioral medicine broadens the view concerning the nature of morbidity and the process of intervention. Instead of confining itself to pathophysiological considerations or to psychodynamic constructs, it emphasizes adaptive and maladaptive function, considered in the context of the system in which the patient lives. Thus, a central notion concerns recognition of the existence of stress, and the capacity to cope with it. However, the idea of organic disease is not rejected. Instead, the concept of morbidity is broadened by distinguishing disease as a concept of organic pathology and pathophysiology from the subjective state of being ill. Furthermore, illness behavior is advanced as a construct describing how people act or communicate concerning their experiences of being ill or their beliefs about being diseased. A practical distinction is generally made between the idea of acute and chronic illness, because the management often differs, and because the problems of the clients referred to behavioral medicine clinics often are chronic.

The dimension of thought or cognition is often emphasized, with the idea that maladaptive behavior often correlates with maladaptive patterns of thinking and with erroneous assumptions about the sickness and symptoms. These cognitions can be corrected through analysis of the incorrect assumptions, awareness of the self-defeating thinking patterns, and education regarding the true nature of the problem. The focus on thought is paralleled by a focus on actions that the patient should take to relieve the stress or improve coping skills. A change in action can be facilitated by the patient's taking an active part in self-monitoring in order to build self-awareness, learning or applying methods for self-control of stress-induced symptoms, and achieving a sense of self-efficacy through use of effective coping strategies.

Chapter 1

A Rationale for Behavioral Medicine

Some theoretical constructs and terminology used widely in behavioral medicine are useful from a therapeutic strategy point of view, and some ideas have even found their way into the everyday conversation of laypeople—words such as coping and stress. Admittedly, some words may be more useful therapeutically than scientifically (Tunks & Bellissimo, 1988). Because we will be using these terms extensively, we will define here what we mean by them.

COPING AND STRESS

The notion of coping with stress is probably paramount. Since the introduction of the term "stress" to the fields of medicine and psychology by Hans Selye (1936), the term has taken on a variety of meanings; this can be disconcerting to the critical reviewer seeking conceptual purity. In its most unambiguous form, stress—as it would apply to engineering—denotes a force that is applied to a material and may thereby produce a strain or mechanical change in the material. By analogy, stress can be taken to mean a physical or psychological challenge to the organism that might force it to change or adapt (or become damaged). Stress is also used as an adjective to denote the effect of the challenge on the individual—stress ulcer or stress headache, for example. The word may also be used to denote the interaction between individual and environment, as in noting that stress is an important element in adaptation. We use stress as a generic term to refer to events in which demands of the internal or external environment challenge or exceed the adaptive resources of the individual. The term enjoys a useful currency among the general public, even among those who might not be considered "psychologically minded." There is apparently less loss of face in admitting to symptoms due to stress. There is also an appealing simplicity to the idea that if one has stress, there are options available such as stress reduction or acquiring coping skills.

The term "coping" mostly refers to the individual's deliberate techniques to effectively respond to threats or challenges. In more general terms, it means that the individual is adapting despite relatively difficult conditions. The meaning, however, is sometimes stretched to denote unsuccessful coping. It may signify coping as a style rather than a chosen strategy. The coping label may include responses that involve the antithesis of deliberate effort to respond, such as denial. The term may encompass a particular coping response that is in one situation effective and in another harmful. Furthermore, the idea is linked to the concept that stress causes symptoms that should be avoided or mitigated by coping. In fact, symptoms may also be a product of the strategy of coping itself, which causes stress.

Some interrelationships between these concepts are illustrated in Figure 1.1. Stress and coping are figured as products of several interdependent factors. They are seen as "whole organism" phenomena. We learn about them through assessment of self-reports, and physiological,

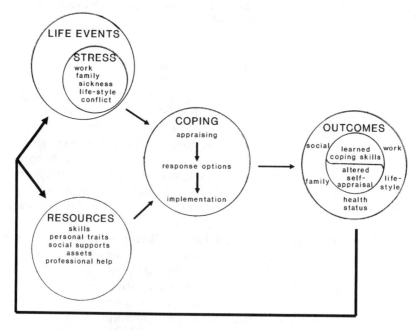

FIGURE 1.1. Stress, life events, and coping.

environmental, and behavioral data. Stress is an essential ingredient in understanding both health and disease, work performance, and satisfaction. Various factors influence others in a dynamic system. (Of course, this does not explain how cognitive, behavioral, or social events actually produce altered functioning and clinical problems.)

ILLNESS BEHAVIOR

"Illness behavior" is a term arising from the work of Parsons (1951) and Mechanic and Volkart (1961), who considered the place in society of those who are sick and those who care for the sick. The individual who is sick behaves in a way that allows him or her to be identified and to have the privileges of a sick person, and to obtain help from a doctor. But what of the individual who acts sick when the clinical investigations fail to define a sufficient medical disorder to explain the sickness? Such a person might then be said to demonstrate abnormal illness behavior (Pilowsky, 1969). The adjective abnormal is used because the sick-role behavior is considered to be maladaptive from the point of view of a normal social need to protect or support the ailing individual, and to exempt him or her temporarily from responsibility during recovery. For example, behavior may be considered abnormal because it is believed that there is some sort of reward for illness, or disincentive for recovery. (However, if the abnormal illness behavior is a response to environmental contingencies, and maladaptive by society's standards, there is also a sense in which it is adaptive with respect to the individual's needs, or the desires of people in the environment to reinforce the illness behavior. Talking about the normality of illness behavior, therefore, is an area of conceptual difficulty.)

Related to the idea of illness behavior is the notion of illness as opposed to disease. To help understand this, one might note, for example, that some people who harbor serious medical pathology may demonstrate few symptoms, whereas others are called hypochondriacs because they worry about their physical health but show no evidence of medical pathology. "Disease" can be used to describe the objective medical disorder, whereas "illness" describes the individual's experience. These distinctions have been useful for the medical sociologists, who have noted that, except in the case of the most severe medical disorders, there appears to be a weak relationship between presence of disease and illness behavior or complaint. The most important determinants of assuming the status of being ill, for many patients, seem to be sociological and cognitive. These ideas of illness behavior and disease are further discussed in relation to treatment in chapter 12.

ACUTE VERSUS CHRONIC

The type of patients who tend to be referred to behavioral medicine clinics are often regarded by the medical specialists as being untreatable by their methods. They are deemed to be suffering from old conditions that are no longer progressive and that are not considered accountable for the patient's symptoms or degree of incapacity.

The distinction between acute and chronic allows the therapist to shift from medical solutions appropriate for acute disorders (such as taking medication and resting until the symptoms resolve) to practical rehabilitative strategies. This shift also benefits the patient who is reassured regarding the reality and legitimacy of the chronic problem.

Of course, distinctions such as these are introduced for their clinical usefulness rather than as an attempt to create a dichotomy. In pathology there is a continuum along which the morbid conditions are spread, from acute to chronic, and the same is true for behavioral phenomena.

In both acute and chronic diseases the symptoms may be modified by emotions and beliefs. Even in the case of acute medical disorders, certain signs such as tenderness or limping might be seen as more or less functional, there may be some discrepancy between detectable disease and reported symptoms, and expression of distress may be modifiable by environmental cues and rewards. The acute versus chronic distinction is useful therapeutically but should not narrow the thinking of the therapist; for example, the therapist should be able to suggest ways in which methods useful for chronic pain patients (such as relaxation) might also be useful for acute pain or childbirth.

Phenomena Characterizing Acute Versus Chronic

There are four fundamental sets of phenomena that distinguish acute from chronic diseases. These are (a) the time frames that characterize them, (b) the expectations about adaptation, (c) the relationship of the disease to the illness behavior, and (d) beliefs that disease is proportional to symptoms.

Time Frame. A fundamental distinction between acute and chronic diseases is the time frame that serves as the bracket for the healing or resolution process. In the acute phase of an injury, there is disruption of integrity and function that is followed by healing and leads to anatomical and functional integrity. Skin cuts close over in as little as 5 days, and regrowth of connective tissue beneath the skin wound takes about 2 weeks. Fractures might be expected to take from 3 to 6 weeks to knit. During the period of healing, there is an inflammatory process that is necessary for healing, which is also the physiological stimulus for pain. The pain has the useful role of alerting the individual to the necessity for rest and protection of the wounded part until the healing is complete.

Chronic illness implies that structural changes, which result from disease or injury, are no longer being resolved, and the disruptions of function and sensation (pain) are persistent. The restorative process in the case of chronic illnesses is aimed at the reorganization of capacities and adaptation. When a problem has become chronic, there is still a great propensity to regard it as acute. Fluctuations in symptoms lead to alarm. Physical guarding, prolonged recumbency, or withdrawal may be evident. All of these might in a real sense increase the disability, promote physical deterioration, and put the individual at risk for the development of other complications (including iatrogenic ones).

Adaptation and Maladaptation. In one way, chronic disorders may be regarded as static, meaning that little spontaneous resolution can be expected from the disease and symptoms. In yet another way, chronic disorder must be regarded as an outgrowth of normal efforts of the organism and individual to heal or adapt. This point was made a century ago by Virchow with respect to pathophysiology and is equally applicable to the domain of behavior and adaptation. In the physical realm, for example, cirrhosis of the liver is considered a chronic condition that slowly progresses until death. At the microscopic level, one finds areas of tissue injury with areas of regeneration of new liver tissue. Unfortunately, the new tissue growth leads to further disorganization in liver structure, predisposing the liver to even further destructive changes, which are again met with further efforts of regeneration. In the behavioral domain, illness and symptoms lead to efforts in coping, depending on the resources of the individual. In some cases the adaptive efforts themselves lead to further problems, requiring further adaptive effort. One could take the example of someone with pain who begins to use opiate analgesics for relief. The opiate analgesics may promote psychological changes such as depression and lack of energy. Excessive bed rest may lead to deconditioning and pain on less activity. Altered rest patterns may lead to sleep disorders. In this way a chronic pain syndrome develops.

One sometimes finds stoical individuals who gradually forego their normal pleasures, family, recreational activities, and even sleep in response to illness in order to preserve their occupational roles, so that they finally live to work. Some individuals respond to chronic symptoms by adopting a chronic illness complaint and cease working, to live on their pension, but maintain their family life and recreation.

Relationship of Behavior to Disease. The popular conception is that pathophysiological disorders determine behavior (and symptoms). This is easily verified if one is dealing with severe and overwhelming problems such as acute peritonitis or acute schizophrenia, for example. However, take the case of chest discomfort due to myocardial ischaemia. The behavior associated with a first episode of myocardial pain could be different from the behavior of an individual who has frequently experienced angina pectoris. In the former case the individual might be anxious and confused (a victim of the disease), whereas in the latter case the individual might have learned to carefully quiet him- or herself (thereby controlling his or her distress and preventing escalation of the angina). One of the transformations of the illness experience over time is that it is modified through learning, and behavioral responses tend to define the illness experience. In the case of low back pain, for example, one individual with time might eventually learn to pace himself well, avoid undue strain, and accept a certain amount of pain in stride. Another person might frequent clinic waiting rooms, abuse medications, enlist family in giving sympathy, and take a totally disabled posture. Either of these examples illustrates that in chronic conditions the behavior increasingly defines the illness experience and what the clinician would label as good or bad coping or adjustment. The task in dealing with certain problems of chronic medical disorder is not to eradicate the original medical disorder (this might be impossible), but rather to alter the behavior associated with the medical disorder. In many cases, the behavior itself is the core of the illness experience and the object of clinical concern.

For our purposes, we might summarize that in acute sickness the state of morbidity tends to determine behavioral function, whereas in chronic illness the behavioral function often defines the state of morbidity. Although an approximation, this idea is often useful therapeutically.

Belief that Disease Is Proportional to Symptoms. From childhood most of us develop notions that link the severity of the wound to the severity of the symptoms. This belief is appropriate in some cases and not in others. It is appropriate and logical to the diagnostician who surveys the patient's history for any indication of fluctuation in symptoms that might pinpoint the change in pathophysiology. It is inappropriate in many chronic conditions. For example, the individual with chronic pain may be suspected of malingering or lying if the complaint of pain cannot be substantiated by a serious and observable lesion that is equivalent to the pain. The individual with chronic illness may also fear deterioration if symptoms wax during prescribed exercise, or may be misled about useless cures as symptoms wane during the inevitable spontaneous fluctuations in the symptom level. The corollaries of the beliefs regarding the equation of symptoms and disease magnitude include the following:

1. The existence of symptoms is a danger sign, to which the sufferer should respond with help-seeking or rest, or ceasing activity while the symptoms last.
2. Symptoms should be treated each time they occur or the patient risks the possibility of physical injury.
3. The former attitude may lead to invalidism, and the latter to abuse of medication.

A classical paper by Beecher (1956) critically assessed this equation in comparing the pain experienced by wounded soldiers on the battlefield with the pain experienced by civilians with similar wounds but in civil situations. He made the assertion, now commonly accepted, that an important determinant of the pain experience is the meaningfulness of the lesion to the sufferer, its likely consequences, and its context. If a wound spells evacuation from the battlefield with honor, it may be experienced in a way very dissimilar to a wound in a workman who is struggling to survive financially. The point is important when dealing with chronic disability and suffering. Patients may never begin to meaningfully participate in rehabilitation until they dissociate the idea of their persistent symptoms from the fear of underlying disease, accept that symptomatic relief may have to take second place to improved function, and believe that recumbency will not resolve the problem but rather aggravate it.

The distinctions here have to do with the assumptions regarding acute and chronic. Behavior biased by either of these illness models may prejudice interpretation of events that pertain to the other model and may lead to inappropriate interventions. For example, it may be anxiety provoking and antitherapeutic to embark on a repeat series of laboratory studies in a chronic headache sufferer who has already had negative results; instead it may be preferable to teach coping with stress.

COGNITION

In the behavioral medicine literature, considerable attention is given to the importance of cognitive (thinking) events as mediating behavioral responses to physical or environmental occurrences. Thought content and the interpretations of events correlate with either adequate or inadequate coping. Coping can be improved by altering cognitions. Some authors reverse the traditional psychodynamically favored hierarchy and assert that cognitions determine affect and that this should be the starting point for therapeutic intervention (Beck, 1976). In practice, there has never been a good clinical reason to polarize affect and thought. From classical Greek to modern times, practitioners have dealt with both the emotion and the meaning in their work with patients. Our understanding is that, although different theoretical perspectives take unique stances on the relative primacy of cognition and affect in clinical work, the cognitive, affective, and behavioral aspects of human experience are inextricably interwoven (Buck, 1985). The cognitive emphasis in recent literature offers a useful avenue in establishing therapeutic work with some patients who, in older psychodynamic frameworks, might have been considered "not psychologically minded and therefore not treatable." There is not actually a unified cognitive therapy approach; some practitioners prefer reasoning with their patients to demonstrate that the assumptions underlying the distress are faulty, others teach methods of coping and thinking more adaptively to ward off distress, and still others offer educational approaches by providing information that permits reinterpretation of the problems in a way that makes the problems solvable. In this text we offer illustrations of educational input, but we do not cling to any particular viewpoint. In general, cognitive–behavioral methods suitable for both individuals and groups of patients are given prominence.

SELF-EFFICACY AND
SELF-CONTROL

The concepts of mastery and self-efficacy are not particularly new in psychological writings, but these terms are common currency in behavioral medicine. The purpose of therapy is to use therapeutic exercises to foster a belief in personal competence in patients who see themselves as being out of control (Figure 1.2). It would not be difficult for any therapist of any therapeutic school to agree with this general idea.

Critically speaking, however, it is likely that coping in some cases does not always involve the achievement of mastery or self-efficacy; one might take, for example, the problem of a patient who is told that he or she is soon going to die of cancer. One individual in such a situation may sometimes find peace of mind by ignoring the threat altogether by using suppression or denial, whereas another might seek control by visiting faraway spas and foreign clinics, and another by engaging in meditation and imagery in which he or she mobilizes his or her body to fight the intruding illness.

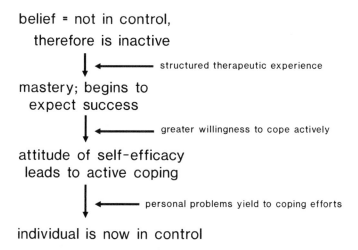

belief = not in control,
    therefore is inactive

        ↓ ←————— structured therapeutic experience

mastery; begins to
    expect success

        ↓ ←————— greater willingness to cope actively

attitude of self-efficacy
    leads to active coping

        ↓ ←————— personal problems yield to coping efforts

individual is now in control

FIGURE 1.2. Control, activity, and self-efficacy.

Patients seek clinical help when they think they have lost control over some aspect of their health. This perception of loss of control seems to mediate motivational, emotional, cognitive, and subsequent behavioral deficits (Seligman, 1975). The process of generalization of loss of control over many situations and over time may confirm and augment the self-perception of illness. There are different ways in which the loss-of-control attitude may do this. It may lead to

- physiological overarousal giving rise to symptoms
- interference with attentional capacities
- overload of memory functioning and problems of retrieval of information
- arousal of conflicts, symbolically or behaviorally
- inappropriate use of information
- helpless behavior that confirms the original loss-of-control attitude.

Individuals facing problems attempt to find a real or symbolic means to assume control. This often takes the form of trying to understand the problem; that is, cognitively imposing meaningfulness and organization. The emphasis of behavior medicine on control and particularly on self-control reflects a therapeutic interest in mobilizing this natural inclination of facing problems.

SELF-AWARENESS

Another important concept is that of promoting self-awareness. This might be done in a variety of ways, such as through an instrumentally produced biofeedback signal, a diary for self-monitoring, or discussions with a therapist regarding one's own coping style or available strategies. The assumption in it all is that becoming aware not only provides a basis for assessment, but also facilitates the capacity for change.

Chapter 2

Basic Elements in Intervention

Having considered the basic concepts in behavioral medicine, we turn now to the most essential factors in behavioral medicine interventions. (These same factors are implicit in most psychotherapeutic treatments.) Salient among these are the role of assessment and formulation in initiating treatment. With respect to behavioral medicine, one must address the distinctions between acute and chronic disorders, the importance of promoting a sense of personal competence or self-efficacy in the patient, the emphasis on management by goals, and the attention to adherence (or compliance) and its management.

ATTITUDES ABOUT ILLNESS AND TREATMENT

Two points of view, like the two sides of a coin, characterize attitudes about illness: the attitudes of the patient and those of the doctor. In general, both tend to endorse the notions that "symptoms mean disease," "disease is the sufficient cause of all the incapacity associated with it," and "symptoms should go away as the underlying disease heals." In general, patients and their doctors influence each other's beliefs and perceptions about illness.

If we were to take the example of a back pain sufferer who believed that all pain meant bodily damage, he or she might avoid activity for fear that the condition might worsen. Furthermore, the person might interpret some of the pain as evidence that he or she has done something to aggravate the condition. This attitude might be reinforced by the oversympathetic physician who writes a prescription or orders a test for everything.

We might also consider a different individual who regards the

15

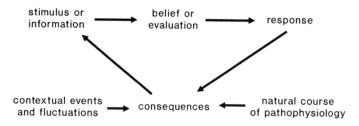

FIGURE 2.1. Illness versus restoration.

symptoms as only one indicator of the overall state of health, and pain as a nonnegotiable element in the state of health, depending on other indicators such as mobility, strength, previous experience, and information provided from health-care workers. The latter individual would be more likely to maintain activity, and at the same time pace him- or herself, and thereby reduce the morbidity of the disease with respect to well-being, personal goals, and quality of life. This attitude also might be reinforced by the physician who advises a rehabilitation program as an appropriate way to manage chronic health problems.

RESTORATION

We can picture the dynamic relationship between illness and restoration in terms of a system in which beliefs affect actions and coping, which produce consequences, further conditioning beliefs (Figure 2.1). Affecting the system are additional factors such as natural fluctuations in sensory-motor events (symptoms) and environmental events. Any rationale for understanding restoration and the resolution of morbidity must take into account the myths about illness and disease that were discussed earlier. One of the most important myths is that the disease that causes the symptoms must be taken away in order for function to be restored. On the contrary, when dealing with chronic illness behaviorally, efforts to restore function may be necessary in order to overcome the illness.

Whereas in acute illness medical intervention likely is employed to reduce pathophysiology (or psychopathology), intervention for chronic problems would have a different orientation. One possibility may be restructuring coping efforts in a more economical and less self-defeating manner. Another may be supporting the remaining strengths of the individual. Energies may be directed to maintaining functional integrity despite ongoing handicaps, learning compensatory functions, or obtaining environmental support. Still another may be restructuring the context in which the individual must cope so that the disability may be circumvented.

The intervention can be conceptualized in terms of the familiar SORC model: "S" is the situation and stimulus, "O" is the belief and cognitive processes, "R" is the response to the stimulus in light of the cognitive processes, and "C" is the consequence in the environment, which in turn becomes further stimulus.

Note that this is a variation of the functional analysis model used to analyze a problem in a situation. The original model is expressed as $S \rightarrow O \rightarrow R \rightarrow K \rightarrow C$. In this formula, "S" represents prior environmental stimulation, "O" the biological state of the organism, "R" the problem response, "K" the contingency relationship of the behavior and the subsequent events, and "C" the nature of the consequences. The complete description of the problem requires knowledge of these elements and their interactions with each other. (See Kanfer & Goldstein, 1980, for details.)

Working from the model, change in any part of the cognitive and behavioral system can be expected to bring about change in the whole system, as in the following examples. The beliefs might be addressed by educating the patient with chronic back pain about his or her problem from a psychosocial and self-care point of view using a back education group. This may lead the patient to fear his or her condition less and to demonstrate less invalidism. Responses may be altered by means of structured therapeutic assignments and exercises. The patient with hypochondriasis and invalidism may be given role-playing tasks of acting unworried and well for specified periods of time and with specific observers such as certain family members, with self-monitoring and then review of the results. The consequences of the individual's behavior may be altered by contingencies manipulated by the therapist or by others. In the latter example, family members can be instructed to first record their natural responses, and then to respond in specified ways to change the reinforcement of the illness behavior. In all of this, the assumption is made that we are dealing with an open system that is continually exposed to influence from others, and that information feedback is one of the variables that helps maintain or change the system's equilibrium. The therapist often works to change self-awareness about beliefs and actions, and to alter responses of the individual and consequences from others (environment). Restoration involves establishing a new self-sustaining system that is less symptomatic.

SELF-EFFICACY AND CONTROL

The idea contained in self-efficacy and control has been given central attention by many writers of different theoretical schools. The psychoanalytic idea of ego effectance and mastery (White, 1963), Erikson's idea of sense of competence (1950), Bandura's idea of self-efficacy (1977), and Frank and colleagues' idea of positive expectations or hope (of one's own success) (1978) are all examples or aspects of it. The presence of this factor indicates the degree to which the individual believes that the problem can be solved or controlled through his or her own efforts. To various degrees, the absence of this factor represents the morale problem of many patients, and the behavioral reflection of a problem in self-efficacy is the style of passivity that inhibits coping.

The elements determining self-control and self-efficacy include beliefs, available coping resources, degree of activity or passivity, and level of motivation. Thinking mediates the relationships between stimuli, knowledge, and action, and forms the belief of what the individual can achieve. All of these elements are subject to clinical intervention and deserve individual consideration.

Ingredients in Self-Efficacy and Self-Control

Beliefs. Beliefs are conditioned by the individual's personality and previous personal and vicarious experiences accumulated over a lifetime. Beliefs exist in part in relation to expectations that have been built up about abilities prior to illness. On the one hand, this can be helpful, as in the case of the individual who remains optimistic about his or her ability to overcome yet another setback. Because such recollections are sometimes faulty, ill people often tend to overestimate their previous function and underestimate their current potential. Beliefs also are in constant relationship with current events and their evaluations, and people may be selective about which elements of a situation they think are important. For example, frequent inconclusive visits to different physicians may not reassure the somatizing patient that nothing is wrong, but rather that the situation is hopeless; whereas limiting visits to doctors may be helpful in treating a problem of somatizing. There are beliefs about one's present abilities to meet a challenge, and about the likely consequences of having to face certain problems. There are often beliefs about cause and effect; for example, that pension applicants will always be treated unfairly, that chest pain means heart disease, or that feeling unwell means that a certain therapeutic exercise has caused harm.

Education or demonstration can be used as explicit therapeutic tools to alter beliefs, as, for example, in the case of classes to prepare patients for hospitalization and unpleasant procedures. However, not all patient education leads to the same desirable result of producing coping behavior. Talking to a patient in medical jargon may be satisfying to the professional, but for the patient it may simply reinforce the sense that the problem is esoteric and strictly in the domain of the professional. A good rule is to limit education to expectations about what will be experienced with a problem and its treatment, and to action that the patient will be able to take on his or her own behalf in mastering the problem. This keeps the focus on activity and mastery rather than on passivity and avoidance.

Available Coping Strategies. In the face of any given problem, the individual usually has a repertoire of possible responses; the style of response of an individual often reflects his or her character. Any one situation usually allows several different possibilities, some better than others. For example, in a supermarket line, someone edging his way into the middle of the line might be dealt with by silence so as to not cause a scene, aggression by banging one's cart into the intruder's cart, assertiveness by showing the offender the end of the line, indirectly by engaging someone else in the line in a discussion about courtesy, or in a conciliatory way after the fact by telling the intruder that he or she seems to have a small amount of items and should therefore go first.

Cues found in the context of a specific coping situation may suggest one way of coping over others; for example, facing a stern judge in a traffic court may inhibit an individual from using a favorite style of bluster, and may instead suggest a more conciliatory strategy. Cues may also come from the effects of modeling by others; group therapy is an effective forum for inducing people to improve their social skills and to abide by group norms, and in families the adage "like father, like son" is frequently true. Coping methods may be verbally communicated, as in exhortation by a coach, suggestion by a psychotherapist, or in confidential conversation between friends.

As with any variable that involves subjective states, it has been difficult to research the area of coping. However, in the research that has been done, several conclusions can be drawn. In the laboratory it is difficult to show the superiority of any one coping strategy over another. People already have their own preferred styles of coping that they use in any event, and the experimental situation does not sufficiently simulate the real problems in which there is more anxiety and less sense of control (Tan, 1982). If one studies poor copers, it is often discovered that they frequently show an excess of coping styles that might be called catastrophizing and avoidance (Crook, Tunks, Kalaher, & Roberts, 1988). In helping people to be better copers, it is necessary to make them aware of effective coping methods and help them to use their coping strategies flexibly and spontaneously, matching the situation to the coping.

State of Activity or Passivity. The patient's state of activity or passivity is an essential element in self-control. Passivity promotes inactivity, which impairs effective response to problems, thereby perpetuating the problem and the passivity. On the other hand, some kinds of activity may also be self-defeating, as in the case of individuals who deal with frustration by impulsiveness, hyperactivity, or perseveration rather than by thoughtful problem-solving. For noncopers, usually the clinical problem is inactivity, and the usual first step in therapy is engaging the patient in some sort of goal-directed behavior. In other cases, it may be necessary to use contingency management or structured assignments of some sort to modify the activity so that coping is possible.

Level of Motivation. The colloquial use of the term motivation makes it rather ambiguous, unless we define it to mean the probability that someone will act toward accomplishing a given behavioral goal. Part of this overall probability depends on the cost to the individual of the situation as it stands versus the risks of change. We might think here of the person with a longstanding problem that results in impairment and symptoms but also results in the receipt of pension and family support. Efforts to improve the disability may lead to greater functional independence and cessation of pension, but not necessarily to financial self-sufficiency.

Social influence, and particularly verbal praise, is a potent reinforcer of behavior toward a selected goal. To the detriment of a patient's well-being, families may also promote illness behavior and negatively influence the motivation to change. All this can happen without the awareness of family members.

There is also a contribution of degree of motivation from the individual him- or herself. We can take the example of someone who becomes depressed and who then withdraws. This same person may improve in motivation when the depression is treated. There is the factor of personality variation; the individual's degree of motivation may vary greatly, from the most energetic and productive person to the most apathetic.

In therapy there is usually the assumption that it will be possible to influence motivation by appeal to reason, by influence of the therapeutic relationship, or by another therapeutic device. Furthermore, success experiences during therapy will promote a sense of mastery and thus enhance the motivation to continue to improve. For this reason, early in therapy many therapists set tasks that can be readily achieved and lead the patient to increased involvement in learning new coping behavior.

Awareness and Self-Control

In various forms, the process of becoming self-aware has been a key element in most psychologically based therapies. Patients generally adopt an explanation for the disorder and for the proposed treatment that implies a personal learning experience and awareness of change.

Various therapies are more or less deliberate in the introduction of means to promote this self-awareness. Dynamic psychotherapy uses the techniques of free association by the patient and interpretation offered by the therapist. In classical behavioral therapy, the patient works out a hierarchy of things that cause anxiety. In group therapy, comembers of the group reflect to each other the parts of the transactions that they perceive in others and in themselves. In biofeedback, the patient attends to signals from a single monitored physical function (such as skin temperature), and links this to other experiences such as the feeling of relaxation. In cognitive–behavioral therapy, the emphasis is on self-responsibility and self-control; thus, the emphasis is on making oneself aware by some form of self-monitoring and/or self-observation. This may take various forms. Patients may be asked to keep a diary of a troublesome symptom in order to gain a better perspective of its prevalence and severity and links to other events. Attempting new behaviors and monitoring the results can promote a sense of competence and control. Having an individual self-monitor or listen to a recording of his or her own self-defeating behavior may make such behavior aversive while alerting him or her to alternatives.

The rationale has to do with the "O" in the SORC model; one's internal self-talk (or thoughts) acts as a stimulus for the individual. Thought stimuli being perceived are evaluated and the response follows. The patterns of such thoughts, evaluations, and responses often have become quite habitual and may operate outside the person's awareness. To break the self-perpetuated problem behavior, the patient is induced to stop for a minute to consider what is transpiring and what is his or her evaluation. The assumption is that awareness and motivation is the key to control. Self-monitoring often has the effect of reducing the tendency to catastrophize; deliberate and systematic observation is a behavior that is contradictory to fearful behavior. In this way it rather resembles systematic desensitization that is used in classical behavior therapy. Self-monitoring may also lead directly to the belief in self-control by altering evaluations, as shown in the case study below.

> A patient complains that he suffers from crying spells that are an embarrassment. The therapist tells the patient that for the next week he is to make no effort to stop crying but only to monitor these episodes exactly. Miraculously, the crying stops. The logic is that although the crying seemed to be beyond the patient's control, allowing himself to cry was under his own control, and the act of self-monitoring was under self-control. The crying itself was reevaluated as being under self-control.

Self-Efficacy and Goal-Directed Behavior

The assumption is made in cognitive–behavioral therapy that people are unwilling to act if they assume that their actions will fail. They will behave in a goal-directed way when they evaluate the problem as solvable and their capacity sufficient for the task. If we were then to enlarge the SORC diagram to focus on the "OR" portion, it could be represented as in Figure 2.2.

This model combines ideas found in control theory with those in self-control (Carver & Scheier, 1982; D'Zurilla, 1986). From control theory is drawn the idea of the negative feedback loop; the patient works toward reducing the discrepancy that exists between the present condition and the desired condition. It is interesting that this alters the usual psychotherapy paradigm; in the situation depicted in Figure 2.2, the patient tests a solution strategy and evaluates the outcome in the real-life setting rather than symbolically in the clinician's office.

Definition of Relevant Goals

When individuals and their families are in distress, with poor confidence in their ability to cope, a variety of problems may be present. Coping skills may not be adequate to achieve the intended goal, or there may be a poor match between the personal resources of stamina, intelligence, morale, family support, or other ingredients to persevere toward the goal. In some cases, no goal has been defined, or the different members of the group (e.g., family) may have contradictory goals, or they may not believe that they will be successful and therefore avoid making goals. In some cases there is a discrepancy between the stated goals and the actual goal-directed activity. For example, an

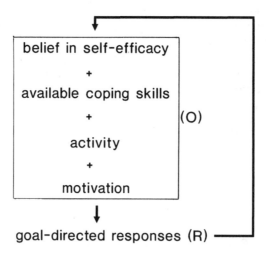

FIGURE 2.2. Self-efficacy and goal-directed behavior.

unemployed person who says he or she is having trouble finding work may have stopped seeking it, or the family who is stating that it wants to have greater harmony may be scapegoating and trying to settle old scores. At times the adaptation of the individual or family may depend on maintaining certain patterns of behavior that accomplish unstated goals, while complaining that other explicit goals are elusive. For example, a warring couple may avoid breakup by projecting the problems onto the defendant responsible for an accident that caused injury and chronic illness of a family member. This supports the illness behavior of one member, while leaving old intimacy and communication problems unresolved. People caught up in these kinds of problems usually feel forever frustrated, as if their problems are not under their own control and they lack the capacity to take definitive action to right their situation.

Dealing with these problems requires that the patient take the following steps:

1. Clearly define at least a few goals that are consistent with his or her real needs and abilities.
2. Ensure that these are stated clearly enough to gain agreement from the most significant others in the environment where that is possible.
3. Share some of these goals with the therapist for the purpose of therapeutic activity.
4. Approach the goals in a series of gradual and workable steps so that a coordinated and logical program toward their achievement can be mounted.

The steps taken to develop self-control are as follows:

1. Performing a task—the action taken to solve a specific problem.
2. Self-monitoring of performance and outcome—the actual observation and recording of the action taken. (Self-monitoring is discussed in detail below.)
3. Self-evaluation—this includes the feedback loop mentioned above, in which the individual revises his or her beliefs in self-efficacy or competence.
4. Self-reinforcement—this means that the individual acknowledges and approves of the accomplishment, which may lead to a tangible reward or a positive self-statement (D'Zurilla, 1986).

COMPLIANCE

The Problem of Compliance

A review by Dunbar (1980) indicates that 20% to 80% of patients drop out of treatment, 20% to 80% make errors in taking their medication, and 20% to 60% stop taking their medication before being told to do so. In medicine, compliance problems are understood to be the negative qualities of the patient that prevent the real clinical problems from being adequately treated.

On the other hand, when illness is formulated in terms of behavior, compliance problems may be seen as part of the illness behavior, and an appropriate target of behavioral intervention. Furthermore, compliance is seen not strictly as a patient's problem but also as the problem of the environment, which may include the doctor.

The traditional biomedical view of compliance would focus on the fact that the hypertensive patient repeatedly omits doses of his or her antihypertensive medication and thus continues on sporadic visits to the doctor to have hypertension poorly controlled. According to the behavioral viewpoint, one may observe that the drug chosen has unpleasant side effects, the patient has had little explanation of what to expect, calls to the doctor are rarely returned, adequate renewals have sometimes not been ordered, the doctor has not established a warm relationship with the patient, the tablets are costly, and the patient is short on cash. In addition, the patient finds that salt avoidance is a nuisance because he or she dislikes the bland taste and must also cook for other family members who like salt, and there may be multiple other similar factors that frame the compliance problem as a multifaceted behavioral issue. Viewed in this way, description and analysis of the illness in behavioral terms would include the factors maintaining and influencing the illness, and likewise the factors influencing the provision, availability, and use of medical treatment. It is also worth noting that compliance is only partly related to how logical the treatment is presumed to be. In the example above, it may seem illogical that a patient would fail to take a drug that may reduce the risk of sudden death through heart disease or stroke. However, on closer analysis, there are factors more influential than logic. Therefore, one cannot hope to rely only on common sense, patient education, and exhortation to ensure compliance, although these have a place.

Improving Compliance

Guidelines for dealing with compliance issues might be categorized as the management of information, behavior, self, incentive, and support.

Information Management. This entails educating the patient about the rationale and regimen, and may include the following:

1. Organize and present information regarding the causes of the disorder, expected outcome, reason for treatment, expectations and collateral effects of treatment, and consequences of inadequate treatment.
2. Entertain questions from the patient regarding the problem and treatment in order to deal with fears and misconceptions. Be available if doubts or questions arise later.
3. Give details of the regimen and important signs to watch for in written form.
4. Present information gradually to prevent overloading.
5. Emphasize the "how to" aspects and avoid the esoteric explanations.
6. Assess the patient's comprehension by having him or her explain or demonstrate.

Behavior Management. This could involve a variety of things, only a few of which are mentioned here as illustration:

1. Tailor instructions to the patient's daily routine.
2. Use stimulus control procedures designed to help the patient to overcome forgetting problems and to develop a habitual routine.
3. When a regimen is complex, introduce components gradually, using shaping procedures.

Self-Management. Self-management techniques are a regular part of most behavior medicine programs, and may be used in managing compliance.

1. Clearly define the behavior change goals that the patient is working toward.
2. Clearly define in behavioral terms the steps that are to be taken as the patient works toward these goals.
3. Use self-monitoring procedures for measuring progress toward these goals.

Incentive Management. The issue of incentive is concerned not only with positive reinforcers, but also with negative ones that may be hidden in the environment.

1. Create a behavioral analysis of the problem in its context (this should be a prerequisite).
2. Eliminate unnecessary hassles in the regimen, or in the treatment setting, such as with clinic organization or time scheduling.
3. Keep the regimen simple. If, for example, several behavioral steps are required, tie them into a sequence that is logistically straightforward and similar from time to time.

4. Build natural reinforcement into the treatment system. For example, increasing the walking tolerance of a pain patient may be tied to the number of holes of golf that are permitted.
5. Give other systems of reward such as rebates, awards, or recognition by a peer group.

Support Management. This is the social dimension of incentive management.

1. Introduce the family to the treatment program to enlist their support, and modify their responses where their behavior could pose obstacles to the patient's behavior changes.
2. Avoid treatment routines that could be interpreted as demeaning.
3. Build in a regular system of review so that behavioral gains can be regularly approved and rewarded by verbal reinforcement from the therapist.
4. Arrange the behavioral program if possible so that it is tied to increasing social contact (or reducing social isolation).
5. Build a good patient–clinician relationship by empathic listening as well as prescribing.
6. Be aggressive about continued follow-up, emphasizing remembering and understanding the various components of the regimen.

From the above, compliance management, rightly conceived, cannot be separated from the entire plan of management. (For more details about cognitive–behavioral strategies to facilitate compliance, see Meichenbaum & Turk, 1987.)

GOAL-ORIENTED MANAGEMENT

The difference between the goal-oriented and the problem-oriented approaches reflects the difference between the rehabilitation or behavioral medicine approaches and most medical or surgical treatment. The crux of it is that in a goal-oriented approach, the thrust of the therapeutic endeavor is to induce the patient to share responsibility in defining a set of goals that he or she is willing to pursue to achieve control over some health problem. In contrast, from a problem-oriented point of view the first task is to define the problems, whether or not the patient takes responsibility for them. A physician may, for example, correctly list smoking, bronchitis, vascular disease, and possible emphysema as elements in a problem list, but the patient might be inclined to deny the importance of the smoking and take no action to curb it, thus refusing to accept responsibility in changing the problem behavior that is at the root of the problem. In a goal-oriented approach, the first aim is to arrive at some common ground for the therapeutic focus. As the therapeutic relationship develops, more goals may be added to the list. The patient is persuaded to focus on self-help—reducing smoking by systematically assessing the smoking behavior and reducing it progressively according to a set of quotas. It is not that the problem-oriented and goal-oriented approaches are incompatible with one another, but rather that in dealing with behavioral change an essential ingredient in strategy is mobilizing the patient's active effort and sense of ownership. This activity helps to minimize the maladaptive stances of avoidance, dependency, and helplessness.

Need for Self-Assessment in Relevant Areas

In behavior medicine, the self-assessment is not usually symptom based. For many patients, the focus on symptoms is part of a helpless and passive attitude that hopes for a cure. Instead, self-assessment is behavior based. The patient has to ask himself, "Just what am I doing that allows this problem to continue? What is the minimum requirement for change to occur in various areas; for example, recreation, family, employment, health enhancement?" The therapeutic impact of the self-assessment process is that a specific therapeutic direction is taken, the patient is recruited into the change process, and change in perceptions and behaviors is facilitated.

Self-assessment needs to be learned. Patients require assistance in learning to single out events and behavior that should be monitored, distinguishing them from other data or symptoms that are not to receive attention. This is often a step-by-step process that takes place under the guidance of the therapist. Three important rules for goal-oriented management are outlined in the following paragraphs.

Avoid Unrealistic Goals. Chronically ill people often entertain a sort of "return to Eden fantasy," in which they imagine that to be well they will be restored to the way that they remember themselves before the illness or accident. Retrospective evaluations of functioning are usually exaggerated, and previous problems are quickly forgotten. Furthermore, previous life-style may no longer be realistic or personally relevant.

Make Specific Concrete Goals. Patients are often overwhelmed with the discrepancy between their current function and the functional level required if they are to be normal. It is necessary to start thinking in terms of short- and long-range objectives. These objectives must be in keeping with the person's life, work, and family situation. They should be simplified by breaking them into component parts and arranging into small manageable steps. The effort and time reasonably required to achieve them must be estimated and built into the goals. For example, in a weight reduction program, it is a necessary component to teach the patient that a large caloric deficit is necessary to lose 1 pound, so that to lose 1 or 2 pounds per week is a good result. Failing to set this expectation will rapidly lead to discouragement and dropping out of treatment.

Objectively verifiable milestones need to be set to quantify and pace progress toward the goals. This is essential as much for the patient's sense of control and morale as it is for keeping the therapy on track.

Encourage Taking Ownership of Goals. This is a valuable attitude that should be conveyed explicitly. The attitude reminds therapist and patient alike that the illness and the solutions ultimately belong to the patient. The patient and clinician must be united in working toward the therapeutic goals.

Behavior Change

To achieve goals in therapy, there are problems to avoid as well as purposes to attain. Self-fulfilling prophecies are the converse side of hopes. Patients often become pessimistic, expecting failure before they start. This may manifest itself, for example, in setting impossible goals, or in retreating to inactivity and passivity, and then interpreting the lack of progress as confirmation of their hopeless situation. Goals have to be scrutinized for such potential problems.

Lack of energy budgeting (or not pacing oneself) is a characteristic of many chronically disabled individuals who respond to their problem with self-defeating behavior and frustration. The pacing has to take into account both the overall number of projects that the patient has taken on (family, work, study, etc.), as well as the volume of activity in any one of these areas. An important skill is learning to break the task down into achievable steps and sequences.

During efforts to achieve therapeutic goals, patients usually manifest the very behavioral problems and attitudes that got them in trouble in the first place. They may overdo their activity, leading to fatigue and frustration, and fail to set priorities, so that some problems still mount up. For example, a patient with back pain who is advised to exercise may decide to cut the lawn that he has not touched for a year. Other problematic attitudes are those of catastrophizing or expecting the worst, and avoiding activity. These have the effect of either leading the patient to panic and stop goal-directed behavior, or to avoid it in the first place. Of all problems, catastrophizing and avoidance are those most important to overcome if therapy is to be successful.

ASSESSMENT AND FORMULATION

Generally, in clinical practice a traditional diagnosis is made on the basis of history, signs, symptoms, and etiological concepts, and this is reviewed from time to time in case a diagnostic change is necessary. On the other hand, in behavioral medicine the assessment represents a detailed analysis of the ongoing problematic behavior and the circumstances that characterize and may have initiated the illness or maintained it. The technical term used in the literature is "applied behavioral analysis." It attempts to look at the patient's problems in a way that can lead to a behavioral prescription and specific remedial steps in treatment. In terms of methods, the usual clinical interview is supplemented by such tools as questionnaires or rating scales, or self-monitoring procedures. This self-monitoring approach will be discussed below.

The assessment process leads to a formulation of the problem in behavioral terms that incorporates information about the problem itself, knowledge of abnormal physiology and behavior, and inferences and ideas that the clinician uses to explain that problem. Whereas medical formulations focus on biological variables, and usually psychodynamic formulations depend on a theory of relationship between mental events and characteristics of personality, behavioral formulations are explicitly related to the interventions that will later be necessary in treatment.

Behavioral Analysis

Behavioral analysis can be facilitated by thinking in terms of the S-O-R-K-C model mentioned earlier (see Kanfer & Saslow, 1965). Such analysis has the purpose of directing the attention of the clinician to optimal intervention strategies. The main focus of intervention is the set of problematic behaviors defined in terms of excesses, deficits, adaptiveness, frequency, intensity, duration, and associated stimulus conditions. The unique characteristics of the problem, the cost of maintaining the same way of coping versus the cost, and consequences of changing it are considered.

Situation. The situations in which the problem arises are catalogued. The life situation of the individual, role expectations, and current pressures are all relevant.

Individual Variables. Inquiry is made into the attitudes, beliefs, and habits of the person, and the pattern of biological and social development, especially with respect to the behavioral problem in question.

Responses. The types of responses most frequently encountered in the patient—deficiencies and excesses of response both in his or her behavioral problem and general repertoire—are noted: The relationship of an individual's responses to self-reinforcement, self-control, or responses elicited from the environment are also considered.

Conditions Associated with the Responses. Of particular interest are factors in the environment that may influence the individual toward adaptive behavior and provide self-reinforcement.

Consequences of the Individual's Responses. For the individual, a list is prepared of reinforcers. The range of consequences includes the individual's own self-perception, responses from family, friends, and professionals, and nonresponses as well. Failure to reward behavior may lead to extinguishing it, and attempts to induce the patient to behave in a more adaptive way may fail if there is inadequate attention to this factor.

The Patient as a Partner

Influencing the patient to become a partner in treatment depends on establishing good rapport. Some of the simple things that build such rapport can be deliberately included in the clinical encounter. These are as follows:

1. Not only is the history of the chief complaint important to the patient, but also the emotional meaning of the complaint to the individual. After listening to the patient, the clinician should repeat the essential parts of the patient's problem, including reference to the fears and frustrations that the patient experiences in association with it.

2. The chief focus of the patient's problem, and the direction that is agreed upon for intervention, should be explicitly addressed. If there is no agreement on the focus of intervention, therapy usually fails.

3. A rationale that allows the patient to see the problem as solvable, and something that he or she can participate in solving, is often not initially part of the patient's understanding, and therefore must be conveyed by explanation and education. This rationale should help the patient understand how the problem has developed and how the problem is now maintained through learning mechanisms.

4. The costs and rewards of entering treatment, the time and effort required, and a time table for accomplishing this must be considered. If possible, likely obstacles that will hamper progress need to be anticipated, with suggestions given to the patient of how they might be dealt with when they occur.

5. Answer any questions the patient may have, provide material when appropriate if the patient wishes to think about it further or discuss it with family, and allow time if necessary before a decision is made to enter therapy.

6. Before finally agreeing to enter treatment, be sure to ask the patient, "Now that you understand what this problem and its treatment are all about, what is it that *you* are prepared to do?"

In a discussion such as the above, it is possible to achieve greater commitment if the patient shares the rationale for behavioral management. This understanding will usually come gradually, and may not occur in every case. When possible, one should attempt to guide the patient to describe the problem in operational terms that encompass the first occurrence of the problem, the surrounding circumstances, and a chronological development within the S-O-R-C framework. Such a framework considers a problem as something that involves an open system with outside influences and the individual's own understanding and action; the problem is reversible, and not simply something that happens.

SELF-MONITORING

Whereas the clinical history taken from the patient gives a starting point in understanding the problem by looking mostly at past experience and recollections, self-monitoring procedures can provide another kind of information that is not readily available to recollections. The history and description of the chief complaint help the clinician focus on areas where such further information would be useful. Another motive for such self-monitoring is therapeutic, since patients do not always have a realistic perspective on the occurrence of their problems and may need to acquire a more objective view.

In self-monitoring, the patient is asked to record specific overt and covert aspects, including, where appropriate, thoughts; feelings; circumstances; and patterns that precede, accompany, or follow the problem in question. As an illustration, a patient with stomach problems may describe it only as pain and diarrhea. Through self-monitoring, the patient is trained to obtain information about the circumstances, onset, frequency, intensity, duration, and contents of the diarrhea; similar information about the pain; and details of the accompanying behavioral responses, thoughts, and remedies sought. If the information sought is drug-taking behavior, the monitoring may instead focus on all drug intake; exact doses and times; and the relation to pain, diarrhea, anticipation, worry, and so forth.

1. Self-monitoring procedures may be used to obtain a baseline of the frequency, intensity, duration, and other characteristics of a presenting problem. It is important to obtain a perspective about the problem itself as well as to quantify some characteristics that may be used as a benchmark for measuring goals and treatment.

2. To make a behavioral formulation of a problem, it is necessary to identify the key controlling variables. Monitoring specific aspects suspected as being important to a problem will permit one to determine which are the significant behavioral antecedents and consequences that best help to understand the problem in behavioral terms.

3. Self-monitoring is used directly as a tool for behavioral change. Such monitoring may have the effect of sensitizing the patient to maladaptive behaviors or may help to reduce anxiety, such as in making the patient aware that a symptomatic behavior has only the appearance of being involuntary, automatic, or out of control. It also provides a form of systematic feedback and encouragement to the patient as he or she moves through treatment.

4. Self-monitoring can be used to show the patient how to link the behavioral problem with the conceptual system to be used in treatment. For example, by monitoring events in the environment that are associated with certain behaviors, it is possible to link the behavior with its context. By monitoring certain physiological processes, one may link attitude or affect with physiological reactions. In these ways, the self-monitoring becomes a window on systems relevant to behavior.

5. Self-monitoring provides a useful and efficient procedure for evaluating either the problem or its treatment in an ongoing way. By being action based, it is easily understood and communicated between therapist and patient.

6. Self-monitoring allows attention to be drawn to the healthier aspects of an event; for example, a chronic pain patient may be inclined to focus on how much pain is experienced with each activity. In a self-monitoring exercise, the therapist may give explicit instructions to monitor only the distance walked on successive days and perhaps the heart rate, but not pain. The patient's thinking and action is separated from pain talk and from reinforcement of pain talk.

7. As a means of gathering relevant clinical data, self-monitoring can, in some circumstances, provide more reliable information than either

self-report (anamnesis), or clinician's history-taking. Patient's recollections may be faulty (Linton & Melin, 1982), the examination situation may provide response cues that distort the patient's behavior, and the traditional hour of clinical history-taking may not allow for detail that may be necessary for some motives such as carrying out a behavioral analysis. Of course, patients may falsify a self-monitoring diary, but for that matter, patients can just as easily falsify the history they give to an interviewer. For the most part, falsified self-monitoring can be suspected when the responses each day are too uniform and stereotyped, or when the patient has a negative attitude toward the treatment process.

8. Self-monitoring minimizes the distortion from intrusion of other influences, such as cues from the clinical examination situation, and it allows one to examine a behavior over a period of time and in different circumstances, where there are differing contingencies operating.

9. In the telling and recording of clinical histories, there may be a tendency for the patient to leave out the things that he or she believes the clinician need not know, or for the clinician to read into the history what he or she anticipates to be implicit. Self-monitoring permits a more inclusive sample of the problems by recording of data, regardless of thoughts about relevance.

10. Because it is "self"-monitoring, it provides a window into private experiences, subjective impressions, cognitions, and feelings, giving an opportunity for the patient to make the associations and linkages that give meaning to the experiences.

Self-monitoring, however, has limitations that must be considered whenever it is used.

1. Depending on how much attention is paid to it, the focus of attention, or the methods of recording, accuracy or details may vary, consistency may be uneven, and the recording may not always validly sample the events of concern. Best results occur when subjects are willing and motivated to use it and are pretrained, and when the therapists use some sort of compliance monitoring during the self-monitoring.

2. When using self-monitoring to assess a cognitive or behavioral problem, the monitoring itself may distort or modify the problems to be studied.

3. Patients may complete the task in a perfunctory way, invent the data as a ticket to the next treatment session, or exaggerate a viewpoint that they wish to impress on the therapist.

4. The self-monitoring exercises must be collected frequently. If not, many patients will fail to do them or will wait until the day of the

appointment and then quickly fill them in for the whole preceding week. The therapist uses the returned diaries to open discussion with the patient, and to identify potential obstacles, conflicting demands, ambiguity of goals, emotional problems, and specific deficits in ability, skills, or information.

Setting Up Self-Monitoring Procedures

Patients need careful instructions on how to self-monitor, with an opportunity for practice before beginning. It is as important to indicate what not to monitor as it is to indicate what to monitor. If you ask someone to bring a diary of foods and headaches, you could end up with an uninterpretable account of various dishes and a litany of complaints about symptoms, what pills they took, and how hopeless they felt about their problem. What you want is an organized recording of selected factors such as frequency, duration, specific elements of diet, and so forth. If you want to use self-monitoring as part of a program to decrease pain complaints or illness behavior, you may undermine the results by telling the patient to monitor the severity of symptoms. Instead, you may want the patient to monitor activities completed or exercise increases, leaving no room in the diary for recording of symptoms.

Most patients are not systems experts. They will usually need a ready-made recording system. The diary should be portable, not bulky or likely to attract undue attention. Times for recording should make the task convenient. In most cases, a set of symbols or brief notations will be preferable to full-sentence narratives. In preparation, the patient needs to be given easily interpretable instructions on how to recognize and label the target events to be monitored. It takes therapist experience to make the best use of monitoring procedures, to be flexible about variations of the procedure to fit the problems, and to choose correct variables such as frequency and duration of self-monitoring, appropriate intervals for recording in order to match the frequency and duration of the clinical problem, and choice of structured or semistructured diaries.

Figures 2.3 and 2.4 illustrate charts that can be used to record symptoms, thoughts, and other events. Figure 2.3 allows the patient to grade the severity of a symptom, whereas Figure 2.4 is used for uptime-downtime monitoring and multipurpose monitoring.

In general, self-monitoring tasks change as treatment progresses. During assessment, the motives are usually to identify the relationship that exists between symptoms, behaviors, and the context in which they appear, and when and how frequent they appear. This provides

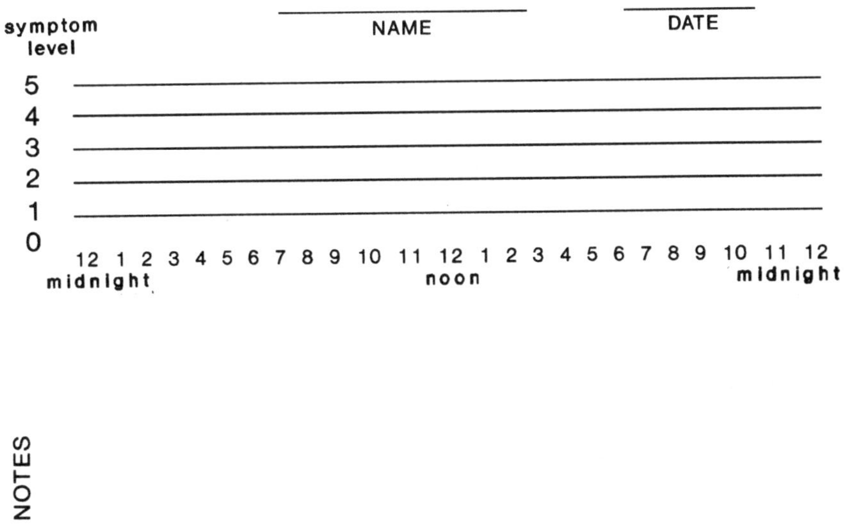

```
symptom
level
5  ─────────────────────────────────────
4  ─────────────────────────────────────
3  ─────────────────────────────────────
2  ─────────────────────────────────────
1  ─────────────────────────────────────
0
   12 1 2 3 4 5 6 7 8 9 10 11 12 1 2 3 4 5 6 7 8 9 10 11 12
  midnight                      noon                 midnight
```

NOTES

FIGURE 2.3. Chart for self-monitoring of symptoms.

diagnostic information to the therapist and makes the patient aware of self-defeating patterns of coping, and the true dimensions of the problem. Figure 2.5 illustrates a self-monitoring form appropriate for the assessment phase of insomnia management. During treatment, however, the motive is to focus the attention of the patient on specific behavioral changes, and to direct the attention away from symptoms, since focus on symptoms can undermine morale and inhibit progress. Thus, a self-monitoring form appropriate for use during the treatment of insomnia is illustrated in Figure 2.6, and an example of its use is demonstrated in Figure 2.7.

Figure 2.8 illustrates a system that can be used to monitor pain or other symptoms over the hours of the day, while at the same time recording other events over the same hours. For example, a patient might record headache triggers, eating or bowel events that coincide with irritable colon, coping behaviors that are used when back or neck pain is a problem, and assertiveness or tension-reduction techniques that are used when anxiety is a problem. See also examples in chapters 4 and 7.

Employing Goals

The more specific the goal, the more satisfactory the outcome. Moreover, when employing goals, one must organize the goal-directed

The date today is _____

NAME _____   DATE STARTED _____   DATE FINISHED _____

| mid-night | 1AM | 2AM | 3AM | 4AM | 5AM | 6AM | 7AM | 8AM | 9AM | 10AM | 11AM | noon | 1PM | 2PM | 3PM | 4PM | 5PM | 6PM | 7PM | 8PM | 9PM | 10PM | 11PM | 12PM |

FIGURE 2.4. Twenty-four-hour chart for self-monitoring.

NOTES

NAME _____ DATE STARTED _____ DATE FINISHED _____

Please fill in this diary for the next three days. Record when you were awake or asleep, day or night. Use the single words shown below. Mark a line to show when these things happened. Fill in your diary each morning as soon as you wake up, at lunch, supper, and when you go to bed. Each morning, answer the questions at the bottom of the page. Hand in each page to your therapist each day as soon as you have completed it.

bed   = I went to bed or was in bed   up   = I got up or was up
nap   = I took a nap when it wasn't bedtime   sleep = I fell asleep
wake   = I woke up or was awake   med   = I took medicine (mark which kind, how many)
coffee = cup of coffee (mark the number of cups)   tea   = cup of tea (mark the number of cups)
alcohol = beer, wine or liquor (number of drinks)   smoke = (mark number of cigarettes)

The date today is _____

mid-night	1AM	2AM	3AM	4AM	5AM	6AM	7AM	8AM	9AM	10AM	11AM	noon	1PM	2PM	3PM	4PM	5PM	6PM	7PM	8PM	9PM	10PM	11PM	12PM

How rested were you when you woke up this morning? Not rested____ Somewhat rested____ Rested____
If you took medicines, mark the time on the line. Write: name of the medicine _____ dose strength _____ Number of tablets _____

Mark down when you had coffee, tea, or alcohol. How much of each? Coffee cups _____ Cups of tea _____ Alcohol number of drinks_____
If you lay awake last night, unable to sleep, write on the bottom of this page what you did.
If you got out of bed during the night last night, what did you do? How long did you spend? Write this at the bottom of the page.
What things could you do tomorrow to have a more regular or less interrupted sleep.

FIGURE 2.5. Wake-sleep chart and questionnaire for self-monitoring.

37

NAME _____ DATE STARTED _____ DATE FINISHED _____

Please fill in this diary for the next three days. Record when you were awake or asleep, day or night. Use the single words shown below. Mark a line to show when these things happened. Fill in your diary each morning as soon as you wake up, at lunch, supper, and when you go to bed. Hand in each page to your therapist each day as soon as you have completed it.

bed   = I went to bed or was in bed
nap   = I took a nap when it wasn't bedtime
wake   = I woke up or was awake
coffee = cup of coffee (mark the number of cups)
alcohol = beer, wine or liquor (number of drinks)

up   = I got up or was up
sleep   = I fell asleep
med   = I took medicine (mark which kind, how many)
tea   = cup of tea (mark the number of cups)
smoke   = (mark number of cigarettes)

The date today is _____

mid-night	1AM	2AM	3AM	4AM	5AM	6AM	7AM	8AM	9AM	10AM	11AM	noon	1PM	2PM	3PM	4PM	5PM	6PM	7PM	8PM	9PM	10PM	11PM	12PM

NOTES

FIGURE 2.6. Wake-sleep chart for self-monitoring.

38

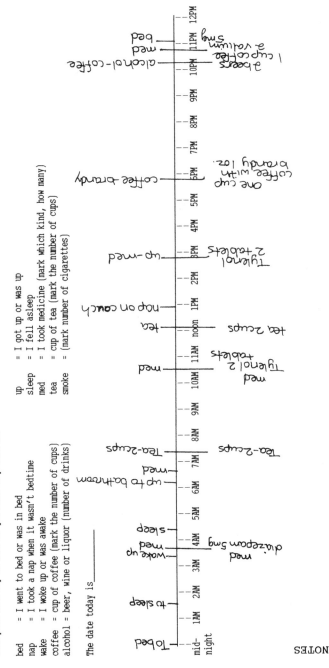

NAME _____ DATE STARTED _____ DATE FINISHED _____

Please fill in this diary for the next three days. Record when you were awake or asleep, day or night. Use the single words shown below. Mark a line to show when these things happened. Fill in your diary each morning as soon as you wake up, at lunch, supper, and when you go to bed. Hand in each page to your therapist each day as soon as you have completed it.

bed = I went to bed or was in bed
nap = I took a nap when it wasn't bedtime
wake = I woke up or was awake
coffee = cup of coffee (mark the number of cups)
alcohol = beer, wine or liquor (number of drinks)

up = I got up or was up
sleep = I fell asleep
med = I took medicine (mark which kind, how many)
tea = cup of tea (mark the number of cups)
smoke = (mark number of cigarettes)

The date today is _____

NOTES

FIGURE 2.7. Example of use of wake-sleep chart for self-monitoring.

39

NAME _____

DATE FROM _____ TO _____

SYMPTOM _____

TIME	INTENSITY (0-5)	SITUATION (place, with whom?)	WHAT WERE YOU DOING? (or taking medicine)	WHAT WERE YOU THINKING AND FEELING?
07:00				
08:00				
09:00				
10:00				
11:00				
noon				
1:00 PM				
2:00 PM				
3:00 PM				
4:00 PM				
5:00 PM				
6:00 PM				
7:00 PM				
8:00 PM				
9:00 PM				
10:00 PM				
11:00 PM				
midnight				

FIGURE 2.8. Self-monitoring diary.

therapy. Chronically ill individuals often have a low sense of self-efficacy; they do not expect that their efforts will be successful, so they do not initiate consistent coping behavior. If such patients can be induced to clearly specify a performance goal, even if the goal is a small one, their actions toward achieving it can be facilitated. When this is done, the sense of self-efficacy also improves, leading them to set further and more ambitious goals, leading in turn to further achievement. When the disability problems are fairly extensive, the success of therapy depends on first starting the process of identifying goals, then working toward some specific goal, and finally widening the focus to a variety of goals that represent a more comprehensive sample of meaningful activities that lead to a better quality of life. These principles are illustrated and elaborated in Figures 2.9 (self-monitoring goal chart) and 2.10 (an example of the use of this chart).

The goals are first categorized within broad groups; for example, health maintenance and promotion, social and family participation, avocational and personal interests, and work. They are then broken down into small steps that can be quantified, and stages; for example, preliminary therapy in clinic; skill acquisition in clinic; skill application at home, and at work without supervision. Initial goals (quotas) are set well within the patient's capacity, and then are steadily increased in a time-contingent manner; that is, not based on symptoms. However, self-efficacy is maximized if the agreement with the patient is that there will be a mechanism for regular review and revision of quotas at fixed intervals, at which time the amounts of the increments will be negotiated with the patient. The amount of the goals also has to bear a relationship to the amount of activity that would be reasonable for that individual to enjoy a good quality of life. It would be unreasonable to set the same walking goal for an elderly amputee bookkeeper as for a young hydro linesman. For example, in negotiating activity quotas for the upcoming week, the patient is told, "Last week, you were walking three blocks and you increased it to six by yesterday. How many do you think you would like to do next week? In the long-term, what is the minimum you will have to do to be satisfied with your function?"

BASIC PRINCIPLES OF
THERAPEUTIC CHANGE

Therapeutic Stance

The therapist's manner, beliefs, and attitude are what make up the therapeutic stance. Four categories of characteristics make up this therapeutic stance (Rubenstein, Bellissimo, & Watters, 1983):

```
GOALS FOR_____  FROM_____ TO_____
              (name)                    (date)        (date)
WHAT I DO NOW          WHAT I EXPECT     WHAT I EXPECT      MY LONG-TERM
                       NEXT WEEK         IN 6 WEEKS         GOALS
FITNESS AND HEALTH




MEDICATION



SOCIAL AND FAMILY



WORK



RECREATION
```

FIGURE 2.9. Goals chart.

1. The therapist's assumptions about the roles, rights, and responsibilities of the therapist and the patient.
2. The personal qualities of the therapist.
3. The theoretical frame of reference the therapist chooses.
4. The therapist's communication skills.

These influence the therapist's executive skills and the development of the therapeutic relationship. The usual doctor–patient relationship is necessary in certain clinical situations, but in others it may interfere with the process of recovery. For example, in cases where hypochondriasis and abuse of the medical services is the presenting problem, seeing a

GOALS FOR_____ FROM_____ TO_____			
(name)	(date)	(date)	
WHAT I DO NOW	WHAT I EXPECT NEXT WEEK	WHAT I EXPECT IN 6 WEEKS	MY LONG-TERM GOALS
FITNESS AND HEALTH			
3 situps 4 warmups 2 min. bicycle at 25 watts 2 laps of corridor weigh 195 lb. sleep 4-5 hours	5 situps 6 warmups 3 min. bike at 25 watts 6 laps of corridor lose 2 lb. go to bed regularly at 11 PM	15 situps 15 warmups 15 min. bike at 100 watts ½ mile walk lose 12 lb. no pills to sleep regular sleep time	keep fit sleep well weigh 160 lb.
MEDICATION			
50 mg Demerol 3X 10 mg Diazepam 3X Tylenol #3 6X Amitriptyline 200 mg alcohol to sleep	25 mg Demerol 3X 5 mg Diazepam 3X Tylenol #2 6X Amitriptyline 150 mg no alcohol to sleep	no pills no alcohol	no pills no alcohol
SOCIAL AND FAMILY			
I want to but I can't do anything at home.	Sit at table + talk to family ½ hr. per day. One card game this week.	Take son to ball game. Help kids with homework. Socialize with family.	Participate like a normal dad and husband.
WORK			
I can't work.	crafts - do ½ hr. twice daily first day and ½ hr. twice daily next week.	Be ready for work ½ time.	Full time work by June 16
RECREATION			
I can't exert myself at all anymore.	Discuss week-end plans with my family. Drive short distance.	Plan a vacation. Drive 50 miles and return.	Vacation together before year end.

FIGURE 2.10. Example of use of goals chart.

doctor in the traditional role will reinforce the dependency, regardless of whether the doctor credits the symptoms or pronounces the patient to be well. The traditional medical stance in which the doctor is the expert may fail to optimally engage the patient actively in his or her own treatment. It may fail to deliver satisfaction to the patient by appearing to promise too much. This may occur implicitly in the medical consultation situation, in which the doctor examines and then states a diagnosis and prescribes a cure. In fact, there are many disorders for which a cure is not possible and in which a rehabilitation model is more appropriate. As an extension of this problem, doctors may overtreat. When the patient is dissatisfied with the results of treatment, regardless of the organic status of the problem, the tendency is to prolong or increase drug therapy and other medical treatment. This occurs particularly with chronic pain patients and those with personality or behavioral disturbances.

If one were to take the example of alcoholism, it would be clear that traditional medicine can offer only supportive medical care, detoxification, treatment of intercurrent problems, and prescription of disulfiram. A different learning paradigm is needed to avoid the attitude of "doctor fix me," and instead to emphasize the idea of learning to take responsibility. Whereas the focus is on correcting pathology in much of medicine, the focus in behavioral medicine is on learning, which lends itself to the idea of gradual emancipation to responsible activity.

The following paradigms can be seen as analogies. One would not expect any of them to completely characterize the therapeutic alliance in behavioral medicine, but each is at various times apropos. In the series of paradigms presented below, there is a gradual shift

- of responsibility for the goals and for treatment from the therapist to the patient
- from seeing knowledge as esoteric to something as shared
- from dependency of the learner on the teacher to mutual cooperation.

The parent–child paradigm invests in the therapist the greatest responsibility for the goals, for the necessary knowledge, and for the solution to the problem. The patient is permitted to be dependent, and sometimes may be excused for his or her incapacity to function or to solve the problem. This paradigm characterizes the quality of roles that are most troublesome in the traditional medical and surgical model.

The teacher–student paradigm assumes that the relationship includes the responsibility on the part of the therapist to establish goals, and to teach and show, and, on the part of the patient, to learn. Failure would be attributed to both participants. It is assumed that the therapist has the greater knowledge. Dependency is permitted to some degree in the interests of learning, but the assumption is that there will be a graduation to a more mature level.

The coach–athlete paradigm allows less dependency, and shifts a greater amount of responsibility onto the patient to practice and master necessary skills. Goals are shared not equally, but mutually. The coach is responsible for guidance, but achievement can come only from the learner.

In the consultant–consultee relationship, the greater knowledge is still attributed to the therapist, but the patient is seen as fully responsible for initiating the learning, identifying the goals, acquiring the skills, and applying the information. The consultant remains responsible for providing authoritative guidance. In some ways, the dependency is even reversed because the consultant is a respected employee of the consultee.

Therapeutic Traps

Considering the above, it is useful to examine some of the situations in which the therapeutic stance is important (see also Sternbach, 1974).

Situation 1. Patients who are chronically symptomatic, such as those with chronic headache, may have hidden reasons for their problems that go beyond the presenting symptoms. The trap is when the therapist assumes that his or her skills are better than those of all the others.

Doctor: You are right, Mrs. A., all the other doctors missed the real diagnosis. You are clearly suffering from a case of. . . . Take this treatment and see me in a month.

This usually leads to a return visit, with an unimproved patient:

Patient: All right, what are you going to do for me now?

If finally every proposed treatment fails, the doctor then can be induced to write a letter to the pension fund certifying the patient's profound and permanent disability. It would have been better if the doctor had reacted in the first instance as follows:

Doctor: Your problem has really become chronic, and trying all the remedies again is only going to make you more frustrated and worse. It's time to work together to start looking at what you can do, rather than expecting that a new doctor is going to do something new to fix you.

Situation 2. A patient presents as angry and blaming other doctors, the Worker's Compensation Board, and so forth. The consultant doctor might perceive the potential for trouble and may also behave in a passive-aggressive manner.

Consultant: I feel so sorry for you! I'll send a letter to your family doctor and to the Worker's Compensation Board.

After agreeing with the patient that the family doctor and others are behaving in a shoddy manner to him or her, the consultant then arranges that the patient not return and writes a consultation letter in which the patient is made out to be a fake and scoundrel. The consultant should have reacted as follows:

Consultant: You are not only having symptoms, but you are also angry to the point that it is making you unhappy. I can't do anything about all the unpleasant things that have happened, but if you are willing, we can set goals for improving your future, rather than getting stuck in all the past problems that make you so angry.

Situation 3. Doctors and therapists enjoy success. A feeling of omnipotence, engendered by a dependent patient, can be seductively attractive. If one takes the example of someone who is not necessarily clinging, but tending to idealize the doctor, it is not hard to see that this could lead to extra visits, and extra attention, as in permitting phone calls for advice, or unscheduled office visits. On the face of it, some of this might seem warranted for a fragile patient, but it may perpetuate the problem that it seeks to resolve and foster a messiah complex in the doctor. This can lead to overtreatment and protection of the patient's fragility, and eventually to the doctor becoming frustrated and abruptly discontinuing the patient's treatment if the dependency becomes too great. There is no quick solution, but the beginning of the right road is for the therapist to recognize the situation.

Patient: Doctor, you are so clever! I feel so much better when I see you. My regular doctor doesn't understand me. What should I do when. . . ?

Instead of falling into the trap, it would be better for the doctor to head off the problem.

Doctor: It is comforting to trust someone, but it is even better to trust yourself. Up to now you have hoped you could depend on the doctor because you certainly didn't have confidence in yourself. If we work together, one of your goals will have to be to gain confidence in your own ability. In your visits with me, we will work on ways for you to become more independent.

Situation 4. Some patients with chronic illness remain somatically focused and refuse to accept the psychological dimension to their disability. They characteristically demand relief and accept only physical and symptom-oriented interventions.

Patient: What are you going to do for my unbearable pain? What are you going to do if that doesn't work?

If the suggestion is made that too many sleeping pills, sedatives, or painkillers are unhealthy, the patient's response may be one of the following:

Patient: Why do you want to let me suffer when all you have to do is. . . ?

Dr. Erudite at the Famous Policlinic in North Overshoe said that I could have codeine (so where do you get off telling me that I can't!)

The doctor may fall into a trap and give an inappropriate response.

Doctor: All right, I'll prescribe it only this once, but you know that this is bad for you!

This scenario can be repeated regularly. It is not easy to get the patient to change his or her focus, but change must begin with the doctor.

Doctor: If those things had been working satisfactorily, you would not have come here. I am willing to help in many ways—to help you attain a better quality of life, to help you become more fit, to help you cope or count on yourself—but I am unwilling to repeat short-term solutions that don't help in the long run.

If the patient insists that it is pain relief or nothing, the doctor can respond as follows:

Doctor: I can understand that what I am saying may seem rather different and hard to accept at first, but I will lay out the options for you, give you a chance to think about it, and see you again.

Situation 5. The anxious patient, overwhelmed by symptoms and multiple coping problems, can sometimes provoke overtreatment by the doctor. Frequently the doctor may panic and abruptly stop seeing the patient, or allow the patient's care to become fragmented by engaging in multiple investigations and specialist referrals. The referrals to orthopedic surgeons and internists may omit critical data regarding the psychological factors in the problem, with the hidden wish that the patient will be placated and suitably occupied with a different doctor for a while. The result of the chain of investigations and consultations is that the patient becomes even more convinced that there is something serious being missed. The consultants are likely to give the patient the reputation of a crank and no longer take the problem seriously, and some of the investigations and treatments may eventually do damage. In the meantime, the original problems of anxiety and coping problems are neglected and aggravated. This confirms the patient as an incurable cripple. The best treatment is prevention, but it is essential to "distinguish the forest from the trees": The real issue is the chronic state of not being in control of one's health.

Doctor: It's evident that your health is no better despite months of looking for the right diagnosis, the right cure, or the right doctor. Given the results you've had so far, if we do more of the same you're going to get the same disappointing results. At this point you have a choice. You can keep getting the same frustrating results from each new doctor, or you can accept the symptoms as chronic and starting getting control of your life, counting on yourself, being free of treatments that don't work, and changing the things that can be changed.

This can lead to a discussion of what behavioral medicine has to offer.

There are seven points to heed if the therapist does not want to self-destruct:

1. The therapist must have enough self-esteem to be able to tolerate frustration in clinical progress. He or she must recognize that it is the patient who has the problem, not the therapist. Otherwise, there may be a tendency for the therapist to require improvement and approval of the patient to affirm the therapist's own worth. Patients are often angry and may provoke a negative counter-transference from the therapist. Likewise, some patients may systematically project all of their anger about failure onto the therapist.

Patient: Doc, I've been coming to your treatment now just like you said, and I feel worse! Are you sure you know what you're doing?

The therapist must respond with discipline and self-esteem.

Doctor: I hear you. It sounds like you are feeling pretty frustrated and are afraid that this is going to be another failure experience. In fact, you were pretty upset about failures even before you got to me. Now hear me. You are less a failure than you sometimes think you are. It feels like failure because you go back to looking at the wrong outcomes. You already knew that you were still going to have your bad times, and if you want to win back your health, it's going to be a struggle, but you are working at what you *can* do and on beating your disability. Look at what your goals are and what you're doing.

2. The therapist then has to be absolutely clear that the criteria for success cannot be subjective. That does not mean that subjective symptoms such as pain do not count, but it does mean that to make progress the focus is on what you do, not on what you feel. The tendency is for the patient to return to the symptoms and take this as evidence for being unchanged or worse. The therapist is always in an educator role, showing the patient that success is not measured in the difficulty of the struggle, but in the real progress of behavior changed, skills learned, and coping achieved.

3. The therapist's position must be completely unambiguous. It includes having empathy for the patient's struggle to become well, not pity for his or her symptoms.

4. The therapist must continually focus the patient's attention on what can be done, not on what cannot be done. You can tell the patient, "To become depressed and feel hopeless in two easy lessons, attend to all the things that can't be changed to the exclusion of things you *can* do, and ignore the small steps toward improvement as being insignificant."

5. Some specific practice is needed in confronting helpless, angry, dependent, invalid, projecting, or similar illness behavior, examples of which are given in the situations above. To a great extent, this requires experience, but the key is recognition of the illness transactions, and a ready response. There is much to be said for the value of rehearsal of scenarios in order for the therapist to learn these techniques. This can be done in seminars, supervision, or inservice supervision.

6. Therapists must be sure not to make a contract for magic. Patients are not cured just because they go along with the therapist and do what they are told. Becoming well depends on the patient's assuming ownership of the disability and responsibility for specific goal-directed action to regain control of health.

7. The control issues need to be given prominence in behavioral medicine. Getting control of one's life and health, controlling one's ability rather than being governed by disability, attributing success to oneself when there is gradual progress, and not interpreting frustration or obstacles as proof of failure are all attitudes that have to be taught. A significant part of behavioral medicine is the molding of attitudes that promote coping. (See also Bellissimo & Tunks, 1984, pp. 158–159.)

Therapeutic Practice

In anticipation of the chapters that address the actual clinical problems and treatment, it is opportune to state some guidelines that apply to all psychotherapeutic practice.

Therapeutic change is based on some kind of learning in the interpersonal situation. This learning occurs through interventions that help to enhance the patient's sense of personal efficacy. Contributions to this sense of efficacy come from actual experiences of accomplishment, vicarious experiences, verbal persuasion or education, techniques that lead to control of autonomic arousal, and interactions of any of the above ingredients (Bandura, 1977).

The patient–therapist relationship is a primary consideration. Therapeutic success does not come from some mechanical application of a treatment prescription. In that sense, we do not believe that self-help programs based on written or taped material alone are helpful unless there is also an ingredient of therapist contact.

Change depends on the opportunity for new learning. Therapy addresses this need by provision of new experiences that are structured for therapeutic purposes. Talk and action are both necessary. Thus, we emphasize the active participation of the patient in every aspect of intervention; from assessment to planning, doing, and evaluating the therapy. Human dilemmas exist in the dimensions of thought, behavior, and emotion. Therapy must affect each of these dimensions.

Symptoms are uninterpretable outside of the context of their psychosocial contexts. Treatment is ineffective unless it recognizes the context and makes use of it. Changes in therapeutic strategy may be necessary. The treatment cannot be approached inflexibly, nor according to the narrow principles of one therapeutic school. However, the general principles of a particular theoretical orientation can help to organize a coherent treatment program.

Part II
Clinical Intervention:
Assessment and Treatment

Authors' Comments on the
Clinical Chapters

The following chapters deal with the assessment and treatment of particular disorders and specific problems that can benefit from behavioral medicine approaches. We have organized the information in each clinical chapter around a common frame of reference. Therefore, each chapter has the same format and subdivisions, which we hope will lead to quicker study and easier recall. We recognize that most clinicians treat a variety of problems and that it is helpful to have a consistent framework to guide conceptualization, data collection and assessment, and the various phases of clinical intervention. Each chapter begins with an illustration of the problem and a summary of relevant data. A chart then sketches the relationships between the cognitive, biological, emotional, and behavioral factors. This sketch is intended to be a conceptual and memory aid in gathering data for assessment and in categorizing the elements in intervention. Through this diagram, we do not intend to be simplistic about the relationship between these various factors. Although a similar sketch format is common to all the chapters, the content in each is tailored to the specific problem. Each chapter details the treatment approach, and gives tables, charts, and material that the patient may use. The overall conceptual framework is summarized in Figure A. A Selected Reading section is included at the end of the book, which provides references of where to find information relevant to individual chapters.

CLINICAL SYNDROME

It is useful to think of a presenting complaint not as an isolated complaint or in respect only to a specific pathological diagnosis, but as

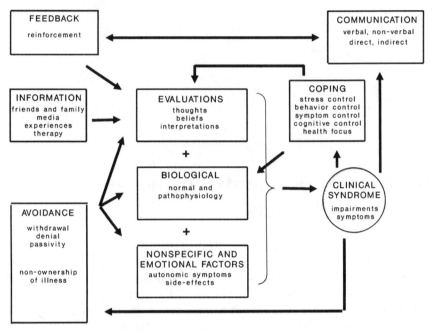

FIGURE A. Algorithm for behavioral medicine.

being part of a system of biological substrates, cognitions, emotions, behaviors, communications, and environmental conditions. A behavioral medicine intervention may address any of these levels, and not strictly the biological level, which is the prime target of traditional medicine and surgery.

The presenting complaint exists as the focal point for the entire illness experience. It is influenced by the interaction of evaluations, biological substrates, emotional state, and nonspecific symptoms.

EVALUATIONS

Evaluations have to do with the cognitive appraisals that an individual has, especially with regard to the illness. This includes self-statements: "I am ill"; "this is/is not serious"; "this is caused by . . ."; "this particular sensation that I am feeling is/is not a part of my illness." Evaluations can be right or wrong and deliberate, more or less consciously held, or automatic. They may be taught or corrected, and might be part of efforts to cope. Much of the therapeutic activity in behavioral medicine is aimed at changing erroneous or problematic modes of evaluating one's illness. There are various techniques to achieve this. The clinician can teach the patient to self-monitor his or her thoughts about the problem, identify which thoughts are self-defeating or anxiety provoking, and then systematically alter them in order to practice a more positive mental attitude. Another approach would be to practice specific coping techniques in a nonthreatening situation, and introduce practice in coping with both imagined and real stressful conditions using these learned techniques. A third method would be to provide information to patients, giving guidelines as to how they can achieve mastery over their problems. This provision of education is an active process in which the patient is engaged in discussion either in a group or directly with the therapist. Doubts and anxieties about the problem and its treatment are exposed, and procedures for self-evaluation and self-monitoring give a sense of ownership and control. The information to patients technique is chosen in this book, but the other techniques could also be applied at the clinician's discretion.

The actual process of using this information can take several forms. One would be to form a patient group in which some sessions are devoted to lectures about the problem and discussions among the members before assigning self-monitoring and behavior-change tasks. Another way would be to provide the patient information as reading material and have the patient return for a discussion of what was learned and understood, using the sessions mainly for exploration and for learning techniques. Still another way is for the clinician to engage the patient in a one-to-one therapeutic conversation. As the patient gives expression to his or her anxieties and recounts the events of the week, the therapist uses these things as stimuli to initiate discussions that reevaluate the disorder.

BIOLOGICAL SUBSTRATES

In behavioral medicine, biological substrate is not limited to the pathophysiological territory usually studied in traditional medicine, but, rather involves the application of relevant techniques that modify the impact of biological and autonomic systems on the experience of being ill. For example, relaxation therapy may be used to modify the physical and autonomic responses that perpetuate distress.

OTHER FACTORS CONTRIBUTING TO THE SYNDROME

Emotional states and motivation affect both the quality and the probability of action. Emotion includes elements of interpretation and thought, motivational arousal, and biological status. In the behavioral medicine perspective, the emotional factors of importance are anxiety, the motivational and evaluative problems associated with depression, and emotional distress resulting from somatic symptoms.

Nonspecific symptoms is a concept intended to mean sources of experience (sensory, cognitive, and emotional) that are not directly related to the mechanism of the clinical disorder, but become part of the whole illness experience and are likely to be evaluated by the patient as part of the illness. A headache sufferer may end up taking large quantities of codeine, which produces nausea and sweatiness. The patient perceives these symptoms as part of the headache. A chronic back pain sufferer has trouble sleeping, and develops a nonrestorative sleep pattern. This results in a feeling of general achiness, fatigue, and irritability, especially in the morning. The patient attributes this to a spread or aggravation of the back pain. Depression, anxiety, or resentment are all strong negative emotions that are commonly found in people who suffer chronic disabilities such as chronic pain, and that modify both the biological substrate of illness and the perception of being ill.

AVOIDANCE OR FLIGHT

Avoidance or flight behaviors are certain behavioral and cognitive events that occur, usually at a habitual level, in chronic illness. They are distinct from attempts to cope, and involve denial, withdrawal, inactivity, avoidance through abuse of drugs or alcohol, physical guarding and spasm, overprotected and therefore dysfunctional movement such as limping or moving stiffly, or avoidance of activity that provokes anxiety. This results in aggravation of the symptoms.

COPING

Coping refers to the specific behaviors that are aimed at stimulus control, behavioral control, and environmental control. It is understood that coping is active, that it may be more or less adaptive or successful, is subject to volition but is not always done with full awareness, may or may not be habitual, and can be learned. These factors affect the illness experience and evaluation.

COMMUNICATION

Communication is a particular part of behavior in which the patient conveys meaning about the illness verbally or nonverbally, and more or less directly or clearly. It is understood that communication is aimed at an audience (but that the patient is also perceiving his or her own communication, and the patient's self-evaluations are affected by perceiving these communications).

RESPONSES

Responses from others may be verbal or behavioral, direct or indirect, and clear or unclear. They are mainly potential reinforcers of the patient's behaviors; verbal responses from others (especially family or doctors) many times influence the patient's evaluation of his or her problem.

INFORMATION

It is important in many cases to recognize that the origin of the symptom complex may have begun with an injury or illness. Although the symptoms and behavioral problems may have become chronic and self-perpetuating, the patient might fear that the original cause is still present and be afraid to abandon the quest for doctors to investigate, or be reluctant to give up inappropriate medication use, unless these fears are put to rest. There is a section in each chapter in which information for patients is given. The purpose is to provide a basis from which the clinician may prepare lecture notes or handouts in layman's language to assist their patients in reevaluating their problems in a more hopeful manner. Provision of information for patients is intended to stimulate the patients to discard their existing fears, beliefs, and feelings of helplessness. The basic concepts of this reevaluation process were discussed earlier in chapter 1 in the section on "Acute Versus Chronic."

Chapter 3

Clinical Procedures: Relaxation, Biofeedback, and Cognitive Coping

We will discuss some specific treatment procedures in this chapter that are applicable to various clinical problems. Three of these procedures—relaxation, biofeedback, and cognitive coping—are discussed briefly. The focus of this chapter, however, is to give clinicians detailed information about the actual process of putting these procedures into practice. It is not our intention to encourage application in a cookbook fashion, but rather to give enough details to permit the clinician to adapt these treatment procedures to a variety of clinical situations.

Patients need adaptive concepts (language) to evaluate their illness and health state, and they need specific procedural instructions to take an active part in dealing with their problems. This education input is not intended to be a substitute for professional help, but to encourage patients to become active participants in their health care. The educational process includes the following four elements.

1. There is an emphasis toward helping patients share the responsibility for health management with the professional. Patients can be maximally helpful to themselves if they have basic knowledge about the problem in question, have some understanding about the purpose and process of change, and implement the procedures for change under the guidance of the clinician.

2. Emphasis is placed on looking for sources of stress both within the patients and in their environment. The patients can be guided to appreciate that their symptoms and distress are not just things that happen to them, but are also thoughts they think and things they do.

59

They can learn that they are part of their own environment, that they are constantly surrounded by stimuli, and that their responses lead to new stimuli. They learn that they become vulnerable by being in excessive and prolonged stress-inducing situations or by not having the physical and psychological resources or techniques needed to deal with the demands.

3. Being well cannot depend just on the physician's cures as traditionally given. Emphasis on health-promoting and illness-preventing activities is the key to wellness.

4. Growth in health depends on learning from one's own experiences and developing one's own coping skills.

RELAXATION EXERCISES

Relaxation procedures are the most commonly used specific treatment techniques in behavioral medicine. They are used either as the main treatment or as an adjunct to other procedures. A state of relaxation or low arousal, usually referred to as the relaxation response, in contrast to the fight-or-flight response, can be achieved using a variety of training procedures. The most frequently used relaxation training methods in clinical practice are as follows:

1. Physical relaxation techniques
   a. Progressive muscle relaxation
   b. Physical exercise (as in t'ai chi for example)
2. Imaginal exercises
   a. Autogenic training
   b. Imagery
   c. Sensory awareness
   d. Passive progressive muscle relaxation
   e. Conditioned cue relaxation
   f. Meditation
3. Hypnosis
   a. Therapist-directed
   b. Self-directed
4. Biofeedback-assisted methods
   a. Electromyography (EMG)
   b. Temperature
   c. Pulse volume
   d. Electroencephalography (EEG)
   e. Galvanic skin response (GSR)
   f. Visceral monitoring

The common underlying features found in these procedures have been summarized by Benson (1975):

1. The restriction of attention to a mental device is characteristic. Patients are guided to attend to specific events such as breathing, biofeedback signal, and physiological sensations.
2. A permissive and receptive attitude is required. Specific instructions are given to attend to the procedure and changes are allowed to happen. Patients are not expected to have identical subjective experiences during relaxation.
3. A quiet environment is the desired setting for training.
4. The explicit goals of decreased muscle tone, relaxed breathing, and quiet mind are pursued. This is either built directly into the actual instructions or is implied by the procedure.

In addition to the above basic concepts, some procedural guidelines help to achieve successful training.

1. Provide the patient with a rationale for the training to be undertaken. This should include the idea that the patient is embarking on the task of learning a new skill, just like playing a musical instrument or learning a new sport. This would explain the need for time and practice in order for the skill to develop. The patient therefore goes through a process of training where the routine entails (a) instructions, (b) concentration and practice, and (c) feedback.
2. Set the occasion for relaxation training as a daily routine. This should include the appropriate time and place that offer comfort and privacy. Patients will not relax and practice if there are curious family and children standing about, or if there are distractions.
3. Prepare the patient for increased awareness of bodily sensations such as floating, tingling, or perceptual distortions. "You will experience in some way a heightened awareness of your body. People experience the relaxed sensations in different ways, but whatever you experience is right for you." For some patients, experiencing deep relaxation may at first be alarming. It may accentuate the drowsiness experienced from medication the patient is taking, and for others may lead to expression of anxiety or tearfulness, or recollection of past distressing experiences, or create altered states of physiological functioning. In all of these conditions the patient is to be reassured that this is a good sign because it means that whereas before a lot of energy was being used to suppress these feelings, now it will be possible to learn to be more relaxed inwardly. The clinician should be aware, however, that occasionally one encounters an anxious patient who is actually on the verge of a psychotic episode. Such a patient might respond to attempted relaxation with a sense of loss of contact with reality, fears of losing control, paranoid interpretation of the relaxation, or other florid psychiatric

symptoms. This type of marked response should prompt the clinician to complete the mental status examination before continuing. After ruling out a serious psychiatric problem, the clinician should recognize that an anxious patient, who reacts with alarm to a relaxation technique, needs more concrete procedures, structure, and support, with relaxation being introduced gradually. For this purpose, the Jacobson technique (1938) is probably most suitable.

4. Address the issue of control. Some patients initially fear that letting go will lead to losing control. They need to be told that relaxing the tension is the best way to control tension and the effects of tension.

5. Model and demonstrate the procedures. Do the relaxation yourself while you are teaching the patient. The patient can observe and then mimic the steps. You can then encourage, reinforce, and give specific feedback to the patient.

6. Set up a series of application sessions in which the patient learns brief relaxation techniques (with eyes open and sitting), and then rehearses how the relaxation might be applied in a variety of day-to-day situations.

7. Through monitored home practice, weekly encouragement, and reviews of progress, transfer the skills to the home for autonomous practice.

SPECIFIC RELAXATION
TRAINING PROCEDURES

In the following section, we present detailed relaxation scripts. In addition, in the Selected Reading section at the back of the book references are given for resources that contain detailed discussions and step-by-step instructions for relaxation training. The first script follows the tradition of Jacobson (1938), emphasizing neuromuscular relaxation. The second illustrates therapist instructions for progressive relaxation, emphasizing breathing, sensory awareness, imagery, and promoting rapid induction in subsequent sessions. Of course, these can be altered or combined to fit the needs of the particular patient and style of the therapist.

The Jacobson technique is the best self-directed method. Patients need to know that they do not have to go through it in any special order, and they can change the elements. The key is to demonstrate it once or twice with the patient, and follow up to make sure there are no problems. Some patients like to have an audiotape. Music without words, or nature sounds with an unstructured, arrhythmic pace and calm associations, are favorites with some people. Some like meditation, focusing on one mental word that they say over and over in their minds.

PROGRESSIVE MUSCLE RELAXATION TRAINING (JACOBSON TECHNIQUE)

Rationale

The skill of relaxing using the progressive muscle relaxation procedure is probably the easiest to teach to patients for home use, and proficiency can be acquired by anyone with sufficient instruction and practice. The focus on physical tension and relaxation gives excellent proprioceptive feedback and helps focus the attention.

Once learned, the technique can be streamlined and varied, condensed, and made portable to a wide variety of situations. Although this procedure has been used to help people overcome chronic anxiety, physical tension and pains, and insomnia, our focus here will be to reduce the effects of everyday stress.

Getting Ready

(The following instructions should be given to the patient at the initiation of relaxation training.)

Place: Find a place where you have privacy and are free from distraction.

Position: Take a comfortable position where you have support for all parts of your body (e.g., reclining chair, bed with extra pillows for the shoulders and beneath the knees, or carpet with two pillows beneath the head and shoulders and three beneath the knees, or lying on your side in a partially curled up position with one pillow between the knees and one or two for the head).

Clothing: Clothing should be loose and comfortable.

Time: You should take 20 to 30 minutes daily at first. Pick a fixed time every day so that it will not be forgotten: morning before rising, coffee break, lunch, before supper, evening, right before sleep.

Attitude: Be open and prepared to experience what is natural and comes spontaneously for you. Do not worry about trying to experience exactly what you hear from other patients. You have your own body and your own experiences. However, the therapist will given you some clues about what to look for.

The key: You will learn to notice the particular sensations that come from letting go of tension; you will do this by tightening muscles and tensing your breathing muscles, and then relaxing everything so that you can feel the difference.

Tightening: Tighten your muscles and hold your breath until you can feel tension in your body and feel like you want to breathe out and relax. Notice what the tension feels like.

Relaxation: Now relax your muscles as you relax and breathe out, and notice the changed feeling of relaxation. Always relax your muscles as you breathe out and notice the feeling.

Awareness: As you continue, notice how the relaxed feeling spreads and increases.

Keeping Track

(Using a diary such as the one illustrated in Figure 3.1, the patient is asked to monitor the use, application, and results of the relaxation procedure.) As you practice, be patient, because everyone learns at a different pace. Keep track of your progress in the relaxation diary. This will give you feedback and clues that will help you to get better at this technique. In this diary, record the rating of your tension (uptightness) before and after each session; 0 means the most relaxed you have ever been and 10 means the most nervous.

Therapist Script

(The script is to be spoken slowly, comfortably, and clearly. This can be facilitated if the therapist is going through the relaxation exercise at the same time. The therapist can remain sitting.)

"Lie back, get comfortable, loosen any tight clothing. You can close your eyes . . . and notice . . . your breathing. Now I want you to give a number to the tension you feel right now; 0 means no tension and 10 means the worst tension, so pick a number from 0 to 10 for your tension. Make a mental note of that number. Later you will probably be surprised to see how your tension changes. Now, I'm going to ask you to tense certain muscles and study the feelings in them. Pay attention to how they feel when they are tense and then when you let the tension flow out of them.

"You may start with making a fist; clenching your right hand and tensing the muscles of the hand and forearm. Keep all the other muscles resting. Notice the feeling in the back of your hands and your knuckles, the feeling of your fingers in your palm, the pressure, and maybe even tension wanting to go

NAME _____

DATE FROM _____ TO _____

DAY	TIME	WHERE WERE YOU?	WHAT WAS HAPPENING?	HOW DID YOU RELAX?	ANXIETY AT BEGINNING (0 TO 10)	ANXIETY AT END (0 TO 10)	HOW MIGHT YOU IMPROVE YOUR RELAXATION NEXT TIME?

FIGURE 3.1. Self-monitoring diary for relaxation exercise therapy.

up your forearm (wait 3 to 5 seconds). Now open your hand and completely let go and notice the feeling . . . as you relax and let the tension flow out of your fist and forearm. Study the feeling in your arm and hand as they relax more and more. Maybe you notice already some warmth, heaviness, or tingling. In a little while you will be noticing that feeling starting to expand through other parts of your body, too (wait 10 to 20 seconds and repeat the above step of tension and relaxation with both the fists and forearms).

"Now tighten the muscles of your upper arms, your biceps, like you were going to make a muscle or lift a heavy weight. Notice the tension going all the way from your elbows to your shoulders. Hold it (5 seconds), and now release it. Relax and notice how good it feels to let that tension go. You may already have begun to notice the growing comfort in the front and back muscles of your upper arm and into your shoulder, just like the relaxed feeling that is growing in your hands and forearms (wait 10 to 20 seconds and repeat the above step for both upper arms).

"Frown and wrinkle your nose as strongly as you can. Notice the tension. Hold it . . . and now release it and notice the difference. Notice how the forehead muscles become smooth and your face and eyes relaxed (wait 10 to 20 seconds). Now gradually let your eyes drift just a little open, and notice how it feels when you control the tension in the muscles of your face. You can let your eyes close gently now, just like you do when you are asleep. Notice your hands and arms, how they are continuing to relax. You will see how this relaxed feeling can spread all through your body.

"Force your tongue against the roof of your mouth and notice the tension all through your lower jaw, into the neck below the jaw, and even a bit into your throat. Hold it . . . and now relax, letting your tongue fall to the floor of your mouth and letting your teeth be a little bit apart with your lips just barely closed (wait 10 to 20 seconds and repeat).

"Raise your shoulders toward your ears as if you were shrugging. Hold them up as tightly as you can, and notice the tension in your neck, shoulders, and upper back. Now relax, letting your shoulder muscles be completely supported. Let them sag down so that there is no tension at all, and feel the difference (wait 10 to 20 seconds and repeat).

"Take a breath now, filling your lungs about 3/4 full, and hold it. Just keep holding it for awhile. You will notice the tension gradually increasing between your ribs in all the chest muscles, into your upper back and diaphragm in the upper part of your belly. In a moment, when you slowly release the breath, breathing quietly through your mouth and nose, you will notice how the tension seems to flow out of you. Now slowly and gently release the breath until your chest seems fully relaxed. You don't have to push the air out – just let it come out until your chest feels perfectly at rest, and notice how for a moment you don't even feel the need to take another breath because your chest muscles have relaxed. Now take another breath, filling your lungs about 3/4 full, and hold it. Just keep holding it for awhile. Notice again the tension gradually increasing between your ribs in all the chest muscles, into your upper back and diaphragm in the upper part of your belly. Now slowly and gently release the breath until your chest seems fully relaxed.

"Now as we continue, you are going to find it very helpful to use this principle. Every time you contract your muscles from now on, take a breath and hold it, too. Then as you relax your muscles, relax your chest and breathe out at the same time. You will be surprised how much this will help you to increase your relaxation. Notice how the relaxation is already spreading through your arms and shoulders, your neck and face, and your chest.

"Fill your lungs half full of air and tighten your tummy muscles and push the small of your back firmly down into the floor or back of the chair, and hold your tummy as tight as you can. As you hold that tension, you can feel it from your chest, through your tummy and lower back, right down into your bottom. Hold it . . . and then breathe out and relax your tummy and back . . . letting go of all that tension, just letting the weight of your body sink down without any effort, and notice the relaxed feeling (wait 10 seconds, then repeat this step with the abdomen and lower back).

"Now take a breath and hold it while you draw your knees up to you, bent at the hips and knees, and tighten the muscles. Hold those muscles as tight as you can. Notice the tension all the way from your chest and waist down to your ankles. You can learn to control this tension. Relax now, letting your knees drop down again as you breathe out, letting your whole body become limp and relaxed, and notice the difference when you are relaxed. I wonder if you have noticed how relaxed your whole body is becoming – your arms, shoulders and neck, head, jaws, and face, chest, breathing, and legs. And with each breath out, you can notice how the rest of your body relaxes a little more. Notice that now, as you breathe in and out, gently and slowly. Each part of your body becoming more relaxed with each breath. In and out. In and out (repeat the above step again).

"Why don't you take a breath and tighten up your toes as if you are picking up a pencil with them. Hold the tension. It is really hard to hold this tension for very long. Relax your feet now, as you also let the rest of your legs relax. Think of how much better you will feel if you find a way to relax your feet and ankles (after 10 to 20 seconds, repeat this step).

"(Quietly pause for 20 to 30 seconds.) Take a few moments now to notice all your muscles . . . and your breathing . . . how each time you breathe out, you can become a bit more relaxed. Notice the relaxed feeling in your hands . . . in your arms . . . in your head and face . . . in your jaws and neck . . . your teeth slightly apart . . . your breath very relaxed and automatic. You don't need any effort. The relaxed feeling in your tummy . . . your back . . . your thighs and knees . . . your legs and feet, and even your toes.

"Use your scale from 0 to 10 to pick a number that reflects your relaxation now, and notice how much you have improved it from the time you started. Think of how much benefit it will be when you have had more time to practice and really make this a part of your life. You might realize that when you get up from relaxing, it can be a bit like waking slowly from a refreshing sleep, so you might want to wake up a bit at a time . . . moving your feet and legs . . . now your hands and arms . . . now your eyes can gently drift open as soon as they wish. Then when you feel like it, you can get yourself up to a sitting position."

THERAPIST-DIRECTED RELAXATION PROCEDURE

Rationale

The perpetuation of tension has much to do with not being aware of it, and therefore not taking control of it. In reality, tension is something you do, but if you simply take the tense feeling for granted and assume you cannot control it, then it is likely that the tense habit will continue. The following relaxation procedures put the focus on imagery, attention to relaxation proprioceptions, and breathing control.

This technique may be preferable for some patients who suffer musculoskeletal pain because the contraction-relaxation routine of the Jacobson technique is avoided. However, other people may prefer the Jacobson technique. For example, an asthmatic may be anxious about his breathing, and focusing on breathing may just make this worse; that patient might prefer the Jacobson technique, which focuses away from the breathing sensations.

An advantage of this next procedure is that it can be practiced in modified and contracted forms without being obvious, even in the presence of observers. This offers advantages to a patient who needs to relax five or six times a day for 1- or 2-minute periods to maintain control over tension.

Getting Ready

The initial conditions are as with the Jacobson technique. The key is that tension is active, and controlling it is also active. The relaxation activity, however, is not an effort. It involves being attentive and permitting the relaxed feeling to develop by setting the right conditions. Along with the comfortable body posture, the subject is instructed to, "Get yourself comfortable and relax." But then the emphasis is, ". . . . to not necessarily move or do anything. You can lie there perfectly still, but still notice lots of things. . . ."

Keeping Track

People who need this technique are often too focused on symptoms. It is best to focus the attention only on the positive aspects of the experience. In general, allusions to discomforts or pains are not made. There is no doubt raised about whether the subject will succeed to relax. There is a permissive set of instructions so that whatever the subject actually experiences is reinforced; feeling heavy, light, distant, floating, and so forth. Any self-monitoring is directed only to two areas. One is the duration and the method of relaxing (sitting, lying, eyes open, eyes closed, etc.). The other is directed at the daily situations in which the technique can be or has been applied, with self-monitoring of what it was that most enabled the application to be successful. Patients are discouraged from recording things such as, "relaxation unsuccessful." Instead, they are encouraged to record what they did and how they might improve it next time (see Figure 3.1).

Therapist Scripts

(The following paragraphs illustrate instructions that may be given to the patient.)

"I'm sure you would like to learn to feel more relaxed. I wonder how surprised you're going to be when you discover how much easier it becomes with a little practice. Perhaps you already know that you can enjoy the feeling that comes with completely relaxing your body and your mind. You don't have to do anything at all; you don't have to move, or even speak. Just make yourself comfortable by sitting back in the chair, or lying back, and in the next few minutes allow yourself to become aware of the relaxed feeling."

First Relaxation Session

"I'm sure you can remember a time when you felt completely relaxed, felt good. You might remember that you were resting, or perhaps just sitting or lying there as you are now. Perhaps you noticed that your eyes were blinking, and each time they blinked, they felt good, so you let them close just a little longer, just as you might want to do now. As you lay there and felt that particular feeling that people feel when they've been sitting back, taking a deep breath, and just relaxing, you might have noticed how good it felt, just for a moment, to let your eyes close, like that. You probably have already noticed the feeling, with your eyes relaxed and closed, that many times you could sit back for a moment and let your tensions go. You likely have realized already that your breathing is becoming more regular and slow, how good it feels to let your breathing become completely relaxed without any effort, to let each breath come and go, coming and going as it seems most natural for you. You may have noticed already that particular feeling that is associated with relaxing, like when you feel drowsy, or when you're sitting there, or lying back, that feeling of your arms and legs being very relaxed, so that with each breath you allow your hands, your arms, your head and your shoulders, your back and your legs, each in turn to become a little more relaxed. You might be aware of that feeling in your right index finger, and as you notice that, in the palm of your hand, too. Then you notice your whole hand, and the other hand, and your hands as far as the wrists; that feeling in your hands, and in your elbow; that particular feeling now, along your arm, and up to your shoulder, noticing it with each relaxing breath, in and out, more and more, becoming more aware. You might be a little surprised in noticing it, and find your mind for a minute wondering, realizing with each thought crossing your mind that it doesn't really matter, because, being aware of that particular feeling now as you become more aware, you realize that your hands, your breathing, your legs and arms can feel very good and relaxed."

Using Imagery for Deepening Relaxation

"I'm sure sometimes you have had a favorite place outdoors where you liked to be by yourself and were really relaxed. It would be hard to stop thinking about a pleasant place like that. You might even see it when your eyes are closed, or just remember how good it felt to be there. If you were in that quiet place by yourself, you might find yourself walking, drifting, past the tranquil familiar things you like to see. The things you feel and hear all seem so clear when you can be there by yourself: the colors, how it would smell, the feel of the air, the dark and lightness. I wonder if you realize how many times you have drifted along and didn't even notice your feet touching the ground. You can still be aware of that feeling of being at peace. And as you quietly passed the tranquil surroundings, I wonder if you noticed below you a small garden with steps leading down into it. You can count five steps. You may realize that when you're in that garden, other things and sounds around you are not important any more: maybe some small sound in the distance, maybe in the distance a voice talking quietly, maybe footsteps, or a breeze, or faint music. You may realize that you feel deeply relaxed when you step down into that garden; you take the first step and find yourself descend a little, and then go on to the second step and go down a little deeper, and going on to the third step you become more relaxed, and feel yourself descend to the fourth step, and going profoundly deeper with the fifth step you go down, down deeply into the garden. When you are deep in the garden, everything seems so very far away. You know how it is, how sounds of voices or children or airplanes or footsteps can seem so far away; you know they have nothing to do with you, so you don't even hear them: you don't need to hear sounds that have nothing to do with you. Even the voice of someone talking to you can seem so far away that you are just aware of that deep, profoundly deep feeling now, just aware of the deep feeling of relaxation in your own mind and body, and realize that that good feeling is going to go with you after, because when you've been in that quiet place, you might be surprised how good you are going to feel afterward. You can take a quiet moment now and just enjoy that relaxed feeling.

"Like many times when you lay back, closed your eyes, and found yourself drifting, allow yourself to enjoy that particular feeling that you are realizing is coming from relaxing, from being drowsy: hearing, almost hearing the sounds of a breeze in the bushes, leaves rattling and swishing, faintly and then more, then faintly; and if you listen, almost being able to hear the tinkling of small bells hung in the branches, ringing randomly, hearing the swishing in the rhythms like the rhythm of your breathing, a drowsy hypnotic sound, with the faint bells so far away that you have to strain to hear, or wonder if you are barely hearing them; hearing your breathing, and feeling far away. If you try to remember the last ten words you hear now, the harder you try, the fewer you can remember—five, or at the most three, and then tinkling and swishing in and out, warm and sleepy. Remembering a word and another tinkling, and thinking, too hard to remember. So you don't have to try, just notice the feeling. Soon, you can just give up trying to remember the last six words, and just enjoy the relaxed feeling. But the important things you still remember, like how easy it is to relax, the more you try. You can remember that, and how you feel right now. But it can seem too much of an effort to remember anything else, to think of anything else. And so you just feel relaxed instead."

Shifting Attention from Bodily Discomfort

"I'm sure you remember what it's like to be in a place where there is so much noise that you can hear nothing plainly. Or a place where there were so many things that you could find nothing. And sometimes that good relaxed feeling can be so strong that it is hard to think of anything else. Maybe there was something you tried to remember, but found that the more you tried to remember, the less you could remember. The more you try to feel something, you think you can do it at first but then you might be surprised that it becomes harder and harder to remember it. Maybe you sometimes have a discomfort, a pain in a particular spot. It's okay right now to try to think about it, even if you can't. If you find that at first you can think about it, but then it seems harder and harder to concentrate on it – something else always enters your mind, perhaps you get distracted by the heaviness, or the lightness, or by that particular feeling you have – you can try again even if your mind seems too relaxed to want to bother. You can try even if you can't concentrate on it . . . can't keep your mind on it . . . like it's getting drowned out by the relaxed feelings. But if it gets too hard to keep concentrating, you can try again, and when you can't think of anything except your relaxed feeling, and that calm feeling in your arms, you can stop trying and enjoy instead that relaxed feeling in your whole body."

Ending the Relaxation Session

"If you were to turn in the garden toward the steps by which you came, you might notice that there were five steps leading up, and as you put your foot on the first step, you can feel yourself going up, getting lighter, from the fifth, to the fourth, and getting lighter on the third, and the second, and alighting on the first, and going up and out of the garden, and drifting back the way you came, and becoming aware that this relaxed feeling is staying with you. It would not be at all surprising that even later in the day, the feeling would remain with you. Now coming to the place where you first started out, where you first began to relax, you might notice how relaxed your breathing is, and your arms and legs, and that special feeling that you know comes from being very comfortable. You might recall that in the morning when you wake up, you first become aware of the light in the room while your eyes are still closed, become aware of the lightness and how your eyelids flicker and move a little; your eyelids can feel light, and with each breath become lighter, and become aware of the lightness. And they want to flicker and open a bit, and open more, and your eyes just fix on something across the room. You don't really have to look around at all to be aware that the feeling of relaxation is still with you. And as you allow your eyes to come open you can still feel that relaxed feeling. If later you want to experience again that relaxed feeling, all you have to do is remember that particular feeling, as you give yourself a moment to sit back, and you'll remember what it means to enjoy the benefits of relaxation."

Promoting More Rapid Relaxation Induction

As skill is developed, the patient may be wise to learn to relax in different situations; sitting, sitting with eyes open, and using progressively briefer techniques, so that eventually it can be integrated into everyday activities without disruption. Five to ten brief relaxations of 1 to 2 minutes may be more helpful than one long period of half an hour in the control of tension. Once brief applied techniques have been learned, occasionally during the week a longer relaxation session can be done, in order to keep the skill fresh. There are two therapist scripts. The first is used within a longer therapist-directed relaxation session to arouse the expectation that the patient will relax more quickly. The second is used to produce the rapid relaxation and can be used by the patient without the therapist's intervention.

Script to Produce Rapid Relaxation

"Think of that feeling that you have now; I wonder if you realize how quickly you will learn to become aware of it again. The next time you sit back or lie back just as you are now, and notice how easily your eyes drift closed, and how regular your breathing becomes when the relaxed feelings begin to spread through your hands and arms and through your body, you can remember that with two or three relaxed breaths it would be hard not to begin to feel the same feeling of relaxation as you do now. In the next day or two, I'm sure you will find a moment to do this, to just sit or lie back, let your eyes close, take a deep breath, and hold it awhile. As you let it out slowly and feel the tension leaving your chest, you will realize that it is already happening, and you need only take a couple more breaths, hold them, and slowly let them out. With each time you breathe out and feel your body relaxing you can remember how it feels to allow yourself to drift into a deeply relaxed state. You know that you can let this feeling go as far as you want, and as long as you want. Even if you want to feel that feeling for only a few seconds, it's all right. You'll realize that you have felt that feeling before. You'll find that the relaxation feeling comes more and more quickly each time you try, so that you will be able to call up this feeling whenever you need it."

The following instructions can be recorded on magnetic tape for home use. Remind the patient to take a comfortable position, that it is unnecessary to move or do anything. Remind him or her that with eyes gently closed, he or she will be taking a few deep breaths and gently exhaling through the nose and mouth, and that the feeling of tension leaving the chest is the sign that the relaxation is already happening. After this, it will be necessary only to notice the relaxed rhythm of breathing and the particular body sensations that come from relaxing. When the patient has learned the relaxation procedure, he or she should practice without the tape.

Script Used by Patient Alone

"You can sit back comfortably and close your eyes, and relax your face and limbs. You can relax your breathing. It really isn't necessary to do anything else, not even to move. Remember last time when you were really relaxed and the relaxation seemed to be greater with each breath. Perhaps you already can clearly visualize how you are going to feel when you take a deep breath, hold it, and then feel the relaxation sweep through your chest and body. So take a deep breath now and hold it (about 15 seconds). And now notice how relaxed your chest became, and that particular feeling in your arms and legs, in your face and abdomen. (Wait a few moments.) You don't have to move your limbs any more if they have begun to get heavy. You can just take another deep breath and hold it (fifteen seconds). And then release it, and notice that feeling again (repeat the instruction after a pause). If you are becoming too relaxed so that it would be an effort to take another deep breath, you can just notice the relaxed and comfortable breathing, in and out, in and out, that relaxes you more with each breath."

BIOFEEDBACK TECHNIQUES

What the various biofeedback techniques have in common is the self-regulation of bodily processes. This is achieved by detecting, amplifying, and displaying specific physiological processes in such a way that the patient can be trained to voluntarily modify these processes. Generally, electrical amplification and visual and auditory displays are used. The most common modalities are listed as follows:

- EMG, monitoring muscle tension
- skin temperature, generally monitoring cutaneous temperature of the finger
- pulse volume, sometimes used over cranial arteries in headache management
- GSR, measuring skin conductance/resistance changes as a function of anxiety
- electrocardiogram (EKG)
- EEG rhythms
- visceral function, as, for example, pressure measurements of the gut.

Biofeedback treatment includes the following elements:

1. People cannot usually control bodily functions over which they have no conscious proprioceptive awareness. One therefore introduces an electrical device for monitoring and measurement of that physiological parameter.

2. Display of this moment-by-moment or cumulative function is provided for the patient in some understandable form, such as tone, reading, or light.

3. An explanation and instructions are provided so that the patient can try to voluntarily alter the monitored function. It is explained that doing so will alter the basis of the illness.

4. Because the monitoring is ongoing, the patient can immediately see the results of his or her efforts to change the function. The therapist also assists by interpreting the task, providing encouragement, and setting realistic expectations.

5. As control is learned over the monitored physiological function, the patient also learns about the relationship between his illness and his actions.

6. Home practice in improving control is assigned, with the patient gradually weaning off the dependency on the biofeedback instrument and finding other means to directly maintain control over the physiological function.

Although there is a significant element of truth in the above conceptual model, it is likely much more complex. On the one hand, there is some indication that in headache cases biofeedback has about the same efficacy as relaxation (Jessup, Neufeld, & Merskey, 1979). On the other hand, there is the clinical impression that biofeedback may often offer something clinically that is not obtained from the more nonspecific relaxation or cognitive therapies. The added element may be a greater facility to acquire control if there is an opportunity to come to terms actively with both physical and mental reactions. Biofeedback may be a better placebo. It may be that biofeedback promotes cognitive change, especially beliefs in self-control, because it gives a concrete illustration of self-control over a function that previously seemed unconscious. The behavior medicine techniques described in this book are completely compatible with the application of biofeedback techniques. However, other references should be consulted for details about the use of biofeedback.

COGNITIVE COPING TECHNIQUES

The literature on cognitive coping is quite extensive and will not be dealt with separately at length here. The various chapters of this book contain cognitive coping elements, especially in the patient education sections, where efforts are made to relabel the patient's problems as being more tractable to self-control. Our aim here is to summarize some coping techniques that may be used to maximize the self-control of problems discussed in this book. In the Selected Readings section at the back of this book, some references are given to manuals that give greater specific detail about cognitive coping techniques. The basic concepts are as follows:

1. Thinking and mental images (cognitions) are a factor in determining how we feel and behave. That is, our thoughts often determine our actions.

2. Therapeutic change can be brought about by reexamining and altering thoughts, images, beliefs, and evaluations. This is an important step in altering psychological distress and adjusting maladaptive behavior. This is the main focus of cognitive coping strategies.

3. How we behave also influences how we interpret events; that is, our actions also determine our thoughts.

4. Change also is facilitated if behavior is prescribed in such a way that dysfunctional thought patterns and images are reevaluated. This is the main focus of strategies such as desensitization, assertiveness training, role-playing, and self-monitoring.

Thus, the cognitive coping approaches attempt to alter maladaptive images, inappropriate beliefs, and expectations, including what has been identified as catastrophic thinking and negative self-talk. The research and clinical literature suggest the following steps for putting this into practice.

1. Use self-monitoring to discover your thoughts and images during distressing situations (see discussion on self-monitoring in chapter 2).
2. Collect further information to reevaluate these images and cognitions in order to see if they accurately represent the situation or whether they represent unjustified apprehensions.
3. Try using alternative ways of interpreting and imagining.
4. Create new coping opportunities by trying out these alternatives in everyday stress situations.
5. Combine the cognitive strategies with relaxation procedures.

There are many specific procedures that can be used by the clinician to help the patient change inappropriate thinking patterns, shifting them from unrealistic and maladaptive to accurate and adaptive. The categories are as follows:

1. *Countering techniques* – identifying irrational thoughts or beliefs, labeling them, showing them to be untenable, and then substituting appropriate thoughts. This tends to be called self-talk procedures.

2. *Perceptual shifts* – changing visual schemata or mental images, because images represent expectations that influence feelings and behavior.

3. *Conditioning techniques* – certain cognitions may have become associated with unpleasant emotional responses; these associations are reconditioned so that the cognitions now have a more neutral or pleasant association.

4. *Paradoxical methods* – patients are influenced to behave in such a way as to contradict previous expectations. In the dissonance that is generated, the patient develops a sense of control, and has less belief that there will be adverse consequences.

5. *Logical analysis* – problem-solving techniques use a step-by-step reality orientation, challenging the beliefs that the problems are beyond personal control.

Chapter 4
Insomnia

DESCRIPTION OF THE PROBLEM

A 40-year-old widow had an 8-year history of chronic insomnia, muscle aches, and fatigue. (The patient's mother had also been frequently hospitalized with painful ailments and insomnia.) After an unhappy childhood during which she was neglected, she eventually married a man who was aggressive and alcoholic, and she was frightened of him. She believed that the demands of her religion and culture left her no recourse other than to suffer his abuse. She remembered lying awake many nights fearing his drunken late homecomings because there would be an argument, after which she might be beaten. Eventually this developed into a pattern of nonrestorative sleep, with difficulty getting to sleep and pain on awakening in the morning. The children became a discipline problem, with her husband undermining her wishes. Her husband developed cancer and died, and she found new friends and help from a social worker. As she became more assertive, she found that her children behaved themselves. However, she still needed help with the sleeping problem and the chronic aches.

A graphic description of insomnia is found in a passage in the Bible:

Woe is me!
For the Lord has added sorrow to my anguish.
I am weary with my groaning,
And I find no rest.
—Jeremiah 45:3

Population surveys indicate that sleep problems are a common complaint. The estimates of the problem from these surveys range from 15% to 42.5% (Cleghorn, Kaplan, Bellissimo, & Szatmari, 1983). Although difficulties with sleep are encountered by people of all ages, they tend to have a higher frequency among the elderly. Classification of sleep disorders is discussed elsewhere (Association of Sleep Disorders Centers, 1979; Cleghorn et al., 1983). Lichstein and Fischer (1985) have discussed the causes of insomnia in terms of psychological, psychiatric, chemical, and medical–biological factors.

Chronic insomnia is a feature of many problems. It may be conditioned, as in the above example, or associated with disturbed emotional states such as anxiety or depression. Many medical conditions, including chronic respiratory diseases, sleep apnea, and the "restless legs syndrome," may impair sleep. Sedatives, stimulants, and alcohol all interfere with sleep and may aggravate insomnia. Insomnia may be created by environmental conditions such as jet lag or frequent changes in shift work. There are some chronic insomnias with uncertain etiology, some with childhood onset, some in association with the fibrositis syndrome, and some with only a subjective element of unsatisfactory sleep.

BACKGROUND

The expression we use of falling asleep illustrates the intuitive notion that sleep is a passive state that happens when someone relaxes, stops paying attention, or becomes too fatigued to continue activity. With the advent of the EEG, the notion that sleep was a passive state was proven wrong; in fact it has been discovered that sleep involves complex changes and patterns of activity of the brain. Sleep is not synonymous with unconsciousness, and thinking does not stop with sleep, even though there are changes in awareness and recollection. Furthermore, dreaming and thinking while asleep is not magical or random, but rather can be influenced by waking thoughts. Finally, sleep is not purely an automatic and involuntary event, but rather can be improved by proper knowledge and good sleep habits.

The sleep cycle is normally composed of a series of changes in the level (or stage) of sleep that occur in regular (approximately 90-minute) cycles. These stages can be recognized by changes on the EEG and in physiology. There are four stages of slow-wave sleep (SWS). In the first stage, there is a feeling of drowsiness, although with awareness of things in the environment, and of the passage of time. In the second stage, the EEG shows slowing of the brain waves and there is the beginning of the sense of being asleep; that is, a good sleeper if startled at this stage will probably declare that he or she had been awakened. However, the sleeper may also have mental activity in this stage, and if awakened at this time may report that he or she was just thinking, although about to go to sleep. The third and fourth deeper stages of SWS involve more of a state of being unaware and are marked by further characteristic slowing of the EEG pattern; there is little dreaming, and these deeper stages of sleep are important for a person to feel refreshed in the morning. The stage of rapid eye movement sleep (REM or paradoxical sleep) is recognized by a marked change in the EEG pattern, which becomes of low voltage and high frequency, much as in an awake individual. However, there is profound inhibition of muscle tone except for rolling eye movements, and marked fluctuations in autonomic activity. This is the stage in which the majority of complex and vivid dreams occurs. When a person begins to sleep, there is progression through the SWS stages for about 1½ hours at which time there is a reversal of EEG rhythms and the first episode of REM. The succeeding cycles during the night repeat these phases of SWS and REM, but feature smaller proportions of stage 4 and 3 sleep. The REM periods became slightly longer and closer together so that, overall, the percentage of REM is about 25%, stage 1 is about 5%, stage 2 about 50%, and deeper, non-REM sleep about 20%.

The sleep pattern is delicate and influenced by many factors. Those having the most influence include disturbances of circadian rhythm, drug effects, effects of activity and exercise, effects of sleep-avoidance behavior, inappropriate sleep habits, effects of "worry" thinking patterns and misunderstanding about the nature of sleep, symptoms such as pain, and effects of anxiety and disturbed emotions. All of these problems can be improved or removed by educated problem-solving.

Circadian Rhythm

Efficiency of sleep is influenced by several factors, the most prominent being the circadian rhythm. We have a built-in internal clock that tends to synchronize itself with the 24-hour cycle of the sun. Within this cycle, there are oscillations of key functions. Body temperature is at its lowest level in the early morning hours before normal waking time, at which time psychomotor efficiency is also at its lowest. There are also swings in various hormones; insulin, cortisol, growth hormone, and others. Pain threshold is at its lowest in the morning before waking, which coincides with the observation that many migraine, fibrositis, and backache patients experience their worst pain at this time.

Major factors that accomplish this synchronization of the circadian rhythm include the daytime exposure to light, mealtimes, and physical exercise. It is possible to change the timing, but it takes an average of 1 day for every hour of change in the circadian rhythm. Travelers often experience this as jet lag, and the same phenomenon occurs in those workers on rotating shifts. It is easier to adjust the timing by lengthening the biological day than to shorten it; therefore, it is easier for a worker to change from day-shift to afternoons to nights than to do the reverse, and it is easier for a traveler to adjust to new time zones by traveling west than by traveling east. At the times of the circadian cycle when the individual is most disposed to sleep (for example, at 4:00 a.m.) there are the greatest problems in mood and mental efficiency, if for some reason the person is wakened or prevented from sleeping. If the circadian rhythm is disturbed by drugs, emotional disorders, bad habits, or illness, the similar adverse mental consequences of poor sleep may also be felt as a chronic situation.

Insomniacs (poor sleepers) often have irregular sleep times. Because of the inability to get to sleep, they may stay up late at night trying to become sleepy. Doing so, they become exhausted, and are even less refreshed the following day. This may lead to daytime napping and further fragmentation of the day and night pattern of sleeping. They may develop the habit of getting up periodically at night because of restlessness so that the sleep rhythm is broken. A key to restoring a normal sleep pattern is to restore consistency to the pattern of sleeping: setting a regular bedtime and regular rising time, keeping the sleeping environment dark, and being in a lighted environment during the day. A good circadian rhythm can be strengthened by partaking of fairly vigorous exercise for 20 to 60 minutes each during the daytime.

Effects of Drugs

It is well-known that there are some drugs patented for use as hypnotics. Most do not realize that there are serious problems associated with the long-term use of such drugs. One is the problem of tolerance and eventual dependency. A more subtle problem is the fact that hypnotics badly disturb the normal pattern of sleep, and eventually lead to more shallow sleep with less of the necessary deeper stages of SWS, and more wakenings. Many sedatives also suppress dreaming (REM sleep), eventually leading to REM rebound, which is very disturbing to the patient whenever he or she tries to eliminate the medicine. This feeds into the vicious cycle of taking more drugs and having more unsatisfactory sleep. Barbiturates have a great potential for abuse and addiction, and aggravate sleep disorders if used on a chronic basis. At one time these were the most popular sedative–hypnotics, but in the past 30 years, benzodiazepines largely replaced them. At this time, the consumption of various benzodiazepines (diazepam, oxazepam, lorazepam, bromazepam, fluorazepam, triazolam, etc.) in North American for the problem of insomnia is enormous. These may have a place in certain acute or overwhelming conditions (acute grief, hospitalization, acute situational disturbances, preliminary treatment for some psychiatric disorders before behavioral therapy is begun), but chronic use is risky. Addiction and withdrawal syndrome can occur. The congeners with a longer half-life (diazepam, chlordiazepoxide, fluorazepam) have a tendency to produce progressive accumulation in the serum. The shorter-acting members of the group (lorazepam, triazolam) have a high propensity for addiction. The withdrawal from these drugs may cause severe anxiety states that may require intensive psychiatric treatment.

Alcohol has the same problems as other sedatives. In addition, alcohol is gradually eliminated in the system during the night, and if used as a nightcap may well cause wakening in the middle of the night as the alcohol leaves the system. Dreams that are suppressed by alcohol will rebound toward morning, further disturbing sleep.

Painkillers containing opiates (such as codeine) have a short duration of action, often about 4 hours, and therefore may disturb the maintenance of sleep. Nonsteroidal antiinflammatory drugs often used for treatment of arthritis may in about 5% of cases have significant nervous system effects, including anxiety, depression, insomnia, or drowsiness, which may directly or indirectly worsen a sleep disorder.

Sometimes it is forgotten that stimulants are found in many things such as coffee (caffeine), tea (theophylline and caffeine), colas (caffeine), decongestants and cold rememdies (pseudoephedrine), and many pain remedies (caffeine). Through multiple sources, an individual can, over the course of a day, absorb enough of these stimulants to seriously interfere with sleep. Anyone with a problem sleeping should take inventory over a few days to determine how much sedative or stimulant is being consumed and when, so that these chemicals can be eliminated. Cigarette smoke, containing nicotine, is a stimulant. Smoking shortly before going to bed, or rising during the night to smoke, is directly antagonistic to sleep.

Antidepressants are sometimes used to offset some of the symptoms that come from nonrestorative sleep. For example, amitriptyline may help fibrositis symptoms by increasing stage 4 sleep and reducing the fatigue and ache that is often associated with the condition. However, it may also cause problems of its own, such as causing nightmares and hung-over feelings the next day, leading to REM rebound problems, which makes it hard to stop taking the medicine.

In short, sleep is such a delicate mechanism that no drug is capable of making it normal, and sedatives, alcohol, and stimulants all seriously disturb sleep in the long term. If someone asks, "What is the best drug I can use to make me sleep better or cure my insomnia?", the answer in most cases is to "stop the drugs you are taking, and take nothing further."

Effects of Activity and Exercise

As mentioned above, exercise has a protective effect on sleep patterns and helps to establish a good circadian rhythm. The mechanism by which this occurs is not clear, but it is known that vigorous exercise has an effect on certain brain functions and can promote a better mental attitude, reduce anxiety, and reduce pain. It is reasonable to expect that such exercise might also influence the brain centers that control circadian rhythm. In helping people with jet lag, prescribing exercise to be carried out during the daytime in the new time zone will hasten the adaptation to the new time. Similarly, people who suffer insomnia benefit from the addition of a daily vigorous exercise regime to their treatment program (chapter 9).

Worry and Misunderstanding

Two common misconceptions are (a) that people stop thinking when they are asleep, or that if one is aware of one's thoughts, one cannot be asleep; and (b) that if one is asleep, there should be no bodily movement, that sleeping like a log is desirable and possible. Sleep, rather than being a steady state of low arousal and unconsciousness, is a state of ever-varying activity of neurological and physiological systems, of mental activity, and of muscular tone.

It is possible to see how insomnia may be a learned behavior. Poor sleepers are more likely to report being already awake if they are deliberately wakened during the first or second stages of SWS; they worry more about sleep; there is more disturbance in the sleep–wake cycles and more daytime napping; more use of drugs and alcohol as sedatives; and more nonsleep behavior in the bedroom. Yet they may fall asleep in the living room or other environments.

The brain is active in one way or another all the time, and thinking also will occur during sleep, either as thinking per se with some self-awareness, as filtering of thoughts with preservation of sleep, or as some form of dreaming. For example, take two hypothetical situations. In the first, someone goes to bed with the realization that tomorrow will be the occasion of a wonderful event (a wedding, an award or honor, a great vacation), and that person's thoughts turn all night in happy anticipation of the event. Although the individual may toss and turn, this restlessness does not have a particularly bad connotation. Such a night is not aversive, and being aware of thoughts during the night would not be feared if it were to occur again. In a second hypothetical situation, if someone becomes anxious or agitated for some reason, (a difficult examination, a court appearance, a family conflict), the result again may be a restless night with disturbed sleep. However, on that occasion, the unpleasant emotional state becomes associated with the act of being aware of thought processes while one is trying to sleep. The result is that thinking or changing position while sleeping becomes aversive, and this thinking may be feared the next night, not for the restlessness alone, but for the quality of the thought content and the meaning to the individual. People try to avoid aversive situations in various ways.

1. One way to avoid aversive situations is to use denial, or, in the above illustration, to try not to think. This is sure to be futile, because one must think about trying to stop thinking, and this serves to reinforce that the thinking is out of control.

2. Another is to stay up late in an effort to become tired enough to sleep. Unfortunately, the ability to sleep is not the same at all hours of the 24-hour period. Despite fatigue, there are certain optimal times to fall asleep, and changing or delaying the bedtime does not necessarily bring one to an optimal sleeping time. Anyone who has ever had to work extra shifts will recall that one seems to be tired, then the tiredness passes and one seems to catch a second wind, and although sleepiness may return, it is not constant.

3. The other problem with trying to stay up later is that it is like changing time zones. We know that it is easier to shift the circadian rhythm by lengthening the day (whereas shortening it is more difficult). By staying up later, one is just influencing oneself to shift the day–night cycle out of phase with the rest of the world.

4. If the individual is less consistent and simply goes to bed at different hours each day, and perhaps naps at different times as well, the circadian rhythm becomes less definite and the hormonal and psychomotor efficiency become poorly regulated. In short, the insomnia and nonrestorative sleep problems are aggravated.

5. Pills or alcohol can be an escape, but this leads to the problems mentioned above, that sleep is eventually made worse by such interference.

6. People often develop a series of inappropriate routines, such as getting up at night to smoke or to look out the window, checking the alarm clock frequently, leaving the television or light on, or sleeping in places other than the bedroom, with the risk of being disturbed by the new environment.

7. It may not be realized that changing position, perhaps 10 to 15 times, during the night is a perfectly normal physiological phenomenon, and is in fact necessary to avoid skin, nerve, and joint damage. The person with insomnia is aware of the desire to move every so often, and may interpret it as part of the inability to sleep; attempting then to suppress movement, or worrying about movement, only serves to make one more uncomfortable.

All of the above routines and sleep-avoidance behaviors serve to perpetuate the insomnia behavior and aggravate the physiological controls that should regulate sleep.

Pain and Illnesses

Insomnia is frequently encountered in certain clinical conditions. Schizophrenia, depressions, and anxiety disorders often provoke insomnia or disorders in sleep duration and maintenance. Chronic pain, especially when due to musculoskeletal problems (fibrositis, myofascial pain, posttraumatic fibromyalgia), is usually associated with insomnia. Whether or not there are medical conditions present, behavioral treatment of insomnia is always relevant because *insomnia is not just something that happens to you, like a disease, but it is also something you do, like a habit.* If there are medical conditions or psychiatric diseases present, they can be treated, but people can be taught to sleep better.

INFORMATION FOR PATIENTS

Sleep is a natural phenomenon, but is so complex that it may be interfered with by drugs, illnesses, misunderstanding, worry, or bad habit. In fact, the majority of people who suffer from insomnia are suffering in part because of bad habits.

There are many misconceptions about what sleep really is. It is not simply "something that happens to you." Your brain is active all through sleep, but in a different way. Thinking does not necessarily stop with sleep; it may go on, and if you are worried, the thinking may even fool you into believing that you are awake when you are not. Sleeping pills do not make you sleep better and deeper. They disturb normal sleep by depressing brain functions, and after prolonged use may actually cause insomnia.

The sleep cycle is normally composed of a series of stages that keep repeating themselves in a specific pattern. The first two stages of sleep involve a feeling of drowsiness with the eyes closed, but you are to some degree aware of things that are going on so that you might have the impression of thinking and might be somewhat aware of the passage of time. If you are awakened during stage 1, and sometimes during stage 2, you might not believe that you were actually sleeping. In stages 3 and 4 there is more of a state of being unaware, and little dreaming, but even then it is possible for the brain to process information. For example, if someone were to come into the room and quietly say a neutral word like book, you would probably stay asleep, but if you were to hear your baby crying, or hear your name, or the word fire, you would tend to wake up. The deeper stages (stages 3 and 4 of SWS) are important in getting the impression of being refreshed in the morning. REM sleep is when most dreaming occurs, and it accounts for about 20% of the night, even in people who do not ever remember their dreams.

When you begin to sleep, you drift through the nondreaming stages of sleep until the REM stage, and then the cyclic pattern of nondreaming sleep repeats itself about every 1½ hours. These stages can be interfered with by bad sleep habits, depression, worry, or medication, for example. People who have chronic muscle discomfort may also sleep poorly. People can become more afraid of being unable to sleep, and may try to avoid it in various ways. They may stay up too late at night trying to get sleepy, or may pop out of bed in the middle of the night if they happen to awaken to take a cup of tea or to smoke and look out the window. Or they may anxiously look at their alarm clock during the night. All of these things are apt to make sleep more difficult rather than better. Some painful problems are aggravated by poor sleeping habits. If you can learn to sleep properly, you are likely to have less pain.

The first thing to do to learn to sleep better is to make a regular bedtime and cut out all of the habits that take you out of bed or that distract you from sleep. Avoid either sedatives or stimulants that may interfere with the natural ability to sleep. Regular exercise during the day is usually beneficial; it will not make you tired, but rather will pick up your energy during the day, and make it easier to relax at night. (Here, the clinician may suggest some reading material from the Selected Readings section at the end of this book.)

ASSESSMENT AND TREATMENT

Assessment is made of the attitudes, physical factors, and behaviors that interfere with sleep. A more normal sleep habit is encouraged, and the circadian rhythm is strengthened. Habits and substances that interfere with sleep are eliminated. Physical exercise and techniques to promote a relaxed and confident attitude cultivate a better disposition to sleep (Figure 4.1).

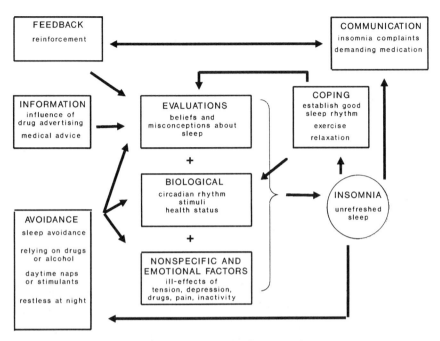

FIGURE 4.1. Algorithm for insomnia.

Evaluations

The individual's beliefs, attitudes, and habits can be ascertained by a combination of clinical interview, self-evaluation, and self-monitoring.

Beliefs and Interpretations. Beliefs about sleep have much to do with creating insomnia. If someone fears the experience of being aware of thoughts, there are times every night during sleep when thoughts will occur, reinforcing the belief that one cannot sleep. If one interprets changes of position to be restlessness, then the obligatory changes of position that occur in everyone's sleep will produce worry. If there is the erroneous belief that readiness to sleep is synonymous with fatigue, then there will be inappropriate behaviors of staying up late in an effort to become fatigued enough to sleep. Intervention must be directed at changing these inappropriate beliefs and interpretations.

Investigating the Problem. If there exists a serious medical or psychiatric disorder causing the insomnia, this will need attention. The focus here is on the questions that are appropriate to investigating insomnia as a problem itself. When there is a complaint of insomnia, the evaluation begins with a survey that is summarized as follows:

1. At what times do you become drowsy? What times do you actually lie down to nap or sleep? What times do you wake up or get up?
2. What medication, prescribed or over-the-counter, do you use? At what times do you take them? What doses? How much cola, coffee, or tea do you drink and when?
3. Do you smoke or drink alcohol before bedtime? Do you awake during the night for a smoke or drink of alcohol? What are the quantities of these?
4. Do you snack before bedtime or wake during the night for a snack?
5. When do you exercise, how long, and with what intensity?
6. When there are sleep interruptions, what are the thoughts, symptoms, worries, or discomforts that disturb the sleep? When do they occur? How do you respond to them?
7. What are the external stimuli, such as noises, people around you, pets, and so forth? When do they occur? How do you respond to them?
8. When you are in the bedroom but unable to sleep (unable to get to sleep or unable to remain asleep), what specific things do you do? Smoke, look out the window, read, munch on snacks, drink tea, or anything else that is incompatible with sleep?
9. What are your beliefs about sleep? Can people think while asleep? Is insomnia harmful? Can people learn to sleep? Are hypnotics a way to restore normal sleep?

Self-Evaluation. After obtaining preliminary answers to these questions by interview, corroborating details are collected by using a diary that is assigned to the patient, using preset categories (see Self-Monitoring in chapter 2; also see Dement, 1985). They can be asked to mark sleepiness, sleeping or napping times, drug doses, eating, exercise, sleep interruptions, and other behaviors on a page marked off into hours of the day. The "Checklist for Sleep Problems" found at the end of this chapter (pp. 97–98) provides a tool for self-assessment and for alerting the patient to beliefs and habits that lead to insomnia. Having the patient conduct this sort of self-assessment is itself therapeutic. Often patients catastrophize, or perceive a problem as being totally outside their control. By self-monitoring, it is possible to demonstrate to patients the true proportions of their problem, and the relationship to what they are doing. It is also possible to convey an attitude that some sort of self-initiated action is possible. Hand in hand with the self-awareness that comes from this self-assessment, the education component (Information for Patients section) is aimed at the misconceptions that perpetuate the insomniac behavior. Diary sheets that can be used for self-monitoring sleep are found in Figures 2.5 and 2.6. An example of their use is shown in Figure 2.7.

Biological Substrates

The neurophysiology of sleep is a subject in itself (Jouvet, 1969). The biological issues we are concerned with are (a) the occurrence of sleep stages, (b) the need for an orderly pattern of sleep stages in order to be refreshed and to feel well, (c) the fact that orderliness of these stages within the sleep pattern depends on a well-established circadian rhythm, and (d) the influence on circadian rhythm of the timing of daily activity, exercise, exposure to light, and intervening factors such as emotional state.

Patients need to be made aware of the nature of sleep, through education and self-assessment, in order to be able to alter insomniac behavior and thoughts. It is also usually necessary to prescribe particular routines that will have the effect of reinforcing a more healthy sleep pattern. This includes establishing a regular sleeping time, avoiding naps, and avoiding nonsleep behavior during the night (counteracting beliefs about fatigue or fears of lying awake). Relaxation exercises may be required to deal with the phobic quality with which some insomniacs approach sleep. Prescription of a regular exercise program is helpful. The expectation is that insomnia is not purely a biological problem or a cognitive problem, but a combination. It is not necessary to create an ideal sleep pattern from a biological point of view, nor is it necessary to have a perfect attitude. It is enough to improve the relationship and the function.

It is not known why regular exercise promotes sleep, but it does so. The layperson often has the idea that exercise causes fatigue, and therefore sleep. In fact, a regular aerobic exercise program increases stamina, reduces fatigue, is usually experienced as stimulating and energizing, and improves the refreshing quality of sleep, probably through neurophysiological mechanisms (see chapter 9).

Nonspecific Symptoms and Emotional Factors

Nonspecific symptoms are introduced into the symptom complex of insomnia most importantly through drugs, but also through other sources. Many sedatives produce REM suppression, which leads to REM rebound, aggravating the dependence on hypnotics while interrupting the sleep pattern. Chronic use of hypnotics leads to disruption of normal sleep cycles, reducing the proportion of stage 3 and 4 sleep, and increasing the number of awakenings. Sleep disturbance is often aggravated by nonsleep behaviors during the night, which might provoke the nonspecific rheumatism pain syndrome, which in turn becomes an irritant that can disturb sleep. Many analgesics that are available as over-the-counter medications contain caffeine. When insomniacs use these medications in order to sleep, they may provoke greater wakefulness. Insomniacs rarely have a satisfactory night's sleep, but may become repeatedly drowsy during the day. This may lead to napping, or taking tea or coffee at irregular intervals in order to fight off daytime drowsiness, but the pharmacological effect of the stimulants continues into the night and interferes with the nighttime sleep habit. With chronic benzodiazepine use, there is a propensity to a dependency syndrome, with anxiety as a predominant feature in any efforts to withdraw; this problem has marked effects on the ability to sleep.

Having become aware of these problems by education and self-monitoring, an insomniac must eliminate the factors that aggravate his or her insomnia. If prescription hypnotic and analgesic drugs are being consumed at the rate that constitutes an addiction or serious abuse pattern, it may be necessary to follow a formal drug withdrawal program (see chapter 8). Otherwise, insomniacs must chart their use of stimulants, sedatives and hypnotics, analgesics, and alcohol, and then systematically eliminate them. Part of this is to prepare the patient for the fact that on withdrawal of hypnotics there may appear to be worse insomnia and distress due to REM rebound and more shallow sleep. However, after a few weeks, normal sleep will begin to gradually return. Usually the best strategy is not to suddenly stop everything, since compliance will be poor. Rather, a quota-based, gradual reduction is employed, using (self-monitored) time-contingent dosing. The latter also permits the growth of a sense of control over these chemicals. Prior to arranging such a program of drug withdrawal, it is necessary to have a physician review the medication and proposal for withdrawal, and give approval. Some patients are not aware of the purpose of the drugs that they are taking. For example, a patient may be taking phenobarbital at night for epileptic seizures and think it is a hypnotic.

The other most important source of nonspecific symptoms is the disturbance in circadian rhythm and sleep readiness that results from an irregular sleep habit. It is not simply that the insomniac has an irregular sleeping time because of insomnia, but also that he or she suffers insomnia because of the habit of an irregular sleeping pattern.

Emotional factors such as anxiety and worry can be both the cause and the result of insomnia. The sleep-avoidance behavior demonstrated by many insomniacs is a good example of this two-way relationship. The emotional factors are dealt with by corrective education and behavioral methods, which increase the sense of self-control.

Psychiatric conditions are not to be overlooked. Serious depressive or psychotic disorders are often associated with insomnia, and usually need special psychopharmacological treatment. The behavioral medicine clinician must be alert to this fact. Treatment of a primary psychiatric condition with the appropriate antidepressant or neuroleptic does not necessarily restore the individual to normal sleep habits; therefore, the other considerations in this chapter about sleep management remain an important element in the overall treatment.

Dealing with Avoidance

Insomniacs must be instructed, "No matter how strange this may sound to you, I am now giving you an instruction which you must follow from now on. You must stop trying to fall asleep. Instead, you must simply create conditions in which the natural thing—sleep—will occur without your interference. Sleep cannot be forced. It must be invited." Insomnia sufferers must become aware that resorting to hypnotic and sedative drugs, insomnia behavior, and self-perpetuating worry are all forms of avoidance behavior that can aggravate the insomnia experience. A checklist for self-assessment is found at the end of this chapter. Having identified the avoidance behaviors, it is opportune to educate the patient about how these each aggravate the problems, which are then labeled insomnia.

Using hypnotics and sedatives to avoid insomnia, the patient makes two assumptions: Insomnia is something medical and therefore outside of one's own control and requires medicine to correct it, and if the medicine does not work, more may be required. When the hypnotics begin to lose their efficacy, or when the quality of sleep is progressively disturbed by chronic intake of the hypnotic, the dependence on the medication increases, and the belief in self-control of sleep or belief that sleep is a natural thing decreases.

Trying not to think and trying not to move are the mistaken consequences of the notion held by insomniacs that they cannot sleep because they toss and turn and cannot get their minds to stop working. This is self-defeating for two reasons. One is that it is natural to expect that a sleeper will change positions periodically during the night and will have mental activity, for some of which he or she may retain awareness. The second is that to try to inhibit thinking is to guarantee thinking. (You can prove to yourself right now that trying to stop thinking actually promotes it. For the next minute, while you have your eyes on this line, go ahead and avoid being aware of your bottom sitting where it is on the chair. If you don't succeed, try harder! When you give up, go on to the next paragraph.)

(You see, you probably weren't even aware of sitting until it was drawn to your attention. Trying to stop thinking does not help because you must think in order to try to stop.)

The insomniac cannot sleep because he or she is trying to avoid insomnia, equating it with thinking and moving. Therefore we tell the insomniac (injecting some humor as we say it), "Do not try to avoid thinking. Do not try to avoid moving. All living beings think and move, even while asleep. If thinking happens, just let it happen, and continue to stay there. It is possible to get refreshing sleep while being aware of thoughts during the night, so long as you do not respond to them by getting up or changing the sleep time. If some night you realize that you are not moving or thinking, you should call the undertaker because you have probably died." We then promote self-awareness of the healthy pattern by asking the patients for one night to prove to themselves that they are really alive by keeping a note pad by the bed, with the instructions that immediately upon rising in the morning, they should estimate and mark on the pad approximately how many times they were aware during their sleep of having a thought and how many times they were aware of having moved. We tell them that normal people may be aware of at least five instances each, and in some cases may double that.

Relaxation. Relaxation exercises are an asset to an individual learning to sleep (see chapter 3). The application to problems of insomnia comes with two explicit instructions. The relaxation exercise is not to be used to fall asleep, since this creates a counterproductive cognitive behavior. Explain this to the patient in the following manner:

"Use a short version (1 to 5 minutes) of this relaxation exercise to help yourself relax sometime before falling asleep. However, try not to fall asleep while you are doing it. If you fall asleep anyway, it's okay, but next time try to stay awake until you have finished the relaxation. Similarly, during the night, if for some reason you have interrupted your sleep with a trip to the bathroom or a phone call, assume a relaxed attitude, and if you have been up for more than 5 minutes, you can do a couple of more minutes of relaxation, but try not to fall asleep until you have finished the relaxation. With time, you will find that you begin to fall asleep quite often while you have been doing the relaxation. When that happens, shorten the amount of minutes of relaxation that you allow yourself, so that you will have time to finish it before falling asleep."

Awareness is then promoted by having the patient self-monitor; in the morning after rising, the patient records approximately how many minutes of relaxation were used. If sleep seemed to cut the relaxation short, then the patient marks how many minutes of relaxation should be shortened in subsequent nights. He or she should be told that it is not at all intended that relaxation should be used every night, because sometimes sleep will come too quickly, and similarly, monitoring needs to be done only occasionally, just to get an idea of how long the relaxation should be done.

Imagery. Imagery can be used anytime. The same imagery that has been learned during relaxation is permissible to use while falling asleep. The following dialogue will explain this to the patient:

"When people are drifting off to sleep, they think both in thoughts and in images. These often will be rambling images and memories of the day and other things. You might begin to realize that the images you have used while doing your relaxation exercises can also come into your thoughts from time to time. You will probably notice though that you can't concentrate completely on them, and no image or thought might stay for very long. Even worried thoughts will tend to come and go and get mixed up with other images. The reason for this is that you are already falling asleep."

Self-awareness is promoted by having the patient record after rising in the morning the images that were most frequent or vivid. They will not always be the same ones, and the patient will not always remember. Nor should he or she try to monitor this every morning. The aim, however, is just to get some idea, and if some image tends to be more frequent just before falling asleep, he or she might then try to recall on subsequent mornings if the same image had appeared. These images might also be incorporated into the relaxation exercises that are done at other times during the day.

Insomnia behavior is a form of avoidance in which the insomniac becomes fearful that he or she is not actually sleeping. He or she then wakes up and begins to do something other than sleep. The analogous thing may happen just prior to sleep onset. Here, the individual may read, smoke, watch television, or "try to get sleepy" in order to avoid the adverse experience of trying to sleep and being unable to do so. We discussed earlier that the insomniac must be carefully instructed to stop trying to sleep. Self-awareness is promoted by using the Checklist for

Sleep Problems. Self-monitoring is done for those items that are most suspected of being insomnia behaviors. If there are relatively few, the patient is instructed simply to be aware of them and not to fall into the trap of sleep avoidance. He or she is asked to monitor in the morning after rising how many times he or she was tempted to give in to the old habits, and what enabled him or her to continue the sleeping attitude. With time, there will be awareness of better coping with the temptations. If on the other hand there are many habits and rituals during the night, and if the person has continued to get up frequently, he or she is asked to monitor *at the time of sleep interruption* the number and type of interruptions (smoking, drinking tea, looking out the window, walking, etc.). After 1 week, an average is taken of each of the key behaviors that have occurred more than four times during the night. The assignment is now prospective. The insomniac is assigned the specific task of rising during the night exactly that number of times to do those specific habits, chart them on the self-monitoring form, and then go back to bed again. The patient must rise exactly that number of times, not one more or less. An alarm may be used for the purpose. This goes on for a week. Then, the insomniac is allowed to reduce the number of awakenings by one (for each habit) every 3 days until there are no more awakenings. The only exception is that if the person prefers to go to the bathroom during the night, he or she may do so if the number is no more than one third the total number of times that he or she goes to the bathroom in the daytime. For example, an insomniac's average may be eight wakenings, with five times to go to the bathroom and three to go sit in a chair and look out the window. He or she would then be assigned to set the alarm for eight wakenings, and on days 1 to 7 would rise five times for the bathroom and three for sitting in a chair. On nights 8 to 10, he or she would be allowed four trips to the bathroom and two to sit in a chair. On nights 11 to 13 he or she would be allowed three trips to the bathroom and one to the chair, and so on.

Coping

There are several possible coping strategies. In broad terms, the elements are as follows:

1. Reevaluate beliefs about sleep.
2. Conduct self-monitoring to determine problems in sleep-wake schedule that may interfere with circadian rhythm.
3. Stimulate behavioral and environmental control. Arrange that distractions such as TV or reading material be moved out of the bedroom. Eliminate chemicals that impair sleep. If detoxification is

needed over a period of time, this can be done concurrently with the rest of the program.

4. Learn a relaxation technique. Integrate it into the daily routine – not as a method to induce sleep, but rather to be more rested and prepared for sleep.

5. Institute an exercise program. This should be done in the day or early evening, not just before bedtime.

More than one approach is possible for stabilizing the sleeping time. Two alternatives are illustrated here. For someone who tends to wake up too early, feels restless and unable to remain in bed, and for whom efforts to stay in bed simply result in increased restlessness and frustration, try giving the following instructions to the patient:

"Keep a diary for a few days. Determine the average sleeping time and take this as the starting duration of sleep. Choose a bedtime that will remain constant. At night, go to bed at that time. Keep the room dark. Chart the number of awakenings, times out of bed, and activities engaged in during the night. Each successive night, eliminate influences that have disturbed the pattern of sleep. Assume the attitude that it is normal to become aware of thinking periodically during the night, and that awareness of thinking is not to be feared. Make it clear that adjusting one's sleeping position periodically during the night is normal.

"The alarm should be set the first few nights for the average sleeping time that was originally calculated. At that time, it is necessary to rise, and no naps are allowed. Do not return to bed for any reason until the following night at the same time. Eventually, you will begin to sleep right up to the time of the alarm, rather than waking spontaneously. When the alarm wakens you on two of three occasions, increase the sleep time half an hour longer. Keep this up until you awaken half the time with the alarm and half the time spontaneously."

Frequently, insomnia involves problems attaining and maintaining sleep. In the following suggestion the objective is the same as above: to avoid worrying and nighttime rituals, and to create a stronger circadian rhythm.

"Agree on a fixed wakening time and set the alarm for that same time each morning. Do not nap or sleep in at any time. The strategy at night is to stay out of the bedroom until you feel drowsy. Go to bed and turn out the light immediately. If sleep does not ensue fairly quickly, get out of bed again and leave the bedroom. Return only when drowsy. Repeat the process until sleep ensues. If you waken during the night, record the activities engaged in, and on successive nights eliminate behaviors that interfere with sleep. After a few weeks, a more definite pattern of sleep will emerge, always with the same fixed waking time. To further increase the sleeping time, the bedtime should be made earlier."

Communication

Communication transactions with prescribing doctors have much to do with the perpetuation of the insomnia problem. The typical transaction begins with an attitude, shared by prescriber and patient alike, that portrays insomnia as a medical problem and puts major emphasis on medication as a solution. This has the effect of reducing the individual's sense of self-control and increasing the probability that the insomnia will be perpetuated through drugs, side effects, and avoidance behavior. The power struggles that ensue perpetuate these beliefs and aggravate the sense of not being in control. Typically, the insomniac complains of the inability to sleep and the physician offers a medication. After a few weeks, the patient returns, still dissatisfied. The physician gives a higher dose or stronger drug, this time with a warning. The patient returns dissatisfied, asking what the doctor is going to try now. The doctor tries again, with further admonitions. This all has the effect of convincing the patient that the insomnia is incurable, even with the use of strong drugs, and the admonitions of the doctor may serve to engender a sense of guilt or resistance and the feeling that the doctor holds the only solutions but is dispensing them unwillingly. There is nothing that can convince the patient that the insomnia is something that can be understood in terms of "what I am doing" instead of "what I am suffering from."

Communication by the insomniac not only gives information to the therapist, but also affects the patient him- or herself through the occasion of "self-talk." Because one perceives one's own behavior and communication, the way one describes a problem has an effect on how one evaluates it. (See earlier sections in this chapter on mistaken assumptions about sleep.)

Feedback

Dealing with insomniacs as patients requires time and a series of steps in which the insomniac can get a sense of competence to change the problem. This means that in the course of visits, the clinician concentrates specifically on homework assignments, beginning with completion of diaries and self-assessments, and going on to gradual detoxification and change of sleep habits, all the while giving clear verbal reinforcement for the positive steps taken by the patient. The patient is encouraged systematically so that the focus changes from the subjective complaint to the coping efforts.

Self-Maintenance

In any clinical problem, the issue of aftercare must be addressed. Aftercare involves follow-up and the patient's commitment to self-maintenance. Self-maintenance is achieved gradually, but is especially guaranteed by integrating the sleep control program with the more comprehensive program of stress control (and relaxation), elimination of drugs and dependencies that aggravate sleep and bring the patient back to the doctor, and promotion of fitness and regular exercise that enhance health. In this way, insomnia control becomes part of a pattern of healthful feelings that are self-reinforcing.

CHECKLIST FOR SLEEP PROBLEMS

Circle the statements that have been true for you in the past week.

A. Habits that interfere with sleep:

During the past week I took a nap during the day because I had not slept well the night before.

I take naps at different times—morning, afternoon, or evening—depending on how I feel.

I often sleep late in the morning because I have not had a good night's sleep.

I often sleep in because it takes so long to fall asleep at night.

Sometimes I like a really big snack before I go to bed.

I often like a mug of tea or coffee before bedtime, or during the night if I wake up.

I go to bed at different times, sometimes early and sometimes very late, depending on how sleepy I feel.

B. Avoidance behavior that interferes with sleep:

Because I can't sleep, at least once a week I end up sleeping in a place other than my usual bed—a chair, a couch, a different bed, and so forth.

If I can't sleep, I prefer to stay up later until I feel sleepy enough to drop off to sleep.

Sometimes I have to watch television until I fall asleep.

When I wake up during the night, I might do one or more of the following: eat a snack; have a pill; drink alcohol, tea, or coffee; smoke; read; watch television; or listen to the radio.

During the night, I usually check the alarm clock or watch at least once because I am having trouble getting to sleep.

Because I can't sleep, I often get up to work or study.

At least once a week, and maybe more, I have some liquor or other alcohol to try to help me sleep.

I need a sleeping pill, a tranquilizer, a muscle relaxant, or a painkiller medication in order to sleep.

Anything is better than lying awake at night, just knowing that I am going to have another sleepless night.

I often can't sleep at night because thoughts keep going on and on in my head, even though I try not to think about anything.

If you have checked off any of these items, you are suffering from poor quality and unrefreshing sleep, and you will benefit from a sleep correction program.

Chapter 5

Anxiety, Fears, and Phobias

DESCRIPTION OF THE PROBLEM

For the past 15 years, Mrs. T., a 48-year-old married woman, has had a fear of thunderstorms. The fear has become so severe that a hint of poor weather is enough to keep her housebound. During actual storms she retires to her bed and hides under the covers. Because of the intensity and duration of the problem she feels distressed and hopeless. All of her daily activities are dependent on the weather. In talking to her family and friends, she is aware that her reaction to thunderstorms is excessive, but the distress and preoccupation does not diminish.

Two years ago, while returning home from work, Mrs. A. had a sudden "attack": she became aware that her heart was pounding, she could not catch her breath, and she broke into a cold sweat. For what appeared to her to be an eternity, things became unreal, she felt weak, and she thought that she was going to die. Within a few months of the incident, Mrs. A. avoided being alone and progressively stopped all activities outside of the home.

For as long as he can remember, Mr. S., a sales manager for a large firm, has been extremely concerned about being embarrassed or humiliated. Because of these fears he has avoided eating or speaking in public. The avoidance of these activities makes it difficult for him to do his work and enjoy social activity. There is an intense sense of shame with this, making Mr. S. very secretive about his problem. With the exception of his wife, no one knows, not even his children.

The most frequent challenge for the clinician consists of dealing with a patient who presents with severe and disabling symptoms but who shows no demonstrable organic pathology. The clinician is left with labeling the problem as functional or indicating that the patient is suffering from a psychological disturbance. The treatment that follows will likely be a prescription of anxiolytic medication.

Epidemiological studies suggest that the most prevalent psychological disturbances in the general population are related to anxiety, fear, and phobias (Myers et al., 1984). Up to 20% of these disturbances are linked to high levels of anxiety and a somewhat smaller percentage qualify for a psychiatric diagnosis of anxiety disorders (Robins, et al., 1984). The most frequently occurring disorders associated with anxiety are simple phobia, agoraphobia, and panic disorder. They are the focus of this chapter. In addition, a less common anxiety disorder—social phobia—will also be discussed.

In clinical practice, anxiety may present in a variety of ways. *The Diagnostic and Statistical Manual of Mental Disorders—third edition, revised* (DSM-III-R) (American Psychiatric Association [APA], 1987) definition and classification will be used here. The classification of these disorders in which anxiety and avoidance behavior are central include:

1. Simple phobia
2. Agoraphobia
3. Social phobia where the anxiety is more or less focused
4. Panic disorder
5. Generalized anxiety disorder, in which anxiety is more pervasive

Anxiety or avoidance also plays an important role in the following:

6. Obsessive compulsive disorder
7. Post-traumatic stress disorder

Although obsessive compulsive disorder is included in the DSM-III-R classification of anxiety disorder, it will not be discussed in this chapter. A manual for the treatment of obsessive compulsive disorder recently has been published (Turner & Beidel, 1988). The post-traumatic stress syndrome is discussed in chapter 12.

BACKGROUND

The concept of anxiety has played a central role in theories of personality development and psychopathology. It has been extensively studied within biological, psychological, and sociological contexts. From the point of view of treatment, anxiety management is described according to psychodynamic, behavioral and psychopharmacological treatment models.

Anxiety is an ever-present clinical phenomenon in emotional problems. Although this chapter attempts to make clinicians aware of the diverse aspects of anxiety, the focus is on the treatment of anxiety disorders, illustrated by the case studies in the chapter opening.

ANXIETY AS AN UNPLEASANT EMOTIONAL STATE

The experience of anxiety is an unpleasant state, that involves (a) what we think (cognitive experience), (b) what we feel (emotional experience), and (c) what we do (action experience). The overall experience may include apprehension, worry, feelings of tension and nervousness, palpitations, sweating, dryness of the mouth, dizziness, nausea, feeling of weakness, hyperventilation, restlessness, tremors, and actions to avoid or escape. In an investigation (Buss, 1962) in which patients were asked their personal definition of anxiety, responses were summarized into the following two categories: (a) autonomic overactivity (e.g., heart palpitations) and (b) conditioned anxiety categories, with subcategories of striate muscle tension, and feelings of anxiety (e.g., inability to concentrate). Normally, a patient presenting with these signs and symptoms is screened for organic disorder because there are many organic disorders that mimic anxiety or that may precipitate or coexist with an anxiety disorder.

In this century, the early clinical studies of anxiety were carried out within the psychoanalytic perspective, and from these explorations came the clinical treatment of anxiety disorders. However, records from Egypt and Greece, biblical times, and other cultures give evidence of the awareness of the experience of anxiety even in antiquity.

Theories have attempted to answer a number of questions about anxiety, from the normal to the pathological:

- What constitutes the experience of anxiety?
- In what sense is anxiety normal?
- What are the biological, psychological, and behavioral components?
- Is anxiety experienced and expressed differently at different points in human development?
- What constitutes pathological anxiety?
- Are there individual differences in vulnerability to pathological anxiety?
- Can abnormal anxiety be prevented and/or modified?

The reader can explore the questions of interest by consulting the texts by Barlow (1988) and Marks (1987).

SIMPLE PHOBIA

Simple phobia is an anxiety disorder that is sometimes referred to as specific phobia because it occurs suddenly when the patient is exposed to the specific phobic stimulus. The basic ingredients consist of intense anxiety associated with circumscribed objects or situations, and a strong tendency to avoid them.

The DSM-III-R (APA, 1987) description of a phobic disorder is

> a persistent fear of a circumscribed stimulus. . . . Marked anticipatory anxiety occurs if the person is confronted with the [possibility of encountering these] situations and the avoidance behavior interferes with the person's normal routine . . . or if there is marked distress about having the fear (pp. 243-244).

The essential features of a phobia are

> (a) It is a fear that is out of proportion to the actual danger, (b) it cannot be explained or reasoned away, (c) it is beyond voluntary control, and (d) it leads to the escape and/or avoidance of the feared stimulus (Marks, 1969, p. 3).

Although simple phobias have been extensively studied over the years, very little is known about predisposing factors. The age of onset of the disorder varies and some types of phobias (e.g., of animals) begin in childhood, some (e.g., of injury) in adolescence, and others (e.g., of air travel) in adulthood. Unlike the simple phobias that appear in childhood and tend to resolve untreated, adult phobias do not improve without treatment. If the phobic object or situation is easily avoided, there is little interference in the person's life and consequently treatment is not sought. However, if the phobic object or situation cannot be avoided, severe impairment in functioning may be experienced.

AGORAPHOBIA

In the classification of anxiety disorder according to DSM-III-R, fear of being trapped or out of control in a situation is distinguished from simple phobia. Agoraphobia is described as

> the fear of being in places or situations from which escape might be difficult or embarrassing or in which help might not be available in the event of suddenly developing a symptom(s) that could be incapacitating or extremely embarrassing (APA, 1987, p. 240).

Agoraphobia, unlike simple phobia, does not present as a single complaint. Patients with agoraphobia present with a cluster of fears that characteristically include public transportation, confined places (bridges, tunnels, stores, elevators), being away from home, and being home alone. The onset of agoraphobia can be sudden or gradual and the symptoms may involve a range of physiological and psychological reactions. Patients with agoraphobia may not be able to give reasons why they are afraid, although they may be aware of the circumstances in which their distress increases.

Data indicate that this disorder tends to begin at 20 to 30 years of age. It tends to persist for decades if untreated. In clinical settings, it tends to be diagnosed primarily in women. The combination of fear and avoidance may lead patients to lead a restricted existence to the point of becoming housebound.

SOCIAL PHOBIA

The central characteristics of social phobia are fear of humiliation, embarrassment, and scrutiny by others. A general fear of negative evaluation seems to be pervasive. In the process of engaging in or anticipating fearful situations, patients may experience physiological and mental distress. Social phobia may range from fear of public speaking, eating in public, using public washrooms, or involvement in a variety of social contacts (APA, 1987).

PANIC DISORDER

Panic is an experience that can occur unpredictably or in particular situations. Clinical and research data indicate that patients experiencing a panic attack can be guided to report cognitive events that are linked to the onset, course, and consequence of the attack. A distinction should be made between panic attacks, which can occur in all anxiety disorders, and panic disorder, which is a separate category in the DSM-III-R classification. The clinical presentation of panic attacks should lead to screening for possible medical problems associated with them. Panic attacks have been associated with hypoglycemia, arrhythmias, transient ischemic attacks, angina, pheochromocytoma, hyperthyroidism, asthma, pulmonary emboli, seizures, and drug intoxication or withdrawal.

Panic disorder is categorized in the DSM-III-R system as occurring with or without symptoms of agoraphobia. As indicated in DSM-III-R, "the essential features of these disorders are recurrent panic attacks, i.e., discrete periods of intense fear or discomfort, with at least four of the characteristic associated symptoms." These symptoms are shortness of breath, dizziness, palpitations, trembling, sweating, choking, nausea, depersonalization or derealization, numbness or tingling sensations, hot flushes, chills, chest pain, fear of dying, or fear of going crazy or losing control (APA, 1987, pp. 237–238). There are clinical and research data suggesting that some of these symptoms are due to hyperventilation during the attack. The emergence of agoraphobia is attributed to the fear of a panic attack in a social situation.

The prevalence of panic symptoms in the general adult population has been estimated from epidemiological studies as being 10%. The prevalence of panic disorders is about 1%. There is a significant level of comorbidity among panic disorders and other anxiety disorders, as well as depression and alcoholism (Weissman, 1988).

GENERALIZED ANXIETY DISORDER

A pervasive feeling of anxiety is the core characteristic of generalized anxiety disorder. The patient's preoccupations, worry, and anxious ruminations tend to be triggered by thoughts and/or mood changes. The DSM-III-R describes the essential features of generalized anxiety disorders as "unrealistic or excessive anxiety and worry (apprehensive expectations) about two or more life circumstances . . . for 6 months or more, during which the person has been bothered by these concerns more days than not" (APA, 1987, p. 251). Apprehensive expectation can be expressed by a variety of symptomatic behaviors that involve motor tension, autonomic hyperactivity, and vigilance or scanning.

INFORMATION FOR PATIENTS

The purpose for giving information to patients is twofold: (a) to teach the patient about what is generally known about the distress the patient is experiencing and (b) to use the sharing of knowledge as a method of initiating the patient into the role of an active participant in the treatment process. The clinician must decide on how much information, and at what rate it is to be given to the individual patient. This decision can be based in part on the type and severity of the anxiety disorder, and the insight the patient has. It is important to keep in mind that high levels of anxiety lead to a dramatic decrease in the ability to take in new information. Structuring of the steps in the learning process reduces anxiety and improves efficiency. Practical exercises are more helpful than information alone. Repetition of material with some rehearsal and feedback helps the process of attending and remembering. In addition, the clinician may have some written material as a handout for the patient.

The content of the information given to patients should include the distinction between normal and problematic anxiety, the process of normal bodily functions, the changes in functioning due to the anxiety disorder, and the issues of coping and control. Some patients need information about normal respiratory functions and the typical changes in body functioning due to hypoventilation and hyperventilation.

The experience of anxiety is a normal part of life. However, anxiety can be seen as potentially having a pathological role in a person's life instead of an adaptive role. In its adaptive role, anxiety seems to function as an energizer of behavior and/or a catalyst that focuses attention and improves functioning on task performance. In its pathological role, anxiety disrupts functioning. Therefore, the goal of therapy may not aim to eliminate anxiety, but to reduce or maintain it within normal limits.

Example of Information for Patients

(The following script is an example of how to provide a general outline of anxiety to the patient.)

"As a patient suffering from pathological anxiety, you experience fear that tends to take over and paralyze you. You may worry excessively or anticipate that something terrible will happen to you. You may experience an anxiety attack that is triggered by stressful events in your life or it may appear to come out of the blue. You may feel anxious wherever you are or you may become anxious only in specific situations. Thinking about upcoming events may make you so anxious that you eventually feel unable to leave home or stay alone in the house.

"We know that you are not alone in this distress, since anxiety disorders are the most common disorders. For some sufferers, the distress can be tolerated and everyday functioning continued. For others, it is so severe that the person can become totally disabled. Anxiety may appear in a variety of ways." (Here the clinician may describe the anxiety disorder that approximates the patient's experience.)

"Some people inherit a certain tendency to be anxious. Learning from frightening experiences may have led to the severe fears and avoidance that makes it hard for you to face certain things. We are gradually coming to understand more and more about the reactions in our bodies that make us feel panic.

"Treatment results for anxiety disorders tend to be good even for the most severe cases. We will discuss a number of methods to help you deal with your problem of anxiety. Our first task in addressing your anxiety is to do some things to get specific information about your distress. You will then learn relaxation techniques, how to control inappropriate thought patterns, and methods to help you get control in the anxiety-producing situations."

ASSESSMENT AND TREATMENT

Our focus is on behavioral medicine measures. The comprehensive treatment of anxiety addresses the specific physiological reactions, thoughts, feelings, attitudes, and behaviors related to the anxiety problem. Our organizing principle is helping patients with anxiety in a specific and directed way to control the symptoms experienced. For example, the agoraphobic patient is helped to engage in performing daily tasks, whereas the patient who experiences panic attacks is encouraged to perform procedures that lead to panic control. This approach focuses on symptom relief as the first goal of treatment.

Because anxiety is an important feature of many psychiatric disorders, the clinician must be prepared for the fact that a particular patient may require different management than is described in this chapter, including the use of psychopharmacology. In the Selected Readings section at the back of the book we give references for clinicians who may want to read about the use of psychopharmacological agents for the treatment of anxiety disorders.

General Principles of Treatment

Anxiety is influenced by the interaction of cognitive, emotional, biological, behavioral, and communication factors (Figure 5.1). The overview of our behavior medicine treatment for anxiety can be summarized as follows:

1. Repeated, systematic, and gradual approach to feared and/or avoided situations.
2. Development of a sense of self control (see chapter 1).
   (a) use of low arousal procedures (relaxation skills)
   (b) attainment of coping skills that address cognition (assumptions and beliefs, expectations and appraisal of the anxiety situation, images, internal dialogue, and self-statements)
3. Guidelines for self-direction throughout the treatment.

Evaluation

Beliefs and Interpretations. Inappropriate beliefs and interpretations are a basic contributing factor to anxiety. The experience of anxiety itself is

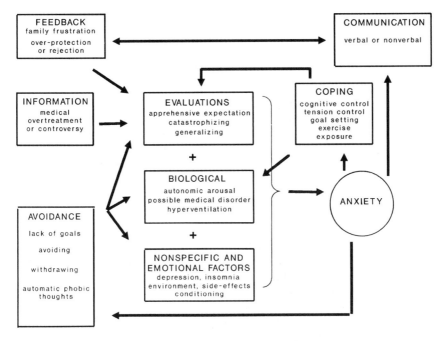

FIGURE 5.1. Algorithm for anxiety.

associated with images and thoughts that exaggerate and/or distort the degree of danger that patients find themselves in. The patient's cognitions are that he or she is in a state of physical, psychological, and/or social danger. The psychological danger may be a fear that the anxiety itself will become unbearable. These cognitions also interact with sensory experiences and emotion in a vicious cycle that escalates the anxiety experience. The other side of the coin is the patient's ever-growing sense of inability to cope. Eventually even everyday experiences are given catastrophic interpretations.

Investigating the Problem. The experience of anxiety must be explored within the context of the patient's life situation. As indicated in the introduction of this chapter, anxiety may be a symptom of physical disorders or it may coexist with organic conditions. Physical disorders that might be causing the problem must be ruled out (Hall, 1980).

Each clinician has his or her own approach for gathering information. Many clinicians find the "graduated funnel" approach helpful (Nelson & Barlow, 1981). By starting with a global question, the clinician explores the patient's presenting problems, the history, and the patient's life situation. This general inquiry is followed by exploring the specific pattern of the anxiety problem.

Self-Evaluation. The patient's self-monitoring helps to identify the specific factors associated with the problem. It may help to delineate the problem's frequency, intensity, and duration. (For guidelines to implement self-monitoring see the description in chapter 2.) Direct the patient to use the standard symptom-monitoring chart (Figure 2.3) to note anxiety on a five-point scale periodically during the day, and write on the left side what was happening, what his or her thoughts were, and what actions he or she took. It also could be used to monitor use of drugs, cigarettes, and tea and coffee. An important dimension in the treatment of anxiety is avoidance behavior. The patient must be guided to monitor what was avoided, and how the avoidance occurred.

Biological Substrates

Traditionally anxiety has been investigated biologically in its role for adaptation and survival. More relevant to the clinical situation is recent study in the neurobiology and pharmacology of anxiety. Underlying biological abnormalities in the anxiety disorders have been postulated from genetic studies and from epidemiological studies about distribution of disorders, biochemical provocation of anxiety, and treatment efficacy of many categories of medications. The medications that have been used to treat anxiety disorders include benzodiazepines, tricyclic antidepressants, monoamine oxidase inhibitors, and beta-adrenergic blockers (Last & Hersen, 1988).

Anxiety is not just something that happens to a person—it is something he or she does. When a person is anxious, his or her body prepares him for fight or flight. Muscles tense, heart rate increases, and blood is diverted to where it is most needed. Adrenaline is poured into the circulation. Breathing becomes more rapid and deep. In a genuine emergency this is good. But when faced with apprehensiveness that does not go away, the person may go through this preparation but have no way to discharge the tension and let the crisis pass. The continued rapid breathing shifts the blood chemistry so that calcium is not able to work properly, and muscles get tighter and go into spasms. The hyperventilation sets off more adrenaline release, which increases the anxiety and makes breathing even faster. The tight chest muscles give the feeling of not being able to catch one's breath, so that the person may begin to sigh more deeply. All of his may occur at a nonawareness level so that the patient may not realize that it is a vicious circle. The object of treatment is to teach tension and breathing awareness and breathing control exercises to get control of this cycle.

Nonspecific Symptoms and Emotional Factors

The complex presentation of an anxiety disorder can become more confusing when subsequent factors become part of the symptom complex. These may be drug related or dietary, or caused by coexistence of a medical disorder. The patient's clinical presentation may be caused or made more severe by drug toxicity due to treatments that the patient may be receiving. These drugs include many prescription and nonprescription drugs and caffeine. The withdrawal of alcohol and sedative–hypnotics may also trigger anxiety symptoms. Although alcohol at first may reduce anxiety, continuous use makes anxiety worse. Environmental factors and working conditions may also influence anxiety symptoms. Patients with anxiety disorders may have disorders of depression, drug abuse, and alcoholism that need direct treatment. Once the contribution of the above factors is identified, corrective procedures may range from educating, to self-monitoring, to withdrawal or stabilization of medication under close medical supervision.

Dealing with Avoidance

People who experience anxiety will develop some degree of avoidance. In simple phobia, the individual may avoid many social situations; in panic disorders, the individual may avoid situations associated with panic attacks; and in agoraphobia, the individual may become housebound. The first step in dealing with avoidance is to identify the unique pattern of avoidance that the individual patient uses in his or her attempts to minimize distress. This includes obtaining information about the role that family, friends, and health-care systems play in avoidance patterns. Once the pattern of avoidance is identified and discontinued, the therapeutic task becomes that of reducing physiological arousal and implementing a program of systematic exposure (see chapter 3).

Guidelines must be given to the patient in order to establish a consistent program of systematic desensitization. Concurrently, instructions should be given to alter maladaptive patterns of thinking associated with the experience of anxiety. The detailed instructions are needed because the patients may not be aware of these automatic upsetting thoughts and images, which go unchallenged by actual data.

The program of direct exposure to the feared event may be undertaken in a rapid or flooding fashion, or in gradual desensitization. This procedure can be carried out in the presence and under directions of the clinician, in the company of the patient's significant other or volunteer, or in a totally self-directed manner by the patient. During these exposure exercises, which should also be carried out between therapy sessions, the patient is asked to remain in the stressful situation for assigned time periods, using relaxation and other coping procedures until the anxiety diminishes.

In the program of indirect exposure, the patient is presented with gradual symbolic cues of the anxiety-producing events, in combination with relaxation. This can be initiated by the therapist and eventually can become self-directed by the patient, who is encouraged to continue regular extensive practices.

Coping

There are many strategies for coping with anxiety and the symptoms associated with anxiety disorders. The first strategy of coping has to do with reducing the high physiological arousal experienced by these patients. The steps are to learn the relaxation skill, make it "portable," become aware of physiological cues of anxiety, and apply the relaxation skills in everyday situations. The second type of strategy is to learn and apply on a daily basis a variety of cognitive coping techniques. These include relabeling and using imagery and altered self-talk. Two additional strategies are the use of systematic desensitization and in vivo exposure. These will be discussed briefly here. Detailed information on how to carry out these procedures is given in "Guidelines for Systematic Desensitization" and "Guidelines for Exposure," pp. 112–118.

Systematic Desensitization

The traditional systematic desensitization was conceptualized as a rather passive counterconditioning procedure. It is better to consider it as an active self-control method that allows the desensitization to become a learned skill that is self-directed and applied to cope with anxiety-producing situations (Goldfried, 1971).

Systematic desensitization appears to work best when the anxiety and avoidance is elicited by specific situations, contexts, or conflicts, even though the patient is aware that there is no actual danger. Examples of anxiety-producing situations appropriate for systematic desensitization include phobias, interpersonal tensions, persistent anxious thoughts and ideas, fear of social criticism, and unpleasant feared bodily sensations. There is a variety of social situations, such as where the patient becomes the center of attention or when a particular person or category of people is present, that systematic desensitization becomes an appropriate coping strategy. This strategy is especially useful where high levels of anxiety prevent the patient from addressing the maladaptive response by direct action, such as problem-solving or assertiveness.

In systematic desensitization, the patient first learns a relaxation skill. Next, a hierarchy of anxiety-producing situations is constructed. Subsequently, the patient is guided to gradually and systematically progress through the hierarchy while maintaining a relaxed state. The patient is directed to determine the pace with which the process occurs. Once the imagery procedure is carried out in vivo exposure exercises are instituted.

Exposure

Using exposure as a coping strategy demands attention both to the high level of autonomic arousal and to the avoidance behavior. The essence of the process of exposure is in guiding and encouraging patients to confront real-life feared objects and situations. The most important variable is the duration of the exposure to the anxiety-producing situation. Inappropriate exposure may lead to the exacerbation of the problem, leading to reinforcement of escape behavior and problems of compliance. Experience shows that prolonged exposure, rather than brief or interrupted exposure, leads to the process of extinction (for details about exposure see the Selected Readings section for chapter 5 at the end of this book).

Communication

Communication plays a part in maintaining the dysfunctional pattern of behavior as well as in affecting the potential for therapeutic change. These interactive systems include the patient's family and the health-care professionals. The aim is to teach the patient and family to alter the communication patterns so that avoidance behavior is reduced and adaptive behavior is encouraged. Thus, it is especially important that the family's help be enlisted to help in the exposure treatment.

Feedback

Feedback is essential for successful completion of various tasks, from appropriate data collecting to the learning of coping skills. The process of appropriate feedback is initiated early and carried on frequently by the clinician, but must generalize to the patient's natural environment. Family members are therefore introduced to the treatment situation and are taught to reinforce the changes made by the patient.

Self-Maintenance

Two aspects of self-maintenance of therapeutic change can be high-lighted. The first is related to regular use of coping skills that are incompatible with the experience of debilitating anxiety and avoidance behavior. The second aspect can be captured by the concept of a "booster shot." From time to time patients may need the help of the clinician to review and reactivate coping procedures that have helped to control anxiety.

GUIDELINES FOR SYSTEMATIC DESENSITIZATION

The following is the step-by-step procedure for implementing a systematic desensitization program. Although the procedure is set to run for ten sessions, the number of sessions as well as the order used can be altered to fit the specific problem.

Session 1. Outline of Introduction to Patient

Objectives of this session:

1. Establish a working relationship.
2. Discuss extent and duration of anxiety.
3. Explain the nature of the treatment.
4. Incorporate relaxation training.
5. Introduce hierarchy.
6. Do homework.

These objectives should be covered using a psychotherapeutic interview format in order to discover attitudes and to show empathy.

Discussion with Patients. The rationale and explanation of treatment should be presented in a format that allows discussion. Feel free to paraphrase the following therapist script and use your own expression and examples.

"So far we have discussed the anxiety you experience in a number of situations. You have also learned how relaxation can help you reduce anxiety. The treatment procedure that we are about to begin is designed to eliminate your fear concerning these situations and reduce anxiety. It is a treatment approach we have been using with people very much like yourselves. The two main procedures are relaxation and learning the skill of self-control. You have been trained to systematically relax all parts of your body. The real advantage of relaxation is that the muscles in your body cannot be both tense and relaxed at the same time. Therefore, you can use relaxation to control anxiety, tenseness, and feelings you experience in feared situations.

"Since relaxation can be used to reduce anxiety and tension, you will be asked to continue to practice it. However, many times it is inconvenient to use relaxation, and it is not a miracle cure to permanently prevent anxiety. We combine the relaxation technique with the self-control skills to actually desensitize you to situations so that anxiety no longer occurs.

"We will help you to make a list of things that make you anxious, from least to greatest. This is called a hierarchy. We will then ask you to imagine each thing, going gradually from the least to the most anxiety-provoking situations, and with each description you will also be given an opportunity to relax."

Relaxation Training. In a discussion with the patient(s), the therapist reviews the role of relaxation in counteracting anxiety. This is followed by actual training of relaxation (see chapter 3).

Introduction of Hierarchy. Identifying stimuli for desensitization and developing a hierarchy requires skill on the part of the clinician. The task involves isolating the most important factor in the anxiety and/or in the impairment and avoidance. The stimuli eliciting anxiety almost always can be categorized around a limited number of themes. An example of this is the theme of fear of rejection for patients who experience anxiety in social situations. By careful data collection and discussions, the therapist must decide on the most relevant parameter of the fear and work toward the most useful hierarchy that considers the facets of person, space, and time. By picking the most important stimuli for desensitization, generalization will often occur so that other related fears will also come under control.

The developed hierarchy should act as a flexible guide in the desensitizations. It should be easily altered to incorporate new data. The hierarchy should consist of about 10 to 15 items selected in such a way as to be graduated along a scale from 0 to 100, where 0 represents no anxiety and 100 represents maximum anxiety. The items should be as concrete and explicit as possible because the patient must imagine each situation as described by the therapist.

To convey what a hierarchy is like, the therapist may illustrate by using a simple hierarchy about the fear of driving or fear of heights, through use of a metaphor, as described by Goldfried and Davison (1976). They suggested that the patients think of their total anxiety as a large balloon full of an infinite number of elements that are associated with a given amount of anxiety. The hierarchy attempts to sample from the balloon in such a way as to have a good representation of all the elements in the balloon.

A discussion on the nature of a hierarchy is carried out beginning with a discussion that links the hierarchy to the desensitization process. As an example of this, the following discussion can be paraphrased and expanded.

"Systematic desensitization is done slowly, step by step in your imagination at first. When this is completed, you gradually expose yourself to a variety of actual situations by starting with those that cause little or no anxiety and gradually moving up to the most anxiety-producing situations. We call this ordered series of scenes an anxiety hierarchy or ladder." (Continue the presentation and discussion illustrating the nature of a hierarchy, and using examples of a hierarchy for simple phobias.)

Homework. Give instructions about home practice of relaxation. Have the patients make notes about their relaxation—what helps them or what inhibits them. Collect data relevant to a personal hierarchy by having patients record situations and events, and thoughts associated with them, in which they experience anxiety symptoms.

Session 2: Focus on Hierarchy

Objectives of this session:

1. Create a high profile for importance of homework.
2. Have a detailed discussion about hierarchy construction.
3. Assign homework that relates to the current session.

Review of Homework. By words and actions we want to convey to the patient that the homework is the most important thing that a patient can do to make this procedure a success. Collect the homework. Discuss the experiences in practicing relaxation and in collecting data relevant to the hierarchy. In giving feedback about the homework maintain a positive stance. If the patient has accomplished little, emphasize the importance of what the patient has accomplished. Also, help the patient find ways to improve compliance and satisfaction in homework activities (compliance is discussed in chapter 2).

Construction of Hierarchy. Highlight again for the patient that the list of tension-producing situations to be developed will help with attaining skills to cope successfully, first in the imagination and then in real-life situations. The current task is to work toward making a hierarchy that has an underlying theme that cuts across the common elements in all of the anxiety-producing situations. Once it has been developed, other individualized hierarchies to be used at home can be developed.

The steps to constructing a hierarchy include the following:

1. Give a brief description of a situation that you find pleasant and free of anxiety. Give it an anxiety/tension scale of 0.
2. Describe a situation that causes you the most anxiety. Give this situation an anxiety scale of 100.
3. Describe 10 to 15 additional situations that vary in anxiety between 0 to 100, with a distance of about 5 to 10 separating the items.
4. Each situation should be briefly discribed, yet have enough information to allow for vivid and accurate visualization during relaxation. It should include, where appropriate, place, people, and distance from the feared thing and duration of exposure to that thing. Each situation should be one that can be realistically experienced by the patient in real life.

Homework. Teach the patients how to practice a method of relaxation and have them practice it at home, keeping a diary of progress. Continue to explore material relevant to the hierarchy by having patients continue to record anxiety episodes, especially noting the thoughts associated with the anxiety.

Session 3: Begin Actual Desensitization

Objectives of this session:

1. Review of homework.
2. Completion of hierarchy construction.
3. Introduction of the desensitization process using mental images.
4. Identification of problems with the desensitization process.
5. Assignment of relevant homework.

Review of Homework. Collect and discuss the daily record on the application of relaxation. Discuss this skill as an aid to coping. Discuss additional data relevant to the anxiety hierarchy.

Completion of Hierarchy. Having collected a series of situations that cause anxiety, have the patient rate each situation for its propensity to cause anxiety. Using the input from the patient, construct a final hierarchy consisting of about 15 items evenly spaced between 0 and 100 on the anxiety distress scale.

Introduction of Desensitization. The exercise is first carried out under full direction of the therapist. The sequence to follow is listed below.

1. Have the patient relax for about 5 to 10 minutes.
2. Give instructions for visualizing the lowest item on the hierarchy, while encouraging the patient to return to the relaxed posture and breathing each time that anxiety increases.
3. Put the patient through two or three items of the hierarchy.
4. Bring closure to the desensitization by repeating the first item, demonstrating that this item no longer produces the anxiety that it once did.

Identification of Problems. Discuss the experience with desensitization, clarify questions, and work out procedural problems. Give tips on how to improve visualization.

Homework. Have patients continue to practice the shortened form of relaxation. Have them pay attention to occasions when they were able to apply relaxation as a coping skill, keeping a record. Have them carry out a daily visualization practice, using a pleasant scene.

Sesssions 4 to 7

Sessions 4 to 7 are desensitization sessions and follow the procedure of practice, identifying problems, homework, and self-monitoring.

Sessions 8 to 10

Sessions 8 to 10 are devoted to the implementation of real-life exposure. Review the rationale of exposing oneself to the feared situation, without attempting to flee. The monitoring procedures include having the patient rate his or her anxiety on a 0 to 100 anxiety distress scale. Have the patient pay attention to the variables of places, people, distance from the feared thing, and duration. Patients should wear a watch to monitor the time. Situations for exposure should be chosen in such a way that the more feared situations are approached slowly and later.

Options available to the patient are to approach the feared situations in the company of a significant other who gives support, in the company of the therapist, or in a self-directed program, which is, however, regularly reviewed with the therapist (see "Guidelines for Exposure" below).

GUIDELINES FOR EXPOSURE

Exposure to feared situations must be set up in a systematic way and should make use of the research findings, which suggest that prolonged exposure is more successful than brief exposure. The exposure tasks may be carried out directly by the patient, in the presence of the therapist, in the presence of the patient's significant other, or with a combination of all three approaches. Another suggestion is to use the help of a former patient who has graduated from an exposure treatment program.

The patient is given support to take on the responsibility of selecting specific daily exposure goals and keeping a diary of the practice experiences. In exposure, the avoidance behavior is addressed directly, and achievement of the goal leads to a decrease in anxiety. However, it may help if the patient learns and practices the relaxation exercise prior to embarking on an exposure program. The principles that guide the exposure strategy are the concept of self-control and efficacy discussed in chapter 2, and the idea that success in exposure is determined by appropriate goals and repeated practices with ongoing feedback. The self-control of exposure time is important, as is specific feedback on each exposure activity. This feedback comes partly from self-monitoring and partly from observations made by helpers or the therapist. In addition, the following points must be considered in guiding a patient through exposure exercises.

A rationale of the exposure treatment must be given to the patient and to the significant others involved. This should include a description of the experience of physiological and cognitive symptoms of anxiety during the exposure practice, and descriptions of the possible emergence of mental or physical avoidance and escape behaviors. Because patients have on their own attempted to overcome the problem with little success, they need to be helped to understand (even if at first they do not totally accept) how structured exposure will alter the maladaptive pattern. The procedure demands that a patient must agree to perform a task while experiencing anxiety. The therapeutic change will not come from logical arguments but only from self-discovery and learning. By agreeing to participate in a series of activities that put the patient in situations that he or she fears, through the application of coping strategies the patient will achieve this self-discovery and learning.

The specifics of the patient's behavior in fearful situations must be explored in order to give him or her feedback on the more subtle ways he or she engages in avoidance behaviors. An example of this could be the patient who is anxious about social interactions, who during the exposure avoids eye contact, or who tries not to think about what he or she is doing.

The structure imposed on the exposure exercises involves regular practice in confronting progressively more anxiety-producing situations. The patient must be guided to implement different coping procedures instead of the previous avoidance behavior while encountering fearful situations. The coping strategies can be based on relaxation or on a variety of cognitive techniques. It is helpful to begin in the clinic to model and practice the exposure strategy before the patient takes on the task in the natural environment.

It is essential that patients are exposed to anxiety-producing stimuli continuously, without escape or avoidance behavior of any kind. This continuous exposure should persist until anxiety reaches its peak in the specific situation and then decreases, thus indicating that extinction is taking place. After this occurs successfully a few times, the patient is ready to take on the next more demanding situation.

Each exposure session should be clearly defined in terms of place, person, distance, and duration, and is aimed at achieving a specific goal. The pace of the exposure process must take into account the unique situation of the particular patient. Follow-through requires that the patient continue to make use of the new confidence after discharge and continue coping skills practice.

Chapter 6

Chronic Back and Neck Pain

DESCRIPTION OF THE PROBLEM

A 36-year-old man presents with a 5-year history of back pain, which began after a fall down some icy stairs while on duty as a security guard. Since then he has been unable to work. He has been seen by numerous physicians and has not benefitted from various attempts at rehabilitation. He has continued to receive Worker's Compensation benefits and is in an adversarial posture with that agency. He makes frequent calls to his physician and the emergency department of the hospital for injections of painkiller, despite the fact that he is already taking acetaminophen with codeine to a total of 300 mg of codeine per day. There is indication from the wife that he abuses alcohol, but he denies it. His background is that he had a very critical father, tried for a time to make a career in baseball and went as far as the farm leagues as a pitcher, then spent time as a police officer, and finally as a security guard. Relationship problems and/or alcohol played a part in the job changes. He has a macho style, not unpleasant, but not given to insightfulness. His wife is very dependent on him, upset about his drinking, and has occasionally left him, but is ambivalent, and always returns unconditionally. Physical examination shows a great deal of guarding in his movements, and there is complaint of tenderness in the lower back and buttocks. He is mildly obese. There are no neurological signs. Radiography shows some narrowing between the fourth and fifth lumbar vertebrae, with some osteophytes.

A 32-year-old woman presents with pain in the neck and headaches she has had for 2 years, following a rear-end automobile collision. This has interfered with her postgraduate studies, and because of her limited activity tolerance she has put many of her plans for her life on hold: starting a business, having children, pursuing social contacts. The consultation is prompted because she wants a second opinion regarding the rehabilitation that has been prescribed for her: aerobic exercise, pool therapy, massage, stretching, and posture exercises. She states that she has improved considerably in function, and less so in symptoms, since she has been following this therapeutic regime. She takes little medication because she finds that it does not help or causes excessive drowsiness. Physical examination shows limitation to half of normal range of neck rotation and pain on extending, and to a lesser extent on flexing the neck. Arm movement is full but with a sense of discomfort and heaviness of the arms. There are no neurological signs, and radiographs of the neck are normal. She is quite content with the verdict you give that the therapy she has been following is appropriate, and she appears motivated to continue with it.

BACKGROUND

Back and neck problems are considered together since they involve similar pathophysiologies and similar patterns of disabilities. Such pains may begin spontaneously or may result from injuries in the region of the spine. They often occur together in the same patient.

The clinical picture is of constant or recurrent pain that may remain localized or be referred. From the back, it may be referred into the buttocks or down the legs, or be radiated up the spine. From the neck, pain may be radiated into the shoulders, referred into the head to produce headache, or into the arms or the chest.

Epidemiology

Epidemiological surveys have shown that the prevalence of chronic pain in the adult population is 11% or 12% (Crook, Rideout, & Browne, 1984; Sternbach, 1986), and that back pain accounts for one third of these cases. More than half of the cases of back pain come from the age 25 to 44 group. Among injury compensation cases, low back pain accounts for 70% of cases compared with 7% for neck and thorax. Of low back sufferers, three quarters return to work within 3 weeks, but 7.4% have not returned before 6 months. The back pain sufferers account for three quarters of total days absent from work, of medical costs for sick employees, and of costs of indemnity and compensation (Spitzer, 1986).

Treatments in General

Several reviews (Flor & Turk, 1984; Turk & Flor, 1984; Spitzer, 1986) have come to similar conclusions. Various treatments that might seem appropriate and helpful for acute injuries are less helpful or sometimes harmful for chronic pain. The most important example is bed rest, which is useful during the period of acute injury healing, but promotes the development of chronic pain if unduly prolonged or prescribed too long after the injury. Thus, bed rest for back pain is best kept to a period of not more than 3 days if the pain is localized and unaccompanied by signs of sciatica. When pain is referred to the knee level or below, longer bed rest may be necessary in acute cases. For chronic pain, however, where there is no objective evidence of progressive nerve root impairment and in cases of more than 6 months postback surgery, regardless of whether the pain is confined to the back or neck or radiated down a limb, a physically active rehabilitation approach is indicated. Physical treatment measures such as heat, cold, ultrasound, shortwave, microwave diathermy, and massage all have transient effects, as is also the case with traction, manipulation, corsets, braces, or canes. Prolonged physiotherapy is associated with a poor outcome in chronic pain (Hohl, 1974). Antiinflamamatory drugs, antispasmodics, and tranquillizers have a role in acute injury management during the first 7 days. Surgery is usually helpful in patients with clear evidence of progressive nerve root injury, or in cases of spinal instability. Operations for pain alone, or in cases of repeat surgery for back pain, often lead to poor results.

On the other hand, patient education, psychological intervention, and active remobilization of the patient with exercise, occupational therapy, work hardening, and emphasis on early return to work have a great advantage over symptomatic treatments. Such active and behaviorally oriented management can even be used to prevent chronic pain (Fordyce, Brockway, Bergman, & Spengler, 1986; Spitzer, 1986; Linton, Bradley, Jensen, Spangfort, & Sundell, 1989). Lately there has been considerable growth of "back schools" and early intervention programs, and some prevention programs have also been put in place.

INFORMATION FOR PATIENTS

Back pain afflicts about one person in 30, and usually starts in young adulthood, although no age group is exempt. Neck pain is less common, but still a frequent problem.

There are many misconceptions about pain in the back or neck. When we hear about back or neck pain, immediately we may wonder if there is a vertebra injury, a "slipped disk," or a degenerative spine. In fact, the majority of pains in the back or neck come on spontaneously, with no obvious injury or spine disorder. Some cases are due to sprains and strains; anything from a minor strain of muscles and connective tissue to a severe accident, with major strains and bruising of the vertebral column, joints and ligaments, and other nearby tissues. Less than half of the cases of back or neck pain occur in people who have some degree of changes in the radiographs of the spine. These changes are a normal part of aging and therefore the vast majority of us will have such changes and never have any symptoms. A rarer occurrence is that of a larger bulge of a disk or a narrowing caused by thickening of joints that gets in the way of nerve roots or nerve pathways. These sometimes have to be surgically treated. People often fear that they will have to have surgery when they begin to have back or neck pain. It is important for back and neck pain sufferers to know that surgery is necessary only rarely—for less than one case in 100—when tests show that nerves are damaged or the spine is unstable. The vast majority of back and neck sufferers will get better with simple treatments. However, when surgery is necessary for these selected few patients, the results are usually good.

What about the great majority who do not need surgery? Most back and neck pains improve spontaneously over a few weeks or months. Occasionally the pain may be more longlasting, but even then the tendency is for the pain to be fairly constant or to repeat itself frequently for the first 1 to 3 years and then to gradually become less constant, with attacks farther apart, until most people recover satisfactorily. However, it is still necessary to learn how to live with the pain or to have some rehabilitation because the pain may be around for quite awhile.

The steps in the process of injury and recovery must be understood. If you are injured, the cells and tissues of your body are damaged and your body immediately sets out to repair the damage and make new cells and tissues. Inflammation is a natural part of this healing process, and it is the inflammation that causes most of the pain. But healing and inflammation do not go on beyond a few weeks. In fact, it is a common misconception that some wounds or operations take many months or years to heal. During the period of inflammation and healing, what is needed is rest to give the injured part a chance to heal, along with painkillers (if needed), heat, bracing or splints, and other things that soothe the pain.

In 2 to 3 weeks (3 months at the very latest), healing is complete and the inflammation associated with it is gone. This usually means that the pain is gone, too, but in about one case in 10 the pain will last longer. Persistent pain can be caused by many things, such as unnatural posture after injury, muscle and ligament weakness, overprotection of the injured area, wasting of the muscle and tissue and other changes due to lack of use, and increases in sensitivity and tenderness of tissues that have been injured previously. Emotional changes such as insomnia, worry and tension, and fatigue or depression may also be associated with pain, and may be present all at once. What all of these things have in common is that rest and time (or medication) will not make them any better. A return to proper use is the best medicine, since the body is made of living cells and tissues, and the only way to be healthy is to encourage proper use and growth.

Here we must mention some more misconceptions. Sometimes people think that if something hurts, it should be visible on radiograph. Most people with neck or back pain have nothing to see on even the most sophisticated radiographs or scans, and many may not even have signs that can be detected by a specialist in neurology or orthopedics. A similar wrong belief is that if nothing shows in the laboratory tests or radiographs, then the pain is imaginary and unreal. The amount of obvious injury relates, to some degree, to the amount of pain, especially if the injury is fairly recent, but the longer the pain lasts after the injury, the less the amount of pain relates to the amount of injury. If the pain has been going on for longer than it takes to heal, often there is a poor relationship between the amount of pain and the amount of obvious or visible physical problem. But the pain is always real.

If pain persists beyond the usual time required for healing and is always present, or frequently occurring, then we call it chronic. Here we have to deal with another misconception, because people with chronic pain are often afraid to do normal things for fear that they will cause further injury or make the pain worse. It is true that in acute pain (soon after injury) the pain usually is a sign that something is injured and that rest will make it better. But in the case of chronic pain, there isn't any healing. Too much rest might just add to the weakness, cause the posture to be more abnormal, or interfere with the exercise necessary to restore function. Pain might occur with activity or exercise, but it might also occur when doing nothing. Remember also that if you are out of shape, it is natural to ache at first as you begin some activity or exercise. Hurt does not equal harm. The pain you feel does not mean that you are injuring yourself, and you should not be using pain as your guide. It is usually necessary to have a more reliable guide.

The guide to activity should be the promotion of good health, and this is done by being attentive to fitness and flexibility, learning to pace yourself (rather than overdoing things or being inconsistent), adopting good postures, and getting rid of drugs and toxins. The guide is to begin with your current level of fitness for activity, arrange for periods of activity and exercise with regular adequate rest breaks, and then gradually increase your activity, the same way an athlete would work on a fitness program—one step at a time, pain or no pain. Doing this does not give a quick solution to the back or neck pain, but it sets the stage for becoming healthy and fit again so that the whole person can function more normally. Experience with this approach has shown that over the next 3 to 6 months on the average, the pain becomes less of an obstacle to normal living, and over time resolves more quickly.

ASSESSMENT AND TREATMENT

Management of back and neck pain entails recognition of the multiple cognitive, emotional, biological, behavioral, and communication factors that interact in the chronic disability (Figure 6.1). The main thrust of intervention is to take the patient's focus off symptoms and instead institute a goal-oriented approach in which the patient actively participates.

Evaluations

Beliefs and Interpretations. The most important beliefs that must be dealt with are that (a) hurt means harm, (b) if it is from a real injury, then a treatable structural problem must be found and remedied, and (c) it is necessary to always avoid activities that cause pain.

Investigating the Problem. It is not just the physical factors that determine differences in susceptibility; beliefs and expectations play a significant role. Magora (1973) found that if workers were dissatisfied or felt more stressed with their jobs, place of employment, or social status, they were more susceptible to back pain. Crook found that patients referred to a

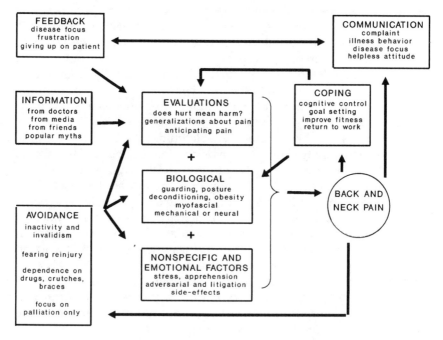

FIGURE 6.1. Algorithm for head and neck pain.

chronic pain clinic had a heavy loading on certain psychosocial factors: work disability, pain originating from work accidents, emotional distress, and use of medical services (Crook, Tunks, Rideout, & Browne, 1986). Those who continued to experience chronic pain on follow-up also had a greater tendency toward coping problems, catastrophizing, resentment, and withdrawal.

There is little doubt that patients with chronic neck or back pain who show the greatest chronicity and disability are often those who are litigating. There is something of a chicken-and-egg problem here. Probably the factor of litigation is correlated with other adverse factors, such as adversarial relationships, injury at work and the direct financial consequences, and obstacles to the resolution of the conflict. These factors are likely to have at least some effect on the chronic pain problems as far as perceived seriousness and emotional significance are concerned. Thus, it is likely that litigation can aggravate the chronicity and seriousness of a pain problem. However, pain and disability are real problems, and injured people have every right to redress; it is illogical to suspect all people who are litigating as having some sort of compensation neurosis. In fact, pain sufferers are rarely the winners in any kind of litigation process, considering loss of quality of life and the uncertain financial outcome. It is unreasonable to equate secondary gain with possible judicial awards or pensions in most cases. Settlement of litigation does not bear a clear relationship to resolution or improvement of the chronic pain complaint (Tunks, Bellissimo, & Roy, 1990). It is unreasonable to take the attitude that patients with back or neck pain should cease their litigation prior to entering rehabilitation because delay is sure to aggravate the chronicity of the problems and sound behavioral rehabilitation has about the same results whether or not the patient is litigating. At this point, the most we can say is that litigation is a factor—be it direct or indirect—in the seriousness of the chronic pain problem, but should not be a barrier to treatment unless the patient unduly invests his or her energy in fighting or attending to symptoms to the detriment of participation in rehabilitation.

Self-Evaluation. There is extensive work available dealing with behavioral measurement in chronic back pain problems (Keefe, 1982; Bradley, 1988). Measures studied have included overt motor behavior, facial motor behavior, coping scales, pain scaling methods, psychophysiological responses, and various personality inventories. These various measures are becoming increasingly sophisticated and the properties of the measures better understood. Their description and use, however, is beyond the scope of this book, where we will concentrate on measurement in the context of managing cognitive–behavioral intervention.

However, the standardized diary form and the goal management forms are relevant here (see chapter 2). The therapeutic focus in cases of back and neck pain is primarily active functional restoration. There are two parts to self-evaluation. One is to have the patient keep a diary for a week to chart downtime, medication use, sleep-wake times, and pain, and then analyze the results with the patient (see Figures 2.3, 2.4 or 2.6). The second step is to establish management by goals, with a regular schedule of review and revision (see Figure 2.9).

Diary. In order to achieve good compliance in the patient's use of a diary, the therapist must secure a commitment from the patient to use it and must explain its importance. If several sessions are being conducted per week, it is wise to hand out only a few pages of the diary at a time each session to ensure that it is not neglected. The purpose of this diary is to answer some basic questions.

1. *How much downtime is there?* Downtime means lying in bed, on a couch, reclining in an easy chair, or any recumbency during the 24-hour day, with the exception of sleeping time at night, which is marked separately. The downtime is marked with a blue or black marker horizontally along the diary (Figure 2.4). The amount of downtime is a fair estimate of the degree of invalidism, and is easier to interpret than the patient's measure of uptime, since it is harder to establish the quality of uptime.

2. *What medication or alcohol is used, how much, and when?* Medications and alcohol are marked by number of tablets and name of drug parallel to the time line. Some chronic pain patients are poor historians as far as giving a reliable account of their drug-taking behavior. Therefore, having them bring their bottles for periodic pill counts may be advisable.

3. *What is the pain level?* Patients are asked to record their pain on a five-point scale (Figure 2.3) in the diary upon rising; at midmorning, noon, midafternoon, suppertime, midevening, and bedtime; and upon awakening any time during the night.

4. *How is the sleep?* As with the insomnia management program (see chapter 4), it is valuable to have the patients mark bedtime and time slept in green, and time awake in bed during the night in red (see Figures 2.5 and 2.6).

Analysis of the charts can lead to useful discussions. Some patients may be surprised to see how much time is spent in invalidism. Others may see that they do not pace themselves. The relationship between not pacing oneself and increased pain often shows. Many chronic pain patients believe that their pain never varies, or that it is always at a maximum, but they will be able to learn that this is not so. They may also believe that rest is the only possible alternative in the case of pain, but may be surprised to learn that increases of pain may occur during or after rest, as in rising in the morning. Sometimes there is an inconsistent relationship between medication and pain; for example, if pain is reported to diminish immediately upon taking the drug, it is unlikely that the drug is responsible because most medications need half-an-hour or more to achieve blood levels. These types of discussions can help to focus the goals that are monitored during the rest of the back pain management program.

Management by goals. See the discussion in chapter 2 and Figure 2.10 for an example of how to set up a management by goals chart. We recommend that the goal-setting not be too ambitious at first. Instead, choose one or two goals from each of several representative categories and break them down into long-range and short-range goals. Then negotiate weekly quotas with the patient to gradually approach these goals. Possible categories are given here as examples.

1. Health
   (a) Fitness—endurance exercise, flexibility exercise, walking, posture correction
   (b) Stress control—relaxation exercise, learning principles of pacing
   (c) Removing unhealthy habits—insomnia control, weight reduction, stopping smoking
2. Medication
   (a) Discontinuing painkillers, sedatives, hypnotics
   (b) Rational use of necessary medications
3. Return to work
   (a) Work assessment
   (b) Work hardening (retraining where necessary only)
   (c) Return to work
4. Social and family function (reestablish roles)
5. Recreational and quality time planning

The key to successful management by goals is realistic quotas, frequent review of increase in quotas, reinforcement and encouragement for success, and application of gains to the "real world."

Biological Substrates

It is a common assumption that when someone begins to suffer back pain there is a slipped or injured disk or pinched nerve. In fact, the relationship between back pain and intrinsic pathology is much more complex. Herniated disks are the cause of pain in fewer than half the cases. Radiographic changes (spondylosis) occur progressively with age, are not well correlated with the degree of pain, and often occur in the absence of pain. Congenital abnormalities such as spina bifida or sacralization of a lumbar vertebra do not correlate with the incidence of back pain. Although spondylolisthesis usually causes back pain and decreased mobility, many people can continue to function without surgery. There is no consistent evidence that muscle spasm in the back is the cause of pain. Phenomena such as myofascial trigger points are well known, but the pathophysiology and relationship to possible underlying conditions is poorly understood.

There is a relationship between the type of work and the incidence of back pain; in the heaviest industries, such as forestry and mining, the incidence is about 5%, whereas in commercial and service industries it is about 1%.

Nonspecific Symptoms and Emotional Factors

There is a multitude of symptoms and functional impairments that arise indirectly as complications in the chronic back or neck pain patient:

1. Inactivity may initially be a response to the pain or to the fear of reinjury, but becomes a cause of deconditioning, which then leads to more fatigue.

2. Inactivity leads to the perception of stagnation or incurability, which leads to depression and increased inactivity.

3. Reduced physical movement aggravates fibromyalgia and myofascial (soft tissue) pain, which leads to the perception that the condition is worse.

4. Chronic use of crutches, braces, or collars leads to immobility, which can aggravate soft tissue pain, and also leads to poor body mechanics, which can provoke pain on movement, convincing the patient that the crutches or collars are necessary.

5. Guarding and avoidance of certain movements leads to stiffness, loss of range of movement, spasm, and reduced function, which provokes more guarding and avoidance behaviors.

6. Apprehension leads to increased pain awareness and tension, which increases apprehension.

7. Many medications, even psychotropic drugs taken for depression, can cause side effects, including fatigue and feeling ill, which can increase the sense of depression and the perception of a worsening condition.

8. Dependence on medical and surgical cures may lead to disillusionment and the belief that one is incurable, which provokes a feeling of helplessness and induces the individual to depend more on external solutions rather than personal coping strategies.

In all of the above vicious circles, the solution is to help the patient to take a more goal-oriented and active approach through goal-setting, coping strategies, and physical exercise, all the while promoting personal activity and eliminating dependency on solutions that are more appropriate for acute pain.

Dealing with Avoidance

In general, avoidance in cases of back and neck pain has several possible motives and several possible forms. Pain sufferers may be afraid of being active because they fear that observers will no longer believe that they have a problem, they fear they may hurt themselves more, or they fear failure. The work they did before their injuries may have been frightening or intolerable, and they may fear the return to an intolerable situation. Avoidance may be passive, as in the case of invalidism and recumbency, or it may be active, as in the case of seeking out ways to avoid pain: abusing medication or alcohol, or depending on braces, collars, or crutches. Avoidance aggravates disability and increases both the symptomatic and the cognitive aspects of the illness. It may also involve inappropriate redirection of energies, for example, becoming completely preoccupied with litigious conflicts.

The primary antidotes for avoidance are as follows:

1. Education that hurt does not mean harm, and that activity despite pain improves health.
2. Quotas for activity so that increasing activity will not be overly threatening.
3. Methods to relieve anxiety, such as applied relaxation techniques.
4. Methods to reduce dependency, such as making medication and activity–rest schedules time-contingent.

Sometimes it is necessary to investigate carefully when a patient fails to progress in a back pain rehabilitation program. There may be evidence that the patient is becoming worse or anxious. The problem may lie in some behavior that is promoting avoidance, which must be corrected.

For example, a chronic pain patient may be preoccupied about back pain and respond by avoiding activity whenever the pain appears. The patient is asked to monitor exercise with the objective of setting increasing quotas of activity. The patient begins to monitor exercise and activity, but at the same time records pain experiences and anxiety about the exercise. As a result, the patient's anxiety about hurting him- or herself becomes accentuated, and the patient begins to attribute the pain to the exercise and refuses to go on. The clinician changes the self-monitoring instruction by using a chart that allows only notations of units of exercise, time, and heart rate, with the explanation that these are the only true indices of improving health. The result is a steady improvement in exercise tolerance, despite persistent pain.

Coping

To assist coping, it is necessary to address both attitudes through education and counseling, and behavior, which conditions and perpetuates attitudes.

Patients need to have a realistic idea about what is the time-frame for improvement. Most back pain programs require 4 to 6 weeks to reduce illness behavior and produce better coping habits. If there is a fair amount of deconditioning and soft tissue pain, an aerobic exercise program can produce progressive benefits over a period of 2 to 6 months. This means that rehabilitation is a fairly long-term endeavor.

Patients must have information concerning how they can deal with any future possible reinjury if they are trying to be active again. In the case of recurrent back pain, if there is no neurological complication diagnosed or if pain does not radiate below the knee, bed rest should be limited to not more than 3 days. Then the patient should begin increasing activity with periods of walking and light exercise alternated with rest, and increasing activity over 3 weeks to begin warm-ups and an aerobic program. The patient must not wait for the pain to go away before becoming active because inactivity may worsen the back pain.

Withdrawal, resentment, and catastrophizing must be addressed by counseling the patient that these attitudes are particularly self-defeating and lead to worse outcomes. Patients can be taught by examples how to recognize these attitudes, and group therapy can be employed to foster and reinforce attitude change.

Communication

We think it might be more helpful here to give a verbatim account of the explanation that we give to our pain patients about the importance of communications. This lecture is usually given as part of a group discussion.

Sample Lecture

"How do you communicate? Think about it. I can come into this room and turn to one of you and say, 'You know, I have back pain today.' That message is clear and direct, and leaves little room for wrong assumptions. But we communicate in other ways too.

"Suppose instead that I come slowly into the room and don't say anything, but I do this. (Here, I simulate a painful back by walking slowly, shuffling the soles of my feet, keeping my thighs and knees stiff and my lumbar spine flattened, stooping at the waist, and putting a frown on my face. Patients usually laugh in recognition of the typical back pain walk.) Here, you see, I have communicated again, but with actions rather than words. The message is still fairly clear but is less direct, and might allow for wrong assumptions. Most of you will still realize that I had a sore back, but maybe someone might think that I rode a horse for the first time yesterday. There are other things that are not quite clear. Am I trying to reduce the painful walk or exaggerate it? Could it be that just today I am beginning to try to walk without a cane? The message is not direct either—no one can be sure whether this display is intended to impress someone in the room, or whether I would walk this way if I were alone. A physical communication alone allows for more assumptions than a direct clear verbal one.

"Now suppose I come into the room and sit down and say nothing, and one of you says, 'Hi doc! How are you doing?' and I answer with a grunt or say, 'Ah, okay I suppose.' Now you know that when someone says, 'How are you' it is intended as a greeting and we expect the answer, 'Fine thank you, and you?' I have just communicated by what I didn't say! That communication is unclear and it is a bit direct. It is unclear because you might think I am sick, in pain, depressed, angry, sleepy, uninterested, deaf, or impolite. It is somewhat direct in that you know that it was you that I did not give a greeting to, but you don't know if it was specifically to you or to other people, too. There is a lot more room here for wrong assumptions.

"Now, again suppose that I am sitting here, and one of you knows that I usually like a game of golf. So you say, 'Hey doc, we're going golfing. Do you want to come?' Then I say, 'Naw, you go without me this week,' or maybe I just keep sitting here and I don't participate. Now, that is communicating by what I don't do. You know that I would normally go golfing, and you now have an unclear and indirect message. You might guess that it means I am sick or mad or broke but you are not sure. You might think the refusal has something to do with you or someone else or possibly no one. There is room for all kinds of wrong assumptions.

"When we communicate, we do it all the time by what we do, by what we don't do, by what we say, and by what we don't say. For all clear verbal communication, there is usually more indirect and unclear communication accompanying it. When there is distress or upset feelings, the proportion of indirect and unclear communication increases even more, mostly because we are uncomfortable about putting our upset feelings into words. We don't want to accentuate the feeling. But that also makes it likely that there are going to be more assumptions made about you by your family and friends. You see, it is your family and friends who are most attentive to nonverbal communication and the subtleties of what you don't do or say, and if they respond in the same manner, the communication problems and the bad feelings grow. They may interpret your pain communication as anger or indifference, and may respond in an irritable way or withdraw from you, which then leads you to do more of the same, and so on.

"Another thing you have to realize is that families and friends will pick up on your communications and give them back to you. For example, you might be thinking, 'My doctor and specialist don't understand my problem,' and you somehow communicate this to family. The next day they say, 'Have you thought of seeing another doctor?' Well, that's the last thing you wanted to hear because of the frustration you have already had with a string of doctors, and you ask yourself, 'Why is my family saying this to me?' Or you might be feeling fed up with your illness, and a friend says, 'What! Are you still sick!?' and your feelings are hurt. But it was really your question. Or you might be grasping at straws for some solution to your problem, and someone brings a clipping to you from a popular newspaper that claims that spine transplants are done in some foreign clinic or that megadoses of rhubarb will cure your headache, and you say, 'I don't need this advice!' But the communication is actually related to your indirect and unclear messages.

"Finally, you must remember some time when you had to do something that intimidated you, such as answer to a complaint from your boss or face an angry teacher, and you found yourself rehearsing beforehand what you would say and how you would do it. Here you were observing yourself communicate, to get up your courage. When we communicate verbally or nonverbally, we are always observers of ourselves. If we communicate fear, we feel more fear. If we communicate confidence, it helps our confidence.

"So what do we do? Begin to pay attention to communicating in a way that gets away from the helplessness. Tell your family, 'Listen, I know you care, but there isn't anything you can do by talking about the pain. That just reminds me it's there. I would feel better if you would ask me what I have done, or include me in any talk about plans, and about what I can do, not what I can't do.' To deal with conflict, make a deal with your family that when there is tension, whoever recognizes it first is to say, 'Stop! There are some assumptions going on here that we're getting upset about,' and then take a minute to explain what you really were feeling, what you wanted to communicate, and what you thought your family was saying, and ask them to tell you what they were really trying to communicate."

At the end of the group session, members can be asked to help each other in their communication. If someone tends to make too many communications that lead to assumptions (by illness behavior, avoidance, or nonparticipation), they should agree to have this pointed out, or if there are communications that remind one of feeling sick instead of feeling hopeful, they should make a deal that the other group members will point it out, until each member becomes skilled in communicating in a healthier way.

Sexual functioning is often impaired in individuals who suffer back or neck pain. Dealing with this problem requires both attention to communication and also practical advice. (See "Guidelines for Sexual Activity," pp. 135–137.)

Feedback

Interpersonal dynamics play an important role in chronic pain. This may be viewed in terms of operant conditioning (Fordyce, 1976), family systems (Roy, 1988; Turk, Flor, & Rudy, 1987), or sociological influences (Eisenberg & Kleinman, 1981). The consensus is that selective attention to symptom complaints and illness behavior in an individual leads to an increase in illness behavior in that individual. The discussion from the section on Communication can be expanded in various ways. One way is to have family members present and have them examine the ways in which they might communicate and inadvertently reinforce perceptions about being ill or helpless. Another is to have the family practice ways to stop conflict patterns and inquire together about hidden assumptions, defusing conflict.

Behavioral feedback must be managed, especially in the case of dealing with back and neck pain patients in physical therapy and occupational therapy, to enable other professionals to deal therapeutically with pain behaviors.

Cognitive feedback must also be monitored for hidden beliefs that might be discovered in conversation so that these can be corrected. An example is given of a patient who was to enter a pain program but who still clung to the idea that there had to be a cure.

Patient: I'm looking forward to this program. I sure hope it works.

Therapist: I can assure you that in the many years I have been with this program I have never ever seen the program work.

Patient: (shocked) What!

Therapist: No. Programs don't work. People work. The program is there to give you information and structure that you need to succeed. But you are the one who will succeed because it is you who will do the work.

Self-Maintenance

The problems of back and neck pain are often long-lasting, and the initial enthusiasm of the pain program can wear thin in the daily grind, months after discharge. To ensure self-maintenance, the patient must internalize the message about ownership. Goal-setting and the techniques of pain and stress management must be a discipline. A positive therapist–patient relationship needs a transition to the patient's relationship with friends and family. A routine of fitness, pacing, productivity, and life-style that promotes a sense of accomplishment despite pain must be cultivated. For this reason, it is essential that the family become involved while the patient is still in the pain program. The family must shift attitudes to foster the patient's change in attitude and illness behavior so that healthy change can be perpetuated. Before discharge, contact must be made with the referring doctor to clarify the new game rules (pain must be accepted) and to ensure that there will not be a return to a cycle of referrals, investigations, and prescriptions. The work setting should be investigated during the pain program and the way smoothed for return to work. Conversations with foremen or supervisors may be necessary to allow a gradual bridging from sick leave to employment. Patients do not change simply out of principle. Usually, positive relationships have much to do with the motivation for change, and therapists must follow up on their patients while they make the necessary links with the community, to give encouragement and support, and to help with troubleshooting.

Many patients feel that stress control techniques (relaxation and pacing) are the most important tools they have in dealing with the day-to-day stress of pain. Therefore, therapists must teach these skills and should query patients on follow-up to ensure that they are comfortable with the use of these skills.

An environment of healthy people does much to guarantee success.

Pain patients sometimes have a habit of associating with other back pain patients when they are disabled. These associations have a depressing effect, and patients need to seek out healthy friends. Sometimes it is good for them to keep contact with other patients who have graduated with them from the pain program.

GUIDELINES FOR SEXUAL ACTIVITY

Sexuality is tied in with your self-image and interpersonal functioning, and there can be significant problems in this area if you have chronic pain or illness. With illness and repeated medical investigations and examinations, there are repeated invasions of your own private body space that can harm your sense of privacy and integrity.

There is also fear of pain during activity, which can extend to fear of pain with sexual intercourse. This fear may be a problem for your partner as well. For example, an individual who suffers chronic migraines may suffer an increase of pain at the time of climax. After intercourse, people with neck and back pain often experience pain later that day or the next day because of the body postures that were taken. Often people with pain will have lost confidence in their own bodies, and this carries over as lack of confidence in their sexuality. Because pain is distracting, it may interfere with the sexual act itself. People may then start to worry that there is something wrong with them, and they become too performance oriented. They may then be overly focused on having a climax and worried only about this rather than enjoying their bodies and their partner. They may feel guilty about saying no to their partner on the one hand, or obligated to satisfy their partner on the other hand.

Many medications given for pain and sleep interfere with sexual drive and sexual functioning. This is true for most analgesics, sedatives, and antidepressants, and also for alcohol. When the spouse tries to help by trying harder to bring on a climax or when there is a great deal of attention and concern shown by the spouse, the person with pain may begin to feel like a cripple. Because it is embarrassing and involves feelings of loss of confidence, there may be difficulty in communicating one's true sexual attitudes, feelings, and worries. Sometimes there is an avoidance altogether of sex by staying up late at night, sleeping at odd hours, or simply being absent or in pain. Because of many frustrating experiences, people often end up feeling so frustrated that they think, "It's no use. I've tried everything already!"

Steps in Helping

The most important steps in helping these problems is to come to accept that we are all sexual people, and that this affects us in different ways. Those of us with sexual partners must realize that having a normal relationship day to day, and having a normal sexual relationship, is part of feeling satisfied about our lives. Those of us who are single or celibate still must recognize our own sexuality. It is important that you see yourself as an attractive person or as being interesting to other people, or simply to like yourself when you look in the mirror. It is important to deal with the fact that in chronic illness, self-image can be hurt.

The next step in restoring normal sexual function is to set nondemanding expectations rather than focus on having orgasms or having sex. The goal must be changed to developing confidence, good bodily feelings, and trust. This can be done by concentrating on making a more conducive atmosphere, changing the pattern of activities that leads to sexual activity or making love, using sexually oriented reading material if this is acceptable to both partners, and introducing affectionate touching without having to feel compelled to have intercourse. Reasonable expectations must be developed. Not everyone has the same rhythm of sexual feelings. Some enjoy the sex act more frequently than others, but this wide variation is normal. It is an important goal to learn again to enjoy each other and your own body, to spend more time caressing, and to come to a mutual acceptance of being good lovers in a good atmosphere and with good communication.

Eliminating drugs or alcohol that change the mood and the drive is a critical element. At the same time, efforts must be made to improve your self-image by paying attention to how you dress and groom yourself so as to feel attractive, and perhaps by going on a diet and having a reasonable idea for target weight over a period of time. Your own sense of being healthy can be improved by daily exercise.

Fears of failure during the sex act, or fear of having pain, must be dealt with. It is helpful to learn a relaxation technique. Gradually introducing sexual play, caressing, and loving touches without feeling performance oriented, and communicating clearly with each other while being intimate is the next important ingredient. The focus must be taken away from being successful at sex and instead be on enjoying being a lover and being loved, and not being afraid to talk to each other about it.

To deal with the fear of pain, postural problems can be corrected. A person with back or neck pain who takes a superior position may find that arching the neck or the back may lead to pain a few hours later. Alternate positions may be possible, such as lying on the side with one thigh flexed forward, and the other partner doing the same, so that a side-to-side position will allow rounding of the back. You might also try lying on your back with a couple of pillows under the shoulder and neck to round the back, and perhaps even a pillow under one knee, lying partially to the side.

1. Find a position that is comfortable for you both and adapt it for sexual activity.
2. Try deep breathing or other relaxation techniques beforehand.
3. If you have joint stiffness, try taking a hot bath or shower or do a few range-of-motion (stretch) exercises before beginning.
4. Have various sized pillows around to help with obtaining different positions.
5. Remember that keeping knees bent automatically flattens the lower back and takes some of the stress off the lower spine. Use this information when experimenting with different positions.
6. Try making love at different times of the day.
7. It is not always easy to avoid extension of the back and neck, especially during climax. Try to keep the chin tucked in closely to the chest.

Focus should be on "Let's experiment and do what we can" rather than on "I can't do much due to my pain problem." Attention also must be given to problems that may arise from previous gynecological surgery or pain in the genital area. Sometimes this sort of pain can be relieved by direct pain-relieving techniques, such as electrical nerve stimulation. Above all, the most important thing is to begin to discuss your sexual feelings, have confidence in yourself again, and do everything possible to build up a good body image and respect for yourself. A sense of health and integrity can be built by healthy habits and frequent exercise.

Chapter 7

Chronic Headache

DESCRIPTION OF THE PROBLEM

A sheaf of notes and investigations from other consultants accompanies the referral of Linda, who is 27 years of age. She is well dressed, polite, and soft-spoken, but her posture, facial expression, and flushing of the face give away the fact that she has a headache. She gives the story of mild headaches after puberty, becoming progressively more severe in the last 5 years. Now, she suffers a daily constant ache over her whole head, and perhaps twice a week a severe exacerbation with prostration a day or more at a time. She has tried numerous headache remedies and currently is taking a mixed analgesic that includes aspirin, barbiturate, caffeine, and codeine four or five times per day, as well as diazepam and dimenhydrinate. She also has a prescription for suppositories containing ergotamine but has found that they no longer relieve her pain. She is able to work part-time, but her employer is losing patience with her sick time. Her social life is also impaired, and she is afraid to accept social engagements for fear that she will suddenly become ill and spoil it for everyone. She says, "I would rather not be taking all these medications, but I can't stand myself when the headache becomes so severe. I don't relish the trips to emergency departments, but there is no other way at times." Beyond her expression of discouragement, she shows little overt emotion other than that of apparent suffering. She admits that with her pain problem she is often sleepless, worries about her health, sometimes feels that her condition is hopeless, or feels desperate and thinks she might be better off dead, although she has never made a plan to harm herself. Her greatest preoccupation is that she will not find her family doctor or someone in the emergency department who will give her an injection when the headaches are severe. She admits that if she worries, her headache gets out of control; for example, on a night or weekend, she might very well have an increasingly severe headache.

Bonnie, a 24-year-old nurse, presents with a 1-year history of pain affecting the ear, forehead, temple, and jaw. Her father is a physician.

One gathers that she is anxious, not sleeping, and preoccupied about the pain. It is learned that a roommate had been suffering from headaches and 1 year ago was diagnosed as having a brain tumor. This roommate has recently died. She admits for the first time that she is worried that she might be suffering from a brain tumor, too. No one has reassured her otherwise, even though she has had a negative neurological workup. She takes no medication. History also reveals that she has pain in the jaw on opening her mouth or chewing, that she has a clicking sound in the jaw on the painful side, and that the problem began soon after having a difficult wisdom tooth extraction. Examination shows that there is a deviation of the jaw, restriction of range of movement in jaw opening, and tenderness over the muscles of mastication.

BACKGROUND

The current literature concerning headaches is voluminous, and there are multiple competing theories. A great deal of the literature concerns pharmacology, which we will not deal with here. Instead, the behavioral medicine point of view is emphasized in this chapter. The reader can turn to other texts and reviews for a more ample description of trends in the current medical investigation and treatment of headaches (see the Selected Reading section for chapter 7 at the back of the book.)

Traditional Classification of Headaches

Muscle Contraction or Tension Headaches. These headaches are provoked by stress and are felt bilaterally in a bandlike distribution, in the temples, or in the back of the head as a steady ache or tight feeling. There are areas of muscle tenderness, especially over the back of the head and neck, and pressure over these areas accentuates the pain and refers it to nearby head regions.

Vascular Headaches. These include common and unusual varieties of migraine, and several varieties of cluster headache. Migraines may be precipitated by various causes, including stress, menstrual periods, certain foods, or changes in barometric pressure, or may come without known precipitant. They may be preceded or accompanied by focal neurological signs such as blurred vision, may be unilateral or bilateral, may change sides, and are accompanied by autonomic symptoms such as nausea and vomiting and aversion to light and sound. There is a tendency for them to run in families. The pain has been thought to arise from algogenic substances released from cranial blood vessels during periods of autonomic instability.

Mixed Headaches. In practice, tension and migraine headache features are usually found in the same patients in varying proportions. Patients who present the greatest clinical problem are usually those who have frequent headaches, with almost constant tension headaches, and migraine qualities to the headache at least once per week. Often these people appear desperate, go to emergency rooms for injections of narcotic, take large doses of medication, and suffer psychosocial complications. This is the main group of patients seen in headache clinics.

Psychogenic Headaches. This designation seems controversial to some clinicians. The clinical features resemble the tension headache. If there is a distinction (and we are not convinced that there is), it would be that the pain experienced with tension headaches is due to tenderness in tight scalp muscles, whereas the pain in psychogenic headaches does not correlate with muscular or vascular events. Instead, pain arises from psychogenic causes in the same way that conversion reaction is a cause of bodily symptoms in the absence of a lesion.

Cluster Headaches. These are a variety of vascular headaches that may have more dramatic presentation. They may have a neuralgialike quality to them and tend to come in clusters of frequent attacks and then leave the sufferer free for months or years. They can also become a chronic problem.

Myofascial Pain Dysfunction Syndrome. This is head pain due to disturbance of the temporomandibular (jaw) joint, otherwise called the TMJ syndrome or the myofascial pain dysfunction syndrome. Symptoms include tenderness in the muscles of mastication, clenching, bruxing, other abnormal degrees of activity in the TM joints causing strain and pain, restriction of the normal range of TM joint movement on account of soft tissue spasm, and other features indicating injury to the joints. This disorder may exist in a pure form or may be part of a larger pain syndrome. It is characteristic to find tender spots in the muscles of mastication, from which pain is radiated in characteristic patterns to the jaws, neck, head, or ears.

Trigeminal and Occipital Neuralgias. A variety of neuralgia disorders arising from disease, injury, and idiopathic causes is represented by tic douleureux, atypical facial pains, and other usually unilateral head pains. These are most often treated medically or surgically, and there is little literature dealing with the psychological management. However, medical and surgical treatment is not always satisfactory, especially with the chronic or atypical presentations, and in these cases psychological treatment is worth instituting.

Cervicogenic Headaches. Cervical spondylosis can produce pain in the neck and referred pain usually unilaterally to the head. In practice, this pain may have many of the features of migraine, although the distinction from migraine is made on the basis of age of onset, association with neck disorders and injury, and whether the headache changes sides.

Post-traumatic Headaches. These will also be discussed in chapter 11. This sort of headache, which may follow head injury or frightening traumatic events, has many qualities of mixed headaches, and may at times resemble cluster headaches, cervicogenic headaches, or psychogenic headaches. The most important feature is that the problem is associated with problems in adjustment after injury, and is usually very resistant to medical management. For practical treatment purposes it should be considered to be in the same category as chronic mixed headaches.

Headaches Due to Tumors and Intracranial Disease. These categories will not be dealt with here except to indicate that they are not the focus of behavioral medicine intervention.

Obviously, medical diagnosis is important when someone presents for the first time with a headache. It may be that medical treatment will suffice in certain cases. However, some patients continue to experience intractible pain despite medical diagnosis and treatment. In practice, the great majority of chronic headache patients that come to headache clinics is made up of three of the above groups; the mixed (tension–migraine) headaches, psychogenic headaches, and the TMJ dysfunction disorders. We find that there is a great deal of overlap between these conditions, and that the psychological treatments that are effective for one are usually effective for all. With this in mind, our emphasis will be on the behavioral medicine aspects of these problems.

Current Hypotheses Regarding Etiology

The traditional positions regarding the causes of headaches come largely from the work of Wolff (1948). More recent theories have likewise gained prominence. Sicuteri (1979) suggested that headaches were due to a disorder of pain processing in the central nervous system. Various sites for this disorder have been proposed, implicating serotonin metabolism, abnormalities in sensitivities of serotonin or opiate receptors, abnormal control of wide dynamic range neurons in the brainstem and cervical spinal cord, or "cross-talk" between neurons in the spinal nucleus of the fifth nerve and the upper cervical segments. Another group of hypotheses concerns the possibility that the intracranial vascular tree and smooth muscle (as in the iris) of headache patients have an increased sensitivity to certain substances such as catecholamines, kinins, or other algogenic influences. These intracranial vessels are innervated largely by the trigeminal and upper cervical segments. When algogenic stimuli affect the intracranial vessels, pain is referred to the corresponding portions of the head and face (Moskowitz, Saito, Sakas, & Markowitz, 1988).

The behavioral medicine concept of headaches is that the sensory component is only one part of the experience of headaches. Other factors are more important in determining if the patient will feel that the headaches are out of control: beliefs and interpretations, coping patterns, emotions, and social reinforcement (Bakal, 1982) (see Figure 7.1).

Current Thinking About Psychological Treatment

There are two major currents of treatment for headaches. The first is pharmacological, which is undoubtedly of value in selected cases. The other is behavioral. The available evidence indicates that on the whole, neither option is significantly superior to the other. Biofeedback became a major tool in headache management with the work of Sargent, Green, and Walters (1972) and Budzynzki, Stoyva, Adler, and Mullaney (1973). These early reports seemed to support the traditional concepts of the etiology of vascular versus tension headache, and the treatment of these disorders with biofeedback conditioning of vascular tone or facial muscle tone, respectively. Handwarming techniques (ostensibly to reduce sympathetic vascular tone) was effective in relieving vascular headache, as was cranial blood pulse volume biofeedback to teach subjects to reduce cranial vessel blood flow. However, it became clear that these treatment effects were not specific (Tan, 1982). Subjects who learned to cool their hands also improved. The degree of improvement often did not match the degree or success in conditioning. The effects of relaxation were found to be at least as good as the more sophisticated biofeedback techniques. Some experimenters found that training the subjects to increase, decrease, or maintain the same muscle tension had no differential effect on the reduction of headaches. Doubts were raised about the contribution of muscle spasm to pain. Cognitive events were found to be important mediators in the outcomes of patients treated by biofeedback or relaxation (Andrasik & Holroyd, 1980). To a great extent, researchers turned their attention to these cognitive variables instead of focusing just on the conditioning of a given physiological variable.

Current Findings Regarding Diagnosis

It has been noted in recent studies that if strict diagnostic criteria were to be applied, it would be difficult if not impossible to isolate cases of tension headaches alone or vascular headaches alone, and that it would be difficult even to distinguish them from certain other headache conditions (for example cervicogenic headaches which resemble migraines). It is also becoming evident that specialty clinics tend to deal with cases that are complicated by nonspecific symptoms and that arise more as a function of psychosocial distress rather than from the disease mechanisms in which the clinic specializes (Kleinnecht, Mahoney, & Alexander, 1987). The current findings have great importance for the clinician because they mean that difficult cases that are referred to a clinic for specialized treatment of headaches are actually most appropriately managed through the perspective of behavioral medicine. These findings also provide a starting point for the behavioral medicine clinician in the approach to the patient. Rather than beginning with the focus on the details of the headache presentation, the focus is on the broader aspects of the patient suffering from headaches, including the psychosocial variables; and rather than presenting a completely different psychological treatment package for each traditional medical diagnosis, a unified approach is possible that will allow patients with headaches to be treated in groups. Traditionally, certain factors have been blamed for causing migraine (see Table 7.1). It is likely that some of these factors trigger headaches in some individuals some of the time, but it is unwarranted to proscribe all of these things. However, there are some factors that are more frequently implicated, especially in patients whose headaches are frequent or continuous.

Psychologically, the state of feeling anxious, out of control of the headaches, and living in apprehension is likely to promote intractable headaches. Helping the patient to achieve a sense of control is a major objective. This can be done by helping the patient to control drugs, learn to relax, learn a biofeedback routine, set goals, and establish control in other ways.

Certain drugs and chemicals have a direct effect in worsening headaches (Kudrow, 1982). Major culprits are excessive or frequent use of ergotamine, acetylsalicylic acid (ASA), acetaminophen, nonsteroidal antiinflammatory drugs, and opiates. In fact, prescription drugs are the major factor in aggravating most intractable headaches of patients who come to headache clinics. Coffee and caffeine-containing substances are also important causes of headache when taken excessively. It is ironic that the most used painkillers are ASA or acetaminophen combined with caffeine and codeine. This combination taken in excess is liable not only to worsen headaches but also to promote stomach ulcers and irritable bowel syndrome.

Lack of physical vigor that comes with chronic headaches, the sedentary or withdrawn life-style, is likely to also worsen headaches.

Table 7.1.   Factors Traditionally Thought to Cause Headaches

Psychological
  Stress
  Resentment
  Fatigue
  Sleeping in or sleeping irregularly
  Overwork for several days followed by rest (triggers a "letdown" or a "weekend
    headache")
Hormonal
  Menstrual periods
  Menarche
  Menopause
  Pregnancy or delivery (implicated either in causing or in reducing headaches)
  Birth control pills
Weather changes
Certain foods
  Chocolate
  Cheese or dairy products
  Liver or kidney
  Yogurt
  Yeast extract
  Citrus
  Processed meats and nitrites
  Ice cream
  Monosodium glutamate
  Caffeine
  Seafood
Alcohol
Cigarettes
Strong odors
Chlorine in the water
Air pollution
Airplane rides
Exertion or sex

Patients fear that exercise will trigger the headache. Instead, they become deconditioned, sleep poorly, and still have the headaches. An aerobic conditioning program makes a great difference in restoring well-being, confidence, and reducing the tendency to headaches.

The correct perspective to engender with the chronic headache patient is to stop worrying superstitiously about multiple environmental triggers, and instead concentrate on promoting resistance to headaches through avoidance of self-poisoning, and through coping skills and health promotion.

A word of caution: No remedy should ever be applied automatically or without adequate assessment of the problem to be addressed. The behavioral medicine approaches here are valuable for a majority of headache patients, but the patients should have adequate medical assessment, since some patients harbor serious physical disorders.

Completing the assessment also puts the patient at ease by making it clear that there is no brain tumor or other condition to be feared.

INFORMATION FOR PATIENTS

Practically everyone has had a headache at some time or another. One survey found that 13% of the population had a headache from 10% to 30% of the time. Some common types of headaches are as follows:

Migraine is also called vascular headache, because blood vessels in the head go through phases of constricting in the initial part of the headache cycle followed by relaxing as the pain sets in. These headaches tend to come and go rather than remain constant. They may be preceded by odd sensations such as visual disturbance. Eventually a throbbing headache begins on one or both sides of the head, perhaps along with nausea, and worsened by light and sound. Migraines tend to run in families. People who suffer frequent migraines may be able to identify certain triggers. The most important of these are stress, fatigue, menstrual periods, certain foods, alcohol, too much caffeine, and other sources of discomfort in the neck and head. Often, migraines are combined with tension headaches. In this case, the pain varies from time to time, and one kind of pain tends to trigger the other. A frequent problem is that many medicines that are taken to relieve the headache may eventually cause worsening of the headache if they are taken too long or in too high a dose. Medicines that can do this include over-the-counter pain relievers, medicines with codeine or similar opiates, with ergotamines, or with caffeine, especially if the person also has the habit of consuming too much coffee.

Tension headache is more constant than migraine, and often is felt as a tight feeling in the scalp, in the back of the neck, and radiating over the head or as a band around the head. These may be triggered by stress or fatigue, or by things that cause discomfort in the neck, jaws, and shoulders. They are also aggravated by taking too much painkiller medication.

Temporomandibular joint (TMJ) dysfunction is the technical way to say that there is a problem in the way that the jaws work. This does not always involve damage to the joint surfaces; in many cases it has to do with soreness in the muscles that are used in chewing or moving the jaws. It can be caused by many things, including uneven teeth that do not come together properly, bad habits like grinding or clenching the teeth, injury to the jaws, or stress. The pain may be hard to distinguish from other kinds of headaches, or it may seem to come right from the jaws and radiate to the teeth. People who suffer this problem also have problems of tenderness of the jaw muscles, reduction in the ability to open the mouth, a feeling of blocking of the ears, and often clicking or cracking sounds when they open or close the mouth. Although antiin-flammatory medicine or relaxant medicine may at first provide some relief, long-term use is usually not helpful. Dentists can often alleviate some of the causes by working with the dental occlusion, which means reducing the stress on the jaw joint, and reducing the tendency to grind the teeth.

Neuralgias are pains that come from injuries to nerves. If these nerves are in the scalp or face, the result is a pain problem that usually is one-sided and may involve burning, aching, jabbing, or painfully altered sensation. As with most neuralgias, emotional upset makes it worse and learning to relax makes it better. Most painkillers are useless against this kind of pain, but antidepressants or anticonvulsant medi-cines and certain other specific treatments may be helpful.

Referred pain means that one painful spot, such as a muscle or connective tissue, causes pain to be felt in another place. A common example would be tenderness at the back of the neck causing a headache to be felt over the temples and forehead. This sort of pain is very similar to tension headache and usually responds little to painkiller medication, but often improves with relaxation methods, and is relieved by im-proving posture and physical fitness.

Although the various causes of head pain are quite different, there are some important common elements for chronic pains in the head.

1. Sleep is often disturbed by pain, and just as often, disturbance in sleep habits triggers pain. A person who keeps irregular bedtime, or who drinks alcohol or takes stimulants or certain other medications near bedtime, is at risk for disturbing the normal sleep rhythm. If this happens, the person becomes more susceptible to pain.

2. Tension is both a mental and physical problem; it causes posture and muscle tightness problems that cause pain and the emotional part also makes pain more intense. Learning and regularly practicing simple relaxation techniques usually provides significant relief or helps reduce the frequency of the problem.

3. As we have mentioned, many chemicals may aggravate headache. Alcohol and smoking are two common examples. Some headaches are aggravated by birth control pills. Painkillers and ergotamine, which are sometimes given to relieve migraines, may actually make headaches worse if the medication is taken for too long at too high a dose. Fortunately, getting these chemicals out of your system soon reverses these harmful effects, and after a few weeks, people who have stopped using a lot of painkillers, ergotamine, or alcohol find that their pain is improved.

4. Active physical exercise has a beneficial effect in improving the sense of well-being, and physical fitness actually reduces the tendency for headaches.

ASSESSMENT AND TREATMENT

Headaches are the product of the interaction of many possible factors. These include genetic predisposition, biological cycles, stress and emotional effects, various kinds of toxicity, coping problems, and even environmental conditions (Figure 7.1). However, two factors are particularly important in patients with headache problems who come to specialty or behavioral medicine clinics. These are the marked anxiety that headaches will recur, and the toxicity from various medications that paradoxically increase the propensity to recurrent headaches. Thus the main thrust of treatment is based on reducing anxiety, and on eliminating harmful habits and substances.

Evaluations

Beliefs and Interpretations. Most of the troublesome beliefs about serious headache pain concern issues of control or harmfulness. Paramount is

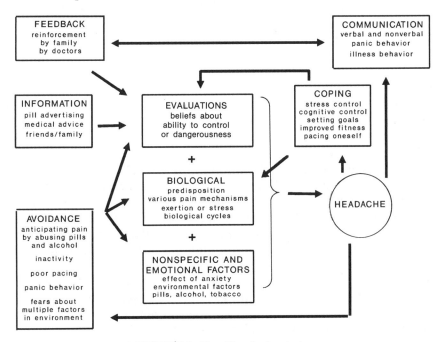

FIGURE 7.1. Algorithm for headache.

the fear of loss of control of the headache; that it may continue to get worse until it becomes unbearable. This apprehension itself may be enough to evoke or perpetuate a headache attack. Another example of anxiety about control is the desperation by which some patients hang onto their prescriptions for analgesics, which underlines the belief that the headache is not within their control, that it may be under control of external causes such as weather or subject to external cures such as pills. The problem with this type of thinking is that it undermines the individual's sense of self-efficacy, thus promoting anxiety and reduced coping efforts. When the pills do not work, as frequently is the case, the anxiety will then be even greater, because this signifies that no control, external or internal, is possible. It is quite understandable that some people will harbor a fear of hidden pathology, such as brain tumor. The neurological symptoms that sometimes accompany migraine may suggest this fear. For some people, the fear arises because the cause cannot be seen, and therefore the patient fears the worst.

Superstitions and fads are a major problem in dealing with headache problems. There is popularly available a host of books, courses, newsletters, alternative medicine practitioners, health food stores, and wellwishing friends, all with versions of headache remedies. Because many headache sufferers end up frustrated with their medical care, they have a tendency to become influenced by these ideas. They may begin to worry about having "the 20th century disease," allergy to peculiar environmental elements, and deficiency of certain body substances, and may be taking nonmedical remedies of various kinds. It can be hard to convince the patient that the remedies are worthless because head pains tend to be intermittent. Chances are that upon taking any remedy during the headache relief will tend to follow; relief is then attributed to the remedy. On the face of it, many of these vitamin cures and nostrums may seem innocent enough, but superstitious adherence to them can promote the cognition that the patient has a disease or deficiency rather than a problem that he or she can address by self-management. The therapist must deal with these superstitious beliefs and patient use of supplements diplomatically. To simply dismiss the patient's beliefs will meet with resistance. It is better to undermine the adherence to these useless remedies by promoting health through other means, improving confidence, and decreasing reliance on medical or nonmedical remedies.

Investigating the Problem. In finding out about the problem, it is necessary to obtain information regarding the origin, development, temporal pattern, symptoms and signs, and family history of the headaches. Some of this has to do with making a specific medical diagnosis of the type of headache. This is, of course, perfectly relevant in the general management and investigation of headaches. However, in many cases, behavioral intervention is warranted, and for this a medical style investigation must be followed by a behavioral analysis. This investigation should pinpoint factors that the patient can change. (Refer to the "Headache Questionnaire," pp. 158–159.) These questions could be either self-rated or included in the examiner's inquiry.

Self-Evaluation. A self-monitoring task is important to create awareness of the factors that may contribute to headaches and to establish the severity of the problem. What is monitored depends on the goal. A simple task might be to have the patient monitor the onset, duration, and severity of each headache to provide a baseline from which a headache index can be calculated: (duration × intensity). This would be used in assessing the efficacy of treatment. Discovery of contributing factors is possible through keeping a diary of headaches and charting certain suspected factors such as coffee or alcohol consumption, stress, sleep habits, or environmental factors, for example. For monitoring the headache pain and events relevant to headaches, the general purpose self-monitoring diary can be used (see Figure 2.3). In the graph section, the patient can be asked to rate the headache intensity on a five-point scale upon rising, and at noon, suppertime, and bedtime, and also if there is a noticeable change in headache level during the day. On the other side, parallel to the hours of the day, recordings can be made of items that the clinician feels should be self-monitored. For example, in determining headache precipitants, one could record working positions, taking breaks, taking medication, eating certain foods, going to bed or rising, or other factors that may be important, as judged by the clinical interview. Promoting awareness of coping factors is achieved through charting the use of key strategies such as relaxation, pacing oneself, and problem-solving while at the same time giving less attention to the details of headache episodes. One might want to take the emphasis off the headaches by noting only the number of headaches in a month, or noting the number of analgesic doses taken. The general strategy is to gradually move away from attention to (and monitoring of) the symptom itself, and instead promote attention to (and monitoring of) the coping. A simple scale can be adapted to all of these monitoring tasks as shown in Figure 2.8 (see the discussion on self-monitoring in chapter 2).

Biological Substrates

As noted in the introduction to this chapter, there are many types of headaches from a medical point of view, and several mechanisms. What concerns us here are the physiological mechanisms that are common in head pain conditions with respect particularly to the mechanisms that are affected by the individual's behavior.

Myofascial pain is characterized by tenderness at specific spots in the soft tissues, usually but not always at muscle insertions, and associated with referred pain from those tender spots. This can be illustrated by the example of the myofascial pain dysfunction syndrome, which is associated with TMJ dysfunction. In this condition, there may be preexisting causes such as injury, malocclusion, emotional tension, or other systemic or local causes of irritation. The patient suffers a variety of symptoms, including restricted or assymmetrical mouth opening, pain in the face, teeth, and jaw, clicking in the jaw, local tenderness over the muscles of mastication, and other problems such as difficulty in swallowing. There is a host of potential contributing factors to myofascial pain, and these have to be dealt with. Such pain may be made worse by (a) abuse of alcohol, painkillers, or hypnotics; (b) emotional tension; or (c) poor sleep habits. Musculoskeletal factors may also contribute to perpetuation of this pain and may include (a) guarded "antalgic" postures or (b) overuse or microtrauma (as in individuals who brux or clench their teeth without realizing it). Those considerations that apply to TMJ dysfunction also apply to other myofascial pain conditions such as those involving trigger points in the back of the neck (occiput) or side of the neck (sternomastoid). In treating any myofascial pain, it is essential to deal with the general perpetuating factors if one is to be successful with a specific pain disorder (Graff-Radford, Reeves, & Jaeger, 1987). Here there is a clear role for the behavior medicine therapist to work hand in hand with the dentist, neurologist, or anesthetist in managing such pain.

To deal with these perpetuating factors, the management should include instruction for and education of the patient, and management targeted at the specific perpetuating factors.

After deciding which medication is inappropriate to the long-term management of the individual's problems, medications can be progressively withdrawn (see chapter 8). At the same time, the patient is taught an applied relaxation technique (see chapter 3), and sleep is monitored and a sleep management program is started (see chapter 4). Posture correction is addressed through demonstration and practice, and reinforced by active exercise and fitness (see chapter 9). In the case of TMJ dysfunction, clenching and bruxing patterns and abnormal jaw postures can be dealt with through relaxation, electromyographic biofeedback, and use of splint therapy (a device inserted over the teeth to prevent clenching and bruxing, and providing proprioceptive feedback to interfere with these habits, and placing the jaw joint in a neutral position where the muscles of mastication are more likely to relax). Such splint therapy must be carried out by a dental surgeon or dental specialist with expertise in this area and requires regular dental follow-up. It may be necessary in some cases for the patient to have more extensive corrective procedures and equilibration.

Vascular mechanisms are those that underlie the migraine symptoms, including visual disturbances, aversion to light, sound, stimulation, scalp tenderness, and pain unilaterally or bilaterally. Daily or frequent headache sufferers rarely experience pure forms of myofascial or vascular headaches; usually the pattern is recognizable as a mixture of myofascial and vascular headaches. The usual story is that these patients originally started to experience a simpler pattern of vascular or myofascial head pains, but that as time went on, the pains became more frequent and the pattern less distinct. The physical findings likewise usually reflect both the features of vascular and myofascial pains. For example, one might find during attacks an unequal pupil, photophobia, and scalp and neck tenderness, and between attacks residual muscle tenderness and trigger points. Some of the acute headache symptoms can return by pressing on these trigger points. The factors that perpetuate vascular headache symptoms include (a) excess of opiate analgesics; (b) excess of caffeine; (c) excess or prolonged use of aspirin or nonsteroidal antiinflammatory drugs; (d) alcohol; (e) certain foods; (f) eating at irregular times; (g) tension; (h) myofascial pain in the head and neck area; and (i) improper sleep. Clearly there are some similarities to the factors perpetuating other head pains. In many cases, the same treatment guidelines apply as for the myofascial pain factors.

Neuralgia features are surprisingly common in chronic frequent headache, even though uncomplicated cases of neuralgia affecting the head and neck are much less common than either vascular or myofascial head pains. One of the most common problems is an element of occipital neuralgia in patients who have had persistent myofascial pain of the head and neck. The typical findings are a complaint of tenderness of the back of the scalp, a tender spot at the entry of the occipital nerve into the scalp, a change in the quality of sensation in this region, and evidence that pain can be triggered by stimulating the affected nerve. Atypical facial neuralgias are another example of such neuralgias of the face. Neuralgia pains can be stabbing or burning, and can be reflected as well into other areas of the head and face. Factors that perpetuate or aggravate these neuralgia symptoms are (a) anxiety, (b) depression, (c) sleep problems, (d) stress, (e) persistent myofascial pain in the neck region, (f) postural problems of the neck region, and (g) pressure on the nerve (as in excessive use of cervical collars, and cervical spondylosis). Except for the last, these factors are all amenable to behavioral treatment.

Nonspecific Symptoms and Emotional Factors

Drugs and chemicals of both the prescription and nonprescription varieties can have an adverse effect in causing or perpetuating headache. In all cases, the aim is to reduce and eliminate medication that in frequent or regular dosing could cause headache.

Caffeinelike drugs are found in many beverages and in some medications. These are caffeine (in coffee), theophylline (in tea), and theobromine (in cocoa). Because they tend to cause blood vessel contraction in the head, there is a rebound effect that gets worse with increased use and leads to headache. The dose of caffeine in a cup of coffee is 60 to 80 mg. A daily dose of 400 mg total over a few weeks can trigger rebound headaches. Considering the fact that many medications also contain caffeine, chronic use of medication combined with coffee, tea, or cola drinks can put an individual far over the tolerable limit. The quantities of caffeine in common headache medications are listed below.

ASA with codeine ....30 mg
acetaminophen with codeine ....15 mg
Fiorinal (butalbital, ASA, and caffeine) ....40 mg
propoxyphene with ASA ....30 mg
Cafergot (ergotamine tartrate and caffeine) ....100 mg

Switching from coffee to tea does not solve the problem, since the quantity of theophylline in tea can be quite high.

Ergotamine is a drug that has the property of causing blood vessel constriction, as well as affecting the neurochemistry inside the head. The administration during the onset of a migraine may prevent the attack, but frequent or prolonged use of the drug may actually aggravate and increase the frequency of attacks. The danger level depends both on the dose and duration but it is fair to say that 7 mg per week on a regular basis can cause increased headaches in some people, and the risk increases with use. The dosages of ergotamine in common headache remedies are listed below.

Cafergot (ergotamine tartrate and caffeine) ....1 mg
Wigraine (ergotamine tartrate, caffeine, and belladonna) .....1 mg
Bellergal (belladonna, phenobarbital and ergotamine
  tartrate) ....0.3 mg

Bellergal Spacetabs (belladonna, ergotamine tartrate,
    phenobarbital) ....0.6 mg
Ergomar (ergotamine tartrate sublingual) ....2 mg

Opiates include codeine, morphine, meperidine, and other natural or synthetic compounds. All have an effect on the central nervous system in reducing the pain experience, but also can aggravate the headache. In fact, the withdrawal syndrome from opiates includes headache and generalized body aches. The risk of increasing the pain, however, does not just come from withdrawal; persistent use of opiates over several months, even in moderate doses, can cause a mixed headache syndrome with both tension and vascular features. This headache is resistant to any cure unless the opiate is withdrawn. It is also important to underscore the fact that opiates are not particularly effective either in migraine pain or in myofascial pain. On the other hand, they can contribute to nausea and vomiting, which often accompany severe headaches.

ASA and antiinflammatory medication all have the propensity to cause headaches. At first it was thought that ASA was the chief culprit in causing a syndrome called salicylism, in which the symptoms are headache, ringing ears, deafness, increased breathing, and nausea. It is now realized that the main symptoms of salicylism can be produced by other antiinflammatory drugs if used to excess, and that headaches can result from prolonged use in a minority of patients who use even low-to-moderate doses on a daily basis over a long period of time.

It is ironic that the mixed (compounded) analgesic drugs are primarily based on combinations of the above medications, and that a high proportion of difficult headache cases are found to be addicted to or dependent on these drugs. It is often difficult to convince these patients that the very drugs that seemed to help them in the beginning have now become toxic, and that the headache problem cannot be resolved until the toxins are removed. The question the patient often asks is, "If you take away my painkiller, what will you give me for my pain?" The truthful answer has to be given, "In this case, taking away those drugs is what will help your pain. Your own body will start to fight the pain again in a normal way once the drugs have been out of your system for 2 to 4 weeks."

Inactivity is a common response to illness, both because of the natural inclination to rest when feeling unwell, and also because of the fear of doing more harm. Inactivity can also promote deconditioning, which then makes activity difficult and leads to strain. Psychologically, inactivity reduces confidence and promotes anxiety and depression. These can add to the vicious circle of further inactivity. In headache sufferers, headaches can be triggered by activity that is strenuous or for which the person is unfit. If there is anxiety, guarding and muscle spasm will cause pain. A return to a healthy level of activity and fitness is part of the prescription for recovery.

Panic occurs frequently in frequent headache sufferers. The anxiety is that the headache will keep spiraling out of control and that there will be no relief. The panicky flight to the emergency room only worsens the problem because of the stress of the emergency room environment, often a suspicious reception by a strange physician, a quick discharge after an injection before the pain has completely cleared, and the lack of provision for preventive measures. The attitude becomes one of just surviving from episode to episode. Each pain leads to anxiety at an earlier stage, and the anxiety itself promotes pain increase. A desperate resort to multiple medication usually has adverse results. The whole attitude of not feeling in control but rather of looking for a cure in a bottle or an emergency department is inimical to gaining headache control.

Dealing with Avoidance

Patients must be taught that they cannot gain control until they realize that trying to deny or avoid pain leads to lack of control. After education about the effects of drugs on headaches, a regime should be set out for gradually eliminating the medications that are likely to be harmful. These include the ones mentioned above, but should also include dependency on sedatives and hypnotics or inappropriate use of psychoactive drugs. Of course, there may be necessary drugs in the mix also, so the practitioner must inquire from the treating physician the indications for the medications and gain agreement for withdrawal. Drugs can then be put on a time-contingent regime and be withdrawn steadily.

Inactivity must be countered with education about the hazards of deconditioning or guarding, giving structure for a plan of conditioning training. This must be matched by self-monitoring and gradually adding home-based activity in the areas that improve quality of life.

Relaxation exercises are a good antidote for anxiety, and panic and management by emergency must be firmly forbidden, giving the option of gradually assuming control using the treatment elements described above. Some patients have a significant myofascial pain component. For them, there will have to be specific training aimed at reducing this component through exercise, posture correction, and possibly some noninvasive physical intervention. The attitude of dependency on doctors rather than on oneself is replaced by emphasis on self-management.

Coping

The main elements of coping are personal active responses to stress (in this case headache), and the elements of management of behavior, thoughts, stress, environment, and health promotion. The individual responds flexibly in such a way as to evaluate (recognize) the problem and context, choose a response, and use the results as feedback in the choice of further coping behavior. In effective coping, these responses may become more or less second nature, but this does not take away from the facts that coping can be learned and that responses can be chosen or changed. (For details about teaching relaxation and coping techniques, see chapter 3.)

Behavior management has to do with active responses to limit the effect of stress or prevent problems. For example, someone may use distraction or engage in pleasant activity instead of being preoccupied with pain or with fear of losing control. Pacing oneself rather than behaving in a panicky way is another example. When faced with a difficult task, one may break it into a series of small tasks, and mentally check them off as they are done to emphasize the fact that it is being gradually accomplished. One may be assertive or role-play someone who is in control.

Cognitive (thoughts) management involves changing the interpretation and approach to thinking about problems in order to cope. A key variable is counteracting the temptation to fear the worst (catastrophize). Strategies can include mental distraction, depersonalizing the pain "as if it were an object to be studied out there, not in me," using mental images contrary to the pain or stress experience, or reinterpreting the pain as something like a challenge, or as a different sensation. There is a subtle difference between distraction or not dwelling on pain on the one hand, and using avoidance or denial on the other hand. The latter is liable to aggravate the sense of having no control, and augment anxiety.

Stress management is directed at reducing the arousal caused by stress and pain. This can be done by using quieting words and phrases as cues to reduce tension, using partial or comprehensive relaxation exercises, modifying posture into a nonguarded relaxed position, or using physical (aerobic) exercise for mental relaxation. An important special case of relaxation is that which employs forms of biofeedback. It is in fact with various kinds of head pain that the use of biofeedback is best developed and documented (Bakal, 1982; Tan, 1982). Biofeedback techniques are a subject in itself, and a summary of the technique is dealt with in chapter 3. However, the principle is that by feedback the subject is given a sense of control over a physiological dimension of the pain problem. The dimension might be hand temperature, blood volume of the head blood vessels, muscle tension, or galvanic skin response. Likely there is also a learned degree of actual physiological control over physiological variables that are linked to pain. Thus, it may be advantageous to a person who suffers pain from TMJ dysfunction to use muscle tension biofeedback (EMG biofeedback) to adjust the jaw postures, bring about awareness of tight jaw muscles, and eliminate habits of teeth grinding. However, it is also reasonable for the therapist to use relaxation therapy without biofeedback devices because the results with the latter may in many cases be equally good (Jessup et al., 1979).

Environmental management involves recognizing that one's behavior affects the environment, and that the environment affects one's behavior. For example, if a person shows apprehension, people nearby may demonstrate anxious concern for that individual, which increases the sense of general alarm. Being aware of nonverbal communication and dealing with assumptions corrects what otherwise could be self-perpetuating behavior.

Health promotion reflects an attitude toward problems. Instead of reacting to symptoms primarily, the aim is promoting both a quality and sense of health by exercise directed at fitness, diet, balance in daily activity, stress management, sleep management, reduction of dependency on pills or professionals, and the engendering of confidence (self-efficacy).

Communication

People communicate verbally and nonverbally through talk about illness and anxiety or through illness behavior. There are two observers of each communication: the audience and the person doing the communicating. Patients often talk themselves into feeling worse. Their nonverbal behavior in abusing pills or panicking is also a communication. Patients must become aware of the effects of their communications on themselves. They then need to consider the effects of their communications on others to avoid being treated as sick and disabled. Patients can learn to disengage others from the urge to rescue or to feel anxious about them. For example, "Yes, I have a headache, but I have been learning what to do for them. You don't have to do anything, thanks."

Patients are taught to take control of the communications among their families and friends to avoid excessive sympathizing or illness discussion.

Feedback

In therapy, the goal is to selectively focus attention on communications that facilitate coping and action. For example, in beginning an interview the therapist would not say, "How have your headaches been?" but rather, "What have you been learning about helping yourself? . . . How have you been using what you are learning?" Families likewise are counseled not to reinforce attention to illness or to feelings of helplessness. For example, they can be told, "Headaches are a kind of disability. It can be reassuring to ask a friend how he or she is recovering from surgery, because that is a temporary thing. But to treat disability the same way is not necessarily kind or reassuring. It is better to keep the conversation on what the person is doing or on hopes and plans, and to show an interest in that person's participation."

Self-Maintenance

In patients who suffer chronic pain, it usually is futile to focus the therapy primarily on eradicating the symptoms. The most common outcome of this is that relief lasts a short time and the patient returns frequently, with an increasing sense of frustration or dependency. However, having completed a behaviorally oriented program with the emphasis on self-management, and having alleviated the factors of anxiety and depression, deconditioning, poor posture, and medication dependency, it sometimes then occurs that conservative biological interventions become effective. In selected cases, one may successfully introduce measures such as splint therapy, transcutaneous electrical nerve stimulation, stretch and spray, or limited pharmacological intervention for specific conditions (e.g., nonsteroidal antiinflammatory medication for TMJ dysfunction). The biological treatment is always given in the context that these things are intended to help but that the real and long-lasting benefit depends on the patient's own activity.

Autonomy is facilitated by therapeutic experiences that gradually promote a sense of control and independence in the person's own work and home environment. For example, self-monitoring of certain coping skills such as relaxation or pacing can be used as the follow-up appointments are spaced farther apart, and the patient can be encouraged to try the new coping techniques in the real work and daily living environment. In the early stages, self-reports of progress in these areas are reinforced by the therapist. Ties of dependency to the medical environment are cut by cutting medications and increasing home exercise in place of physiotherapy and prescription treatment. The therapist must ensure that the self-management regime is tolerable and palatable. An onerous and unpleasant exercise program will not be followed for long. Compliance is improved if a group can be found to share an exercise program. If a patient is being ridiculed by family members for cutting out alcohol abuse or for exercising, family members will have to be dealt with in family interviews.

HEADACHE QUESTIONNAIRE

Headaches are a common problem. If you usually or frequently suffer from headaches, have never been examined by a physician for this problem, or if you have recently begun to experience headaches as a new problem, you should consult a physician. If you have been examined by your physician but treatments have not controlled your headache, then answer the following questions.

- Do you suffer headaches 3 days or more per week?
- Are you ever nervous about having enough painkiller at home in case you come down with a headache?
- Do you take a painkiller most days of the week?
- Do you take pain relievers when you do not actually have a headache but fear that you could suffer one?
- Counting painkillers, tranquilizers, sleeping pills, or other pills for your nerves, do you take at least six tablets per day?
- Do you awaken with a headache most mornings?
- In the last month, have you made an emergency visit to any health-care professional or clinic on account of a headache?
- Is your headache problem getting worse?
- Are you ever afraid that there might be some serious disease causing your headaches?
- On account of a headache, have you canceled plans you have made during the past month?
- Do you avoid making plans because headaches often interfere with your engagements?
- Do you have insomnia (trouble sleeping through the night and feeling unrefreshed in the morning)?
- Do friends or family ask you how your headaches are doing?
- Do friends or family often offer you advice about your headaches?
- Do friends or family ever seem irritated with you because of your headaches?

- Do you ever drink alcohol to relieve the stress or pain of a headache or to help you to sleep?
- Do most of these factors seem to trigger headaches for you: odors, weather, menstrual periods, foods, air outside, lights, exercise, sex?
- Are you ever afraid that your headaches will never get better?
- Have you seen more than two specialists about your headaches?
- Have the headaches caused you to become depressed for as long as 2 weeks or more?
- During the past month, have you ever thought of harming yourself because of your headaches?
- During the past 2 months, have you wished you were dead because of headaches?
- Are you afraid to exercise for fear of provoking headaches?
- Do headaches ever make you feel panicky or helpless?

If you answered "yes" to more than five of these questions, you likely have a problem with control of your headaches, and would probably benefit from a behavioral medicine treatment program.

Chapter 8

Addictions (Drugs, Food, and Tobacco)

DESCRIPTION OF THE PROBLEM

A 72-year-old man complained of headaches, and chest wall and abdominal pain. He was unsteady, having falls at home, and was becoming confused. He had been taking ASA with codeine for several years. This state of health had existed for several years since he had had heart disease, bypass surgery (after which he had begun to suffer chest wall pain), and partial obstruction of the graft. Attempts had been made to relieve the pain by removal of surgical wires from the sternum, and by medication and injections, and he now had a gastric ulcer. He walked slowly, and with a cane, and appeared sad and slow in responses. He became tearful at the suggestion that his medication might be discontinued. However, he agreed to be given a flavored elixir containing all his analgesics, and during the next 2 weeks his medication was slowly withdrawn in this masked solution. By the end of this time, he looked better, was getting some pain relief using small doses of antidepressant and acetaminophen only, was physically more active, and was learning a relaxation technique. One month later, he was planning to take his wife on a vacation. She said that this was the best she had seen him in health, mood, and pain control in many years.

BACKGROUND

Medications are not inherently bad. They have contributed much to reduction of disease and suffering. There are some patients who have attitudes and behaviors around drug-taking that are clearly problematic. Principally the problems fall into the areas of (a) having excessive dependency on drugs without appropriate medical indication, (b) having drug-induced symptoms that in turn become the focus of illness, (c) having frank addiction along with withdrawal symptoms on at-

160

tempting to stop the drug, and (d) having maladaptive attitudes that are reinforced by drug-taking and by having drugs prescribed. The mechanisms that perpetuate these problems are as follows.

1. Learned illness behavior that is reinforced by the effects of the drug or of the drug prescriber.
2. Conditioning based on using a drug as a means to escape or avoid anticipated pain and anxiety.
3. Illness role behavior that represents beliefs about being ill, and about cures.
4. Erroneous notions about the relationship of drugs to health.
5. The behavior of physicians who try to avoid dealing with the complex problems of their patients by writing prescriptions for everything.

The other chapters of this book also contain useful information about medicine. See chapter 4 for hypnotics and stimulants, chapter 5 for anxiety and its treatment, chapters 6 and 7 for painkillers, chapter 10 for drugs that act on the gut, and chapter 12 for consideration of the "Worried Well," who may abuse medication. The following Information for Patients section deals with these main issues.

INFORMATION FOR PATIENTS

How could my medication be bad for me? It was prescribed by a doctor. Of course, the doctor would be crazy to give you something that he or she thought would harm you. Good health can be promoted by good use of medication. Medications are like powerful tools. Once you take them home, they belong to you—not to the doctor! You have to be responsible and informed about what you are putting into your body or they will not work properly and can injure you.

How do medications work? Your whole body is made up of cells and tissues, and each cell has processes that make it live, grow, and carry on certain specialized activities. Mostly, drugs work by altering the functions of the body. They do this by interfering with the processes that control the growth or the activities that are natural for cells and tissues. There are only two exceptions to this.

Exception #1: Sometimes the problem is that the body has something growing in it that it should not have, like an infection or a tumor. Antibiotics in normal doses work by interfering with growth of germs, because they are more toxic to germ cells than human cells. Antitumor drugs are more toxic to tumor cells than to normal cells. However, the medications can still cause toxic problems and must be taken carefully.

Exception #2: Rarely, people do not have enough of certain hormones, vitamins, or nutrients. If they are replaced to normal levels, the health may improve, but high amounts of these are useless at best, and can often be poisonous. Even vitamins and iron supplements in excess can lead to serious poisoning.

Apart from these two exceptions, all other drugs have to change the natural processes in your body in order to have an effect on you.

How do medications cause trouble? We should think of all drugs as having a range of effects, in which tiny amounts produce little or no effects, moderate quantities produce a medically useful effect but at the same time interfere with the body so that side effects are also possible, and high amounts are toxic. The side effects or possible adverse reactions are something that one also must be aware of when an illness does not seem to get better despite medication; in some cases the problem is due to the drug itself. Some painkillers can cause pain, some sleeping medications and alcohol can cause insomnia, and some laxatives and medicines for the gut can aggravate gut symptoms.

The doctor is the professional, and I'm just a layperson. What do you expect from me? The whole subject concerning being informed about your drugs is an important one, and laypeople should have access to reliable literature about the medications they are taking (United States Pharmacopeial Convention, 1989). However, you can start with attitudes. It is the doctor's business when he suggests a drug and explains what is recommended. However, it is your business as soon as you accept the prescription. It is your drug that you put into your body—no one else's. Your doctor is not going to be upset about your efforts to be well informed. In fact, it makes the doctor's job easier.

Types of Medication

We must restrict our discussion now to the three most important kinds of medical drugs that patients tend to have troubles with: analgesics, sedatives, and hypnotics. We will not be discussing alcohol or illicit drugs, even though those are also important topics.

Analgesics. Analgesic means painkiller. There are two kinds of painkillers. Some work by reducing inflammation and altering the body chemicals that are responsible for producing pain. Other drugs work by interfering with the pain messages as they pass through the nerves on the way up the spinal cord to the brain.

Thousands of years ago, Druids in England would go down to the riverbank and get some willow bark, from which they would make a potion that relieved fever and aches. Last century, scientists were able to crystallize that substance which we now know as acetylsalicylic acid (ASA or aspirin). That drug is still the best example of the group of antiinflammatory drugs. This is how it works. When you are injured, cells are damaged. The wall of the damaged cell is broken down by enzymes in your body. One of the byproducts of that breakdown is a form of prostaglandin. This chemical participates in making inflammation and it also works together with other chemicals at the site of injury to make pain nerves become more sensitive. The inside of the damaged cell also releases chemicals such as histamine and kinin, and they too make pain nerves sensitive and help produce inflammation. The nerve endings nearby also get involved. They are stimulated by the swelling, the chemicals from the damaged tissue, and the tissue injury to begin to react and send pain messages to the brain. At the same time, the nerve endings release chemicals near the site of injury to increase inflammation. Inflammation is a good thing. Without it you would never heal. The pain is good too because it warns you to be careful until the healing is well underway. However, we do not like to hurt and are likely to be glad to have a painkiller if the injury is very painful. ASA and drugs like it interfere with the production of prostaglandin so that the pain nerves become less sensitive and react less, so the inflammation is reduced. It does not stop inflammation altogether, as the healing still happens. ASA works to a lesser extent on the chemicals in the brain that help us experience pain and fever; therefore, the ASA works at two spots—at the injury if there is inflammation, and in the nervous system to a lesser extent. Naturally, it will have less of a painkiller effect if the injury is old and the healing and inflammation have settled down. Because the prostaglandin is responsible for making a mucus coat to protect the stomach, ASA can reduce this protection and cause ulcers. It has other adverse effects, too. It can interfere with the little cells in the blood that make clots (platelets) so that you bleed too much. That is a problem for the athlete who strains his knee, takes some ASA for the pain, and goes out to play some more; he could risk bleeding into the joint. ASA can provoke allergic reactions and asthma. In high doses over a long time, it causes kidney damage. Prolonged use of too high a dose causes salicylism—a syndrome of headache, ringing ears, and deafness, and changes in blood chemistry. Sometimes people who have a headache and take medication for it are actually suffering this syndrome, and will not get better unless they get the medicine out of their systems. Lately ASA has become suspected of causing Reye's syndrome, and it is better to avoid this medication for young children with flu or viral illness. In older people who are at risk of stroke or heart disease, ASA in small quantities (two every 2 days) may prevent stroke or heart attacks. Overdoses of ASA are often serious and even fatal. The most common problems occur in people with persistent pain who medicate themselves with over-the-counter ASA products. They run the risk of sudden bleeding ulcers, asthmatic attacks, and kidney disease. It is ironic that some of these people would not have pain if they would stop taking ASA long enough to get over the side effects.

Many other antiinflammatory drugs are now on the market. Usually, they can be obtained only by prescription. They work in about the same way that ASA works and tend to have the same side effects. Some are more or less hard on the stomach, some last longer than others, some affect the brain with drowsiness or mood change, some cause liver problems, some might possibly interfere with blood production in the bone marrow, and some interfere with platelets more than others. Still, what is true for ASA is usually true for them, too. Many antiinflammatories are enteric coated, meaning that there is something on the tablet that prevents it from hurting the stomach, but this is not a guarantee. Acetaminophen relieves fever and has the same action on the central nervous system for pain relief as does ASA. However, it has no effect on inflammation at the site of injury. It is safe in asthmatics, is less likely to upset the stomach, and does not risk Reye's syndrome in children. On the other hand, overdoses with acetaminophen, or even excessive use over several months, can damage the liver.

In short, antiinflammatory/antifever drugs are good pain relievers in the acute stage while an injury is healing and inflamed, but in excessive doses can cause serious problems. For prolonged use they have less than optimal effects and there is an increased risk of adverse effects, including aggravation of pain.

Opiate drugs work on the brain. The nerves are not connected directly with the brain but pass through many connections called synapses. The first synapse is at the level of the spinal cord. At this point, a number of things may happen to the information. It may simply be blocked by release of chemical messengers, such as endorphin or serotonin. It may be passed on to various nerve channels, and some of the channels to which it may be passed carry pain information. Drugs related to morphine and drugs related to the antidepressants may suppress pain information transmission at this level. As the painful information passes up the spinal cord, it reaches the base of the brain. In the region of the mid-brain there are connections that may filter the amount of pain information that goes through. Some of the chemicals involved in this filtering are endorphin and serotonin. These chemicals can be affected directly by certain drugs. If the amount of serotonin or endorphin available is increased, or if some drug is introduced into the body to simulate these chemicals, the result of it may be a reduction in pain. As the information passes up higher, some if it passes through centers in the brain that control emotions, mood, and energy. Opiates affect these centers and reduce the amount of anxiety, tension, and pain. The opiates include meperidine (Demerol), morphine, codeine, oxycodone and ASA (Percodan), pentazocine (Talwin), and other drugs. All work by masquerading as the body's own supply of endorphin, which is normally found all along the spinal cord, at the level of the brain stem, and at higher nervous system centers. The problem is that opiates work for only a short period of time against unpleasant mood, and after about 4 hours the pain and the unpleasant mood returns and there is a tendency to increase the dose. A further problem is that the body recognizes it as a chemical signal that is found normally within the body, and if there is too much of that signal, the body will get used to it (become tolerant) so that higher doses are necessary and eventually addiction can occur and lead to the danger of overdose. These drugs have unpleasant side effects, such as nausea, constipation, loss of appetite, cramps, sexual impotence, sweating, unpleasant moods, confusion, and craving.

Opiates are helpful and sometimes can be given in high doses to cancer patients, and are important in managing acute injuries or pain after surgery. If they are used under these conditions, they should be taken regularly and consistently. For some serious pain problems such as postoperative pain and cancer, there are patient-controlled automated analgesic systems that allow the patient to take the medication by injection whenever pain is experienced.

On the other hand, for chronic pain long-term use of opiates in some people can lead to chronic migraines, irritable bowel pain, and increased generalized pain problems. Fortunately, the body can get over the dependency and after 2 weeks of abstinence, the body is well on the way to recovery again. (However, the habits often remain and might lead to relapse.)

Sedatives. Over the years, a multitude of different kinds of drugs have been used as sedatives, but now almost all are members of the family of benzodiazepines, which are related to diazepam (Valium). Examples of the family are diazepam, chlordiazepoxide, flurazepam, clonazepam, oxazepam, lorazepam, bromazepam, alprazolam, temazepam, and triazolam. Alprazolam also has been tried as an antidepressant. As you can see, the names sound alike, and a layperson can often recognize the type of drug just by the "-epam" part of the name. At first it was recognized that drugs of this kind calmed anxiety while still leaving the patient awake, and that there was a great gap between the effective dose and the lethal overdose. But then it was found that people who took serious overdoses often included these sedatives along with other chemicals, which together made a dangerous combination – for example diazepam and alcohol. It was also found that some of these, such as diazepam, flurazepam, or chlordiazepoxide, tended to accumulate in the blood over several nights' use, posing risks especially for the elderly.

There are subtle side effects of these drugs that may be hard to spot even though they are serious. One problem is increased depression or suicidal behavior. Another problem is memory loss, which the patient usually does not even recognize until he or she has stopped the drug and then finds his or her mind clearing up. The trouble with these side effects is that people might misinterpret these mental symptoms as only a nervous problem and take more of the drug.

It was thought that these medications would not be addicting. Gradually it came to light that these drugs could be very addicting, even at low doses (Noyes, Garvey, Cook, & Perry, 1988). For example, 15 mg of diazepam daily for a year can lead to a withdrawal syndrome lasting a month or more. The shorter-acting members of the family, such as triazolam, are the most addicting, even though they are the least likely to accumulate in the blood. Dependency on these drugs is treacherous because the withdrawal syndrome includes severe anxiety and possibly epileptic seizures, which are relieved temporarily by taking some more of the drug. The withdrawal syndrome takes a long time to overcome and many people relapse. Many addicts become addicted to multiple drugs, but this may go unrecognized for a long time because the prescriptions are obtained "legitimately" from a doctor.

Contrary to the ideas held by many doctors, these drugs possibly can relieve muscle spasm, but they do not relieve pain. They have the most profound effect in the first few weeks and then tolerance starts to develop. In most cases they should be given for no more than 2 months if one is to avoid the risk of tolerance and a withdrawal syndrome.

Hypnotics. For a long time, barbiturates were the main hypnotic. They proved to be addicting and are prone to lead to overdose (even by accident), and now are used mostly as anticonvulsants. There are still several hypnotics on the market, such as ethchlorvynol or methaqualone, but the main hypnotics now belong to the benzodiazepine series. Although they cause sedation, they do not provide a satisfying sleep. In fact, there is no drug on the market that produces a natural sleep. Sleep is so delicate a mechanism, that any drug, stimulant, sedative, hypnotic, analgesic, or alcohol runs the risk of making insomnia worse.

How People Become Dependent on Drugs

Euphoria. We all know the expression that "so-and-so has been drinking and is feeling good." Now, we know that this does not mean feeling good in a normal sense, but rather that somehow the alcohol has altered the brain so that the mood is out of keeping with the situation. The word for this is euphoria. Many drugs that interfere with the brain can produce this effect, including analgesics, hypnotics, and sedatives. Not everyone feels this effect, and it does not happen with every drug, but it is one of the things that may make people depend on the drug. The danger is especially great if the person was feeling bad in some way — discouraged, sad, or worried. The euphoria may be a welcome change, but before you know it, the drug becomes an escape and the person is addicted.

Escape. Even if the drug does not provide euphoria, as long as it interrupts the sense of worry or feeling bad, the person may still become dependent or addicted to it. For example, many alcoholics experience depression, nausea, and other physical symptoms when they drink. Yet, the alcohol's interference with normal brain functions provides enough of an escape that they are willing to be sick in order to have this escape.

Reduced Anxiety. Some chemicals — benzodiazepines and alcohol especially — have a specific effect in reducing anxiety and fear. Often, for example, you see it when someone has had too much and then begins to act in a way that most of us would be afraid to act. People can begin to depend on that in order to deal with unpleasant situations. In the end it may worsen the situation, and provide even further enticement to continue abusing the chemical.

Curiosity. Simple curiosity stimulates many people to take a chemical, in order to have a different experience, or to try to repeat an experience that they have had before.

Fear of Withdrawal. It is true that many drugs have unpleasant withdrawal effects. If someone has depended on a drug for a long time, that person may not want to risk feeling withdrawal, and will postpone coming off the drug. Sometimes a person will fear withdrawal symptoms and will misinterpret normal things like a slight headache or indigestion as withdrawal, and will take more drugs. The fear of withdrawal can get greater until that person takes the drug to try to ward off everything, even the anticipation of symptoms or withdrawal.

Habit. It is difficult to break a routine once it has become regular. After a while, even the time of day will start to remind you of the habit you have. You can feel out of sorts in not having the security blanket. That explains why people can sometimes go on taking a drug forever that does absolutely nothing for them.

Damage to Self-Concept. If people take a chemical like alcohol or a drug for a long time, they begin to believe that that drug is necessary for their functioning. Every time they see the bottle, they say to themselves, "I need this." They begin to feel as if life would not be normal without it. It undermines their sense of healthiness or self-sufficiency. Then, when troubles or symptoms occur, it is harder to resist the urge to take something.

How to Regain Control. To regain control, it is necessary to get rid of a lot of errors in thinking.

1. Drugs do not make people more healthy and normal—they have to interfere with normal body processes in order to have an effect.
2. Bad reactions are not the rule in drug withdrawal. Usually, the unpleasant effects of stopping are short-lived, whereas the long-term results of quitting are feeling more healthy and normal.
3. Except for a few conditions like diabetes or thyroid deficiencies, people generally do not have some kind of deficiency that makes drug taking necessary for a long time.
4. Drugs do not improve sleep; they cause unconsciousness or impair the arousal functions of the brain.
5. For disorders such as schizophrenia, some kinds of tranquilizers are helpful. Other than in the case of severe psychiatric disorders, drugs do not control anxiety; they interfere with the normal appreciation of emotion and restrict motivation to react to the real world.
6. Although there are painkillers (which are valuable in the case of cancer, acute injury, or short-lived pain), in general they do not help you cope with chronic pain. They actually can interfere with learning to cope.
7. It is incorrect to fear that, "Now that I have become dependent on the drug, I can never live without it again."
8. Drugs do not control you unless you give up control.

The next step is to gain control by establishing a set time for taking drugs. This breaks up old habits. It also reduces the problem of side effects mixed with withdrawal effects when you establish a regular pattern and get a steady blood level. Then start a steady pattern of withdrawal, giving your body adequate time to function normally again.

Normally, we control anxiety through coping thoughts, activity, and exercise. We sleep by having a normal routine of day and night, and have physical workouts mixed with rest times. As drugs are withdrawn, it is necessary to reestablish these normal routines. The basic recipe is to have a regular exercise program, a relaxation routine, and a sleep-management routine, and to become informed about your health and about drugs.

ASSESSMENT AND TREATMENT

Dependency on drugs takes many forms. Some patients abuse painkillers and sedatives because of another problem such as chronic pain. Some patients are addicted, and despite their attempts to quit, frequently relapse. In other patients, the chronic illness behavior has led to the accumulation of prescriptions, so that medication dependency is iatrogenic. Biological, cognitive, emotional, behavioral, and coping factors contribute to the problem (Figure 8.1). Helping the patient to conduct an honest self-assessment, and providing patient education, sets the stage for treatment. However, in most cases of drug dependency and addiction, education is insufficient. The problem has to be addressed by new learning. This is accomplished by drug withdrawal and changing the contingencies and reinforcers that affect the drug dependency. The treatment can be based on self-medication or a time-contingent dosing schedule.

Evaluations

Beliefs and Interpretations. Poor health attitudes can lead to unhealthy medication use, as exemplified by the following.

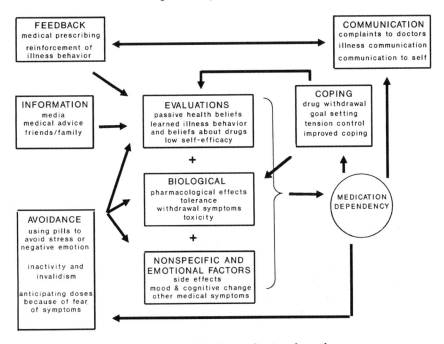

FIGURE 8.1. Algorithm for medication dependency.

1. "A pill for every ill" — the adherence to this idea comes from a passive belief about health, that illness and symptoms are external to the self, and that an external agent can be taken without personal change.
2. "Symptoms mean disease" — this idea involves a fear of symptoms and unwillingness to accept them. An individual with this belief may continue to try remedies until the symptoms are gone.
3. "I take drugs because I am sick" — this simple equation ignores the relevance of specific drugs to specific illnesses and is rather treacherous because it implies its converse; "I am sick because I take drugs." In this way, taking drugs influences beliefs and sustains illness behavior.
4. "If one is good, two must be better" — this attitude leads to escalation of dosage.
5. A tendency to catastrophize about symptoms, and a poor sense of self-efficacy, make it tempting to rely on drugs more than on efforts to cope.

Various learning mechanisms entrench drug-taking behavior. These including the following:

1. There may be operant conditioning of drug-taking. This learning is most likely due to attention given by family and friends who notice and reinforce the illness behavior by their solicitous comments. (Perhaps the euphoriant or anxiolytic effects of the drug could be reinforcing, but remember that these effects usually take the better part of an hour to be felt, unless the drug is taken by injection or sublingually.)

2. If the drug has become associated with a belief that it will relieve distress, there could be a kind of avoidance learning in which the individual engages in anticipatory drug-taking to avoid feared symptoms or unpleasant feelings. There is similar avoidance learning when there is a real risk of drug withdrawal symptoms.

3. If someone has been able to put up with some anxiety or stressful situation while impaired by a drug, there can be state-dependent learning in which resisting the anxiety or having the subjective impression of coping can be repeated only in the presence of self-intoxication.

The "Medication Questionnaire" at the end of this chapter (pp. 180–181) is a good attitude checklist that can be used to sensitize patients to beliefs and attitudes that foster medication dependency.

Investigating the Problem. A first step is to have the patient make a diary for a few days of the number of tablets, kinds of drugs, and times of dosage. These then need to be reviewed. A decision must be made about what is essential versus what is being taken for symptoms or fears or is being abused. For this it may be necessary to get the patient's permission to speak with the family doctor. Some conditions, such as epilepsy, heart disease, hypertension, diabetes, or rheumatic disease, require ongoing use of medication for the person's safety. Otherwise, sedatives, analgesics, hypnotics, laxatives, and most over-the-counter medications can be discontinued.

Self-Evaluation. The diaries described in chapter 2 can be used with the simple instructions to write down everything that was taken over a several day interval. This by itself may reduce the drug-taking behavior, and for some patients is a useful intervention when they come to face how they actually take their medications. However, there is also a significant risk of noncompliance, with the patient neglecting to enter data or doing nothing for several days and then filling in all of the diaries a few minutes before the next session. A strategy to tighten this up is to have the patient bring all of the medications in their original bottles on the first interview, making note of the number of tablets in the bottle, the date of the prescription, and the number of tablets originally dispensed. On the second day, when the diaries are returned, have the patient bring the bottles and check the number of tablets and dates again. This gives a way to cross-check the accuracy of the self-report. Another strategy is to obtain the patient's permission to call the pharmacy and the family doctor to find out how much medication is being prescribed and how many prescriptions are being filled.

Biological Substrates

The biological phenomena of importance are as follows:

- pharmacological effects of the drug, which might reduce some un-pleasant psychological or physical state
- pharmacological side effects that are interpreted as symptoms, giving a stimulus to take more drugs
- tolerance, so that larger doses may be needed to achieve the same effect
- withdrawal effects on any system, which serve as a stimulus to take more of the drug.

Note, however, that a drug does not have to be a euphoriant or anxiolytic, or cause withdrawal in order to cause dependency or addiction. Usually it is enough if the drug reinforces attention paid to symptoms or illness. In that way, all drugs can lead to abnormal dependencies and addictions.

Nonspecific Symptoms and Emotional Factors

Affective disturbance such as anxiety or depression can be interpreted as illness, providing a stimulus to take more medication. Likewise, irrelevant physical or emotional stimuli may be interpreted as due to illness, leading to taking more drug.

Dealing with Avoidance

Avoidance is associated mostly with anticipatory drug-taking. Avoidance may be associated with a desire to have an emotion-altering experience. Self-monitoring is one way of gaining a personal sense of how much and when drug-taking is occurring. The drugs are then taken on a time-contingent rather than symptom-contingent schedule, which allows the individual to disassociate the drug-taking from the illness behavior and the cues that perpetuate attention on the illness. Control is obtained by reducing the drugs while adding behavioral techniques for coping with stress.

Coping

There are various models for getting control of drug-taking behavior. All are based on using some form of time-contingent dosing, withdrawing drugs, and replacing them with other coping methods: exercise, relaxation, sleep control, or pain control techniques.

In the technique originally described by Fordyce et al. (1973), all of the patient's medications were given in a color- and flavor-masked solution, at a constant volume, and on a time-contingent schedule, with the quantity of active ingredient reduced in a stepwise manner until only the masked solution remained. This is useful when dealing with anxious individuals who are afraid of doing without their medication. The downside is that some medications cannot be mixed together because of their chemical nature. Also it takes a great deal of pharmacy time to make up the solutions and mask them (especially when the concentrations are changed constantly), the patients sometimes see the drug withdrawal as having been done to them rather than seeing themselves as having gained control, and it requires a fairly large nursing component in monitoring the strict 4-hour dosing schedule.

A cognitive–behavioral model is based on education regarding drugs, teaching techniques of relaxation and stress control, and then making a contract for taking the drugs on a time-contingent basis and slowly withdrawing them according to a quota. In this system, the patient is aware of what he or she is taking and must be compliant with the idea of medication control. An advantage is that it gives more emphasis on the patient's decision-making rather than imposing a withdrawal schedule. It still requires nursing supervision for the strict time-contingent dosing. In any drug withdrawal program, one must remember to be vigilant about the patient's use of over-the-counter medications or alcohol.

A self-medication program can also be used for chronic pain patients. Self-medication has generally been thought to be inadequate for patients who are habituated or who use excessive medications, but our experience is that with adequate self-monitoring and support, it is as effective and less labor intensive than other drug-withdrawal methods. On admission, patients are allowed to take their own medication for 3 days, and a baseline is established for quantities of all medications. A contract is made for withdrawal of all nonessential drugs within a specified time frame. Patients meet directly with the doctor and pharmacist who describe the dangers of long-term medication intake (see Information for Patients section). Reading material is available. The rationale for time-contingent dosing is explained. The daily average of all drugs is calculated and dosages are worked out for a time-contingent schedule. Patients learn to keep a daily self-medication record, which becomes part of their permanent chart. Medication is obtained directly from the pharmacy; it is given in dose-reminder boxes with all the ingredients clearly marked, enough for 24 hours at a time. Each day the empty box is exchanged for a new full box. Each week a written agreement is made for dose reductions according to the established goals until the medication is stopped. In a group setting, this is quite effective because of the group participation. It lends a strong sense of personal accomplishment, and although there is plenty of support from staff in staff–patient encounters, and from direct contact with the pharmacist, the amount of staff time is less than in a hospital model.

To keep the perspective here, it should be noted that in chronic pain the goal is to stop medication, but in some conditions, such as cancer pain and postoperative pain, the goal should be symptom control. Here, too, the best models will be either regular dosing to keep a good blood level, or self-medication, perhaps with an automated system. Efforts must be made to avoid misguided rationing based on fears of making the patient an addict. In fact, inconsistent dosing in such cases is more likely to generate abnormal clinging to analgesics, which is prevented by regular and adequate provision of analgesics.

Communication

Patients must learn that their nonverbal illness behavior when they take medications also has an effect on their self-concept. The scenario is presented of what they think when they get up in the morning, walk into the bathroom, and open the medicine cabinet to see an array of pills, and what they think about seeing it for the rest of their lives, every morning.

Patients are alerted to the transaction that they create when they visit their doctor. The following scenario is given of picking the "ideal doctor": the choice is given (a) of a doctor who takes a look at them and always gives a prescription, or (b) one who might give a prescription for some things but usually gives advice and support about becoming more healthy. If the patients' statements to the doctor convey only that the symptoms are not adequately relieved, the doctor may prescribe further medication. If instead the patients want to know what is in their best interests—pills or other management—the doctor may feel less constrained to write a prescription. Doctors are much influenced by the demands and requests of their patients.

Feedback

It is enjoined on family to encourage non-drug-taking behavior by praising well behavior. The attending doctor must be fully aware of the program and its goals so that after discharge the prescriptions will not be restarted. A personal conversation with the doctor is usually much appreciated and if the psychologist offers to give back-up to the doctor after the program is finished, compliance will likely be improved.

Self-Maintenance

To improve follow-through, the patient needs to replace the drug-taking with something more successful. The essential elements are stress-control techniques and other health-maintaining activities such as exercise, smoking cessation, improved sleep habits, and restored role function. Reinforcement for healthy behavior must be taught to the family and/or significant others.

OVEREATING AND OBESITY

Several studies demonstrate that in obese people, there is an alteration in the way that appetite relates to internal events and cycles, satiety mechanisms, and environmental cues. (For a discussion on the interaction of metabolic and psychological factors in obesity, see Sahakian, 1982.) Furthermore, there are attitudes that foster the perpetuation of this situation. Family plays a significant role in the maintenance of obesity (Pearce, Lebow, & Orchard, 1981). The factors that have been identified as contributing to the problem of overeating include eating habits, quality and quantity of food eaten, and quality of interpersonal interactions (or eating transactions).

Internal Events and Cycles

Stunkard and Koch (1964) found that stomach contractions coincide with self-reports of hunger in normal people, but that there is a poor relationship between hunger and stomach contractions in obese people.

Satiety

Schachter, Goldman, & Gordon (1968) studied normal and obese people who were hungry or who had eaten before the experiment. In the experiment, the subjects were given crackers with instructions that they should rate their taste and that they could eat all they wanted. Normal individuals ate far more if they were hungry and far less if they were already full, whereas the amounts eaten by obese individuals were unaffected by whether they had full or empty stomachs.

Cues

Nisbett (1968) arranged a situation in which either one or three sandwiches was placed visibly near the subject, with a supply of sandwiches placed out of sight in a refrigerator across the room. Normal and obese subjects were assigned tasks in the room, were allowed to eat freely, and were told that they could find more in the refrigerator. Obese subjects tended to eat mainly what was visible, eating less if they were presented with one sandwich and more if presented with three. Normal subjects tended to rely more on internal signals of satiety, eating about the same amount in either stimulus condition and looking for more if presented with only one sandwich, or leaving some food if presented with three sandwiches.

Cognitions

Attitudes and beliefs about oneself as an obese person who cannot control eating perpetuate the feelings of helplessness and discouragement that interfere with dieting. There is a tendency to make generalizations about any setback or failure to keep on a diet to lose weight. The generalization is that "the situation is hopeless," and this leads to giving up, which confirms the beliefs about hopelessness. There is also a tendency to cling to theories that make the overeating seem to be irreversible; for example, the idea that the number of fat cells is fixed and that they will necessarily fill up again no matter what the food intake.

In becoming an obese individual, it is likely that the eating has a positive reinforcing value, that it may relieve anxiety or dysphoria, and that an irregular eating pattern may strengthen the drive to eat, dissociating it from internal cues, such as cycles of gastrointestinal activity and stomach contractions, and associating the desire to eat with external cues.

Correction of Abnormal Eating Habits

The strategy for correcting eating habits associated with obesity is aimed at establishing a greater dependency on internal cues and satiety, regulating the cyclical rhythm of the gut, and changing attitudes.

Information for Patients

To increase the awareness of how the factors discussed above apply to you, begin by monitoring what you eat, and when and under what circumstances (see Self-Monitoring section in chapter 2). Be aware of the mathematics of caloric intake and expenditure. To lose a pound, there must be a deficit of about 3,500 kilocalories from your diet, about 2 days' worth of food, or there must be increased calories burned, on the order of 2 extra days of moderate activity. Therefore, a weight loss of 1 to 2 pounds per week is really quite satisfactory. When you are burning up fat, there may also be shifts in water and salt balance, which make your weight fluctuate and may give a false impression. To avoid discouragement, weighing should be done only once per week, always on the same day and the same time of day. Your weight must be charted so that it can be seen as a pattern over several months. The goal in the first few weeks is only to establish a pattern of sensible eating that will allow you to gain control of it and to determine the direction of weight change. There should be no discouragement if the actual weight loss does not begin for a few weeks.

Perhaps you do not eat all your meals, but may nibble frequently and eat excessively. Maybe you omit a meal altogether, thinking that this will help you lose weight. Instead, the irregular pattern weakens your responses to your normal body cycles, and omitting meals or starving yourself increases the likelihood of binging later. To establish a good appetite rhythm, you have to eat regularly three meals per day at fixed appropriate time intervals.

Cues have to be controlled, since people with eating problems tend to eat more when food is visible or when there is little obstacle to obtaining it. At eating time, make an attractive meal setting. Prepare all of the food that will be needed, and distribute it directly to your plate rather than leaving it in serving dishes on the table or counter. Before sitting down to eat, all the food that you intend to eat must be on your plate, and all other food should be put away out of sight. If someone in your family does not finish his or her meal, do not play seagull and gobble up the remains; if you worry about the "waste," you will have to worry about the "waist." After your meal, there should be no snacks until the next meal. Do not nibble when you prepare food for the table.

Between meals, do not leave food and munchies lying around. If you can, make a rule that the family will not buy snack food except under strict circumstances (i.e., taking something to a party). Encourage other family members to cooperate by never eating snacks in front of you. Television commercials can provoke nibbling. We suggest that you give preference to channels that have no commercials or that you rent movies rather than take a chance on tempting yourself.

Once the daily pattern of eating is stabilized, look at the trend on the weekly weight chart. If you are already losing 1 or 2 pounds per week, you are on target. If you are gaining or staying steady, make the following change. Keep the balanced diet and the same eating times, but put one fifth less food on your plate, reducing all proportions accordingly. After 3 weeks, if the weight does not change make a similar size reduction. Eventually, the food eaten will be less than the energy needed, and weight will be lost.

Of course, exercise is an essential element of the problem of obesity. Regular exercise with a gradual increase in effort that is adapted to the level of fitness and physical limitation (see chapter 9) is an essential component of the program. An organized fitness program can burn off as much as 500 extra calories per day (1 hour workout), which can make the difference between a successful and tolerable diet or a failure.

Many diets are designed to fail because they are often punitive, unpleasant, or boring, or because they are based on caloric exchange charts that are hard to calculate. The diets or the calculations become too much of a hassle and the individual gradually loses interest. In healthy dieting, there is no miracle substitute for a healthy and balanced diet. Fats and oils have 2½ times the caloric energy of carbohydrates; minimizing oils, fried foods, and foods that are high in fat content will make it easier to lose weight. Chicken should be eaten without the skin.

Butter can be eliminated. Red meat is healthy, but good red meat contains a fair amount of fat between the meat fibers, and therefore portions should be moderate. The diet should contain a good mixture of protein, carbohydrate, vegetable, and fiber.

People who are overweight often dress self-consciously, worried about looking fat. If you are afraid of showing your bulges and dress yourself in a large bag to hide them, you will dress like the stereotypical fat person and make yourself look and feel even fatter. The problem is that being fat hurts the self-image, and you can improve the self-image only by working on flattering yourself. Buy and wear nice clothes, use makeup, and fix your hair. Look at yourself in the mirror often enough to make improvements during the day, and especially to adjust your posture. Practice standing in the posture you will want to have when you have a good figure, with your head straight, shoulders comfortably back, and posture relaxed.

Nagging or reminding hurts the cause. An agreement needs to be made with the family that there will be no joking, nagging, or reminding about weight. A meeting with your therapist will help in this regard. Above all, do not nag yourself about your weight. Take a week at a time. The program is best if it is done in association with the whole health-promotion program; for example, exercising, stopping smoking, and taking time for relaxation and tension control.

TOBACCO DEPENDENCY

Dependency on tobacco involves two factors: habit and chemical addiction.

Habit

As with overeating (see the section on Overeating and Obesity), it is not easy to break a tobacco habit if there is no alteration in attitude, schedules of smoking, and smoking cues.

Addiction

Nicotine is a poisonous substance with strong effects on the body and brain, and the great likelihood of producing dependency and withdrawal syndromes. There is enough nicotine in only two cigarettes that if it were taken into the body all at once it would be fatal. It is only because the fire in the cigarette destroys most of the nicotine or that the smoke escapes that the smoker is saved from death. The addiction is so strong that the smoker is willing to ignore the high risks. These risks include the high probability of contracting cancer of the lung or bladder, the greater rate of onset of cardiovascular disease and sudden death by heart attack, the possibility of causing peptic ulcer or vascular disease of the limbs (so severe at times that gangrene is the result), and the aggravation of obstructive lung disease. Nicotine has numerous potent actions. It causes an increase in mental alertness, reduction in appetite, fast heart and breathing rate, some muscular relaxation, and increased bowel activity. The first two are the effects that are most responsible for the addiction. Nicotine is a fast-acting drug that is also rapidly eliminated. It is a well-established fact that the most addicting substances are those that have the most rapid effects. The irritability and dysphoria that result from withdrawal usually provoke the smoker to have another one, and thus the interval between cigarettes gets shorter and soon loses all association with the situations in which the smoking initially began.

Correction of Smoking Habit

The strategy is aimed at taking control of the schedule of smoking, restricting the cues to fewer situations, and weaning. There is a strong analogy to the program for controlling overeating.

For one week, carry a small pencil in your cigarette pack and mark the number of cigarettes smoked. Divide the weekly total by seven to get the daily average. Increase the number by 10%. Use this number as a baseline. The next week, establish a system of two packs. The smoking pack is to be labeled with a magic marker or adhesive tape and is to be carried with you all the time. You are to smoke cigarettes only from this pack; never lend them. The source pack or carton is used only to fill the smoking pack; you are never to carry it with you, never smoke a cigarette directly out of your carton, and never borrow or accept a cigarette from anyone else. Now set as your quota for the second week the average plus 10% that you calculated the week before. Each morning, load into your smoking pack the number of cigarettes that you are allowed for the day and smoke only these. You must not smoke from any other source or load extra cigarettes into your pack. There are no exceptions. Every day all of the cigarettes must be smoked; if you arrive at the end of the day and have not finished them all, you must finish them before going to bed. (Knowing that nicotine causes mental alertness, it would be wisest to plan ahead so that the cigarettes will be finished for the day at least 4 hours before you try to go to sleep.)

Start planning ahead to try to establish specific times and places that you will allow yourself a cigarette. Remember these times and places and try to repeat them as much as possible on successive days. Each new week, decrease the quota by no less than 10% and no more than 25%. Long-time heavy smokers would be wise to take it a bit slower, whereas an occasional light smoker who has nevertheless had trouble quitting could take it by reductions of 20% or 25%.

Cue control becomes progressively more important as you continue with this program. As the number of cigarettes becomes small (e.g., seven per day), you will get the best results if you smoke them only at specific times and situations; for example, in a specific room in your house after breakfast, in a specific lounge at work during coffee break, in a specific part of the street if you go for an after dinner stroll, and so forth. You have to plan ahead for this. The other cue control has to do with the fact that most of us are bombarded all day by reminders to smoke; commercials, cigarette smoke in restaurants or places of work, and friends who smoke and may offer you a cigarette. Begin to treat yourself as a nonsmoker even before you have completely finished the program. In restaurants, agree beforehand that you will not smoke and ask for the no smoking section. In travel, ask for nonsmoking seats. In hotels, stay in no smoking rooms. Try to avoid smoking environments with your companions; remove ashtrays from your home and ask friends to respect your need to avoid tobacco smoke. Wear a pin that says "Thank you for not smoking."

A smoke withdrawal program is most effective if it is integrated with a whole health promotion program of exercise, sleep control, stress control and relaxation exercises. Because some people come to depend on nicotine to suppress appetite, it may be necessary to implement the weight reduction program at the same time (see the section on Overeating and Obesity).

MEDICATION QUESTIONNAIRE

If you take sedatives, sleeping medication, or painkillers, you should answer these questions.

1. Have you been taking these medications on a regular basis for 3 months or longer?
2. Has the number of different medications increased over the last 6 months?
3. Since you started taking these medications, have your symptoms been increasing?
4. Since you started taking these medications, have you begun to suffer regularly from any of the following new symptoms?

headache   confusion
memory loss   depression

blurred vision	constipation
fatigue	poor appetite
dry mouth	bloating
indigestion	

5. Do you think that your health would suffer if these medications were no longer available to you?
6. Have you tried to stop your medications but were unable?
7. Have you ever been afraid that your doctor would cut off your medication?
8. Do you think that the particular symptoms you have could be cured if only you could get the right amount of the right medication?
9. Is your doctor unwilling to give you enough medication?
10. In the last week, have you taken either sedatives, sleeping tablets, or painkillers on most days?
11. Has the amount of your medication increased in the past 6 months?
12. If you suddenly ran out of sedatives, sleeping medications, or painkillers and could get none for the next 3 days, would that worry you?
13. Do you ever take your medication because you are worried that you might develop symptoms or that your symptoms could get worse?
14. Do you need your medications in order to get through the day?
15. Have you ever canceled your plans on account of not being able to get enough medication?
16. Have you ever been afraid of taking a vacation or have you ever cut a vacation short for fear of not being able to get enough medication when you were away?
17. In the last 2 days have you taken more tablets than is suggested on the medication label?
18. Do you have to take more medication to get a result than you did a year ago?
19. Does it seem to you that the medications do not work as well as they did a year ago?
20. Most days do you suffer constant headache?
21. Do you suffer inability to sleep most nights?

If you answered "yes" to five or more of these questions, you may be having a health problem due to your medication, and a medication self-management program would be helpful to you.

Chapter 9

Fatigue

DESCRIPTION OF THE PROBLEM

A 35-year-old woman presented with fatigue and palpitations on doing anything requiring physical exertion. This problem of about 1 year duration began with the experience of muscular aches and "feverish skin feelings." In time she began complaining of muscular pain, numbness, and weakness in specific body parts such as legs, toes, and neck. The clinical investigation had been carried out by the family doctor, two internists, two neurologists, a psychiatrist, and a psychologist. Although no physical disorder was found, the patient and her husband continued to search for a physical explanation for the fatigue.

BACKGROUND

One of the most common clinical problems in either medical or psychological primary care practices is the complaint of fatigue. This problem might be deemed to arise from a host of possible sources, including excessive physical demands on the body, disease or the long-term sequelae of it, stress, or multiple or undetermined causes. There is also a large group of important illnesses that include fatigue as a cardinal symptom: major depression, chronic fibromyalgia (fibrositis), and Epstein-Barr virus, just to name a few. Fatigue is a broad term that might mean different things. Usually we think of it in terms of physical exhaustion due to hard work, but this accounts for a small minority of fatigue complaints that come to the clinic. There is the simple lack of fitness, or boredom and understimulation that might be interpreted as fatigue. Certain discomfort, especially chronic muscle aching, tends to be described in terms of fatigue, even though it may have nothing to do with exhaustion or work. Poor energy may be found as a symptom of various diseases, both physical and psychological. Elsewhere in this book the

182

symptom of fatigue is relevant to several other chapters: insomnia, the worried well, chronic headache, back and neck pain, post-traumatic syndrome, and often the problem of medication dependency. In medication dependency, the overuse of drugs is a risk factor leading to fatigue, and the fatigue is a stimulus leading to the desire to take medication. The same might be said for the invalidism associated with chronic pain, in which the fatigue is dealt with by avoidance of activity, but the avoidance of activity leads to deconditioning and fatigue.

In a few cases, specific diagnoses will be found, but in the majority, the causes may seem vague. Appreciating this apparent vagueness is necessary to intervention. The most useful way to consider the symptom of fatigue that presents to psychological practice is as follows. There is a nonspecific psychobiological state marked by low energy and probably other symptoms such as insomnia, tension, or vague discomforts. The individual interprets these ambiguous experiences according to certain beliefs or expectations. It is the interaction of the ambiguous biological state and the cognitive events that give fatigue its character.

INFORMATION FOR PATIENTS

In giving information to patients, it is important that the problem of fatigue is discussed within the context of common human experiences. Avoid emphasis on medical issues only. The content of the didactic session should include the following.

1. Fatigue is a subjective experience that may result in the individual not initiating important activity or discontinuing once it is started.
2. The fatigue experience has a mental fatigue component of poor attention, which interferes with performance.
3. Fatigue sometimes, but not always, results from decrease in neuromuscular capacity.

The aim of the didactic sessions is to give the patient a perspective that is receptive to self-help. An example script of a didactic sessions follows.

"If someone says to you, 'I am fatigued,' what does it mean to you? Usually you will take it to mean something like, 'I have been working hard and am now physically exhausted.' It might mean that you should avoid further work for the present, and that you need rest.

"Take the example now of going to a lecture that you begin to find long and boring, and you can't get out so you just sit there. Soon, your mind wanders, your eyes feel heavy, and you feel as though you are going to fall asleep. You say to yourself, 'I am fatigued.' But you won't be able to make this fatigue better by resting and avoiding activity. The best thing you can do, in fact, is to get up and leave to do something active. In this case, the fatigue meant boredom.

"Now, take the example of someone who is no longer physically fit, maybe due to having been away for a long vacation or illness. This person tries to do some task and finds it much harder than it used to be. He might call this fatigue and say, 'I need to rest some more.' But it was all the rest that caused him this problem in the first place. The fatigue here means deconditioning.

"Perhaps you can remember someone who was in a state of grief, having lost a loved one. That person may move slower, have less energy, and be unable to keep up with a normal day. The apparent fatigue here has to do with the emotional state of sadness.

"We can take another example, of someone who is sick with the flu, and who has muscle aches all over. The muscles have not been overworked, the patient is neither depressed nor bored, and it is not lack of physical fitness. Yet there is a feeling of fatigue in everything that the person does, especially in the limbs and muscles. Here, the fatigue means discomfort. Maybe that same individual takes some medication for the flu and has a side effect of drowsiness. Likely the patient will interpret this also as fatigue.

"There are other situations where fatigue might be a complaint. The point is that people usually think of the first meaning, that it means overwork or strain, and often they assume that they need rest or that they should avoid activity for fear of making themselves worse.

"So far, we can see that the thing we call fatigue might be due to different things and that the physical part of it by itself is somewhat hard to distinguish in different situations. What about the mental part of fatigue? We all recognize that there is indeed a mental part: poor concentration, sometimes worry or lack of sleep despite tiredness, irritability, maybe loss of a sense of humor, and other things. We can take two more scenarios. Imagine someone who goes to workout in exercise and competition for several hours and returns saying, 'Boy am I bushed! Everything aches. It's great to have a thorough workout. If I keep working out like this, I'm going to lose weight and get into great shape. I'm really going to sleep well tonight.' Why does this person interpret it so positively? The coach and fellow participants encourage each other, the sporting environment is a cue to think about health rather than strain, the coach may be actively promoting a positive attitude, and there is the sense of wanting to do this for oneself, not being obliged to do it. A neighbor comes home from a new job, and says, 'Boy, am I bushed! Everything aches. If I have to keep working like this, it's going to kill me.' And that night, he or she can't sleep for worrying about this experience. In actual physical terms, there may be little difference in how much effort these people have experienced, and the physical result of this strenuous activity might indeed be to build up strength in both. Yet, the fatigue is interpreted as a positive experience in one and as a negative experience in the other. The deciding factor is how the person interprets the fatigue, the sense of control, and what he or she expects will result from this experience.

"What often makes fatigue such a negative experience is not the physical feeling of exhaustion or tiredness itself but the interpretation (and often misunderstanding) that is associated with it. So now fatigue involves a nonspecific physical sensation that might be the same in good or bad experiences, and a specific mental attitude. The management of fatigue takes into account the fact that fatigue is not just something that happens to you, but that it is something you do and think. Controlling fatigue involves a structured and disciplined physical approach combined with promoting a healthy mental attitude.

"Controlling fatigue may involve getting physically fit, learning how to sleep properly, reducing the harmful effects of drugs, alcohol, and other chemicals, setting goals, improving participation in things that help the quality of life, and finding better ways to respond to stress."

ASSESSMENT AND TREATMENT

The assessment and treatment of fatigue considers its multidimensional nature, including biochemical, physiological, psychological, and social dimensions. The main parts of the practical conceptual model that we use come from the Schachter and Singer (1962) model of emotion; there is a nonspecific state of physical arousal of which the individual may be more or less aware. There is an interpretation of this state, based on expectation, environmental cues, coping style, and other factors (Figure 9.1).

Evaluations

Beliefs and Interpretations. When fatigue is a chronic symptom, sufferers become vigilant about the experience, tending to interpret it in ways that confirm their fears about it. For example, there may be the fear that the fatigue will be made worse by activity; then on attempting to do

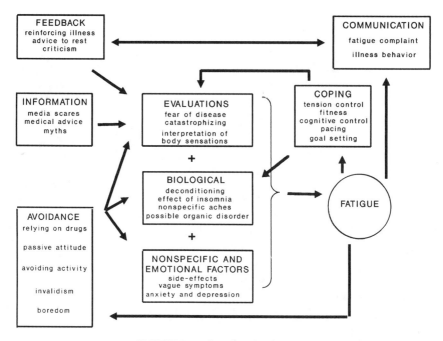

FIGURE 9.1. Algorithm for fatigue.

something, the feeling of fatigue is interpreted as evidence that the fears are correct. This might be followed by stopping the activity, confirming the original beliefs. If the individual does in fact carry out some activity, he or she does not tend to take this as proof that things are getting better, since the expectation is focused on what he or she cannot do rather than on what he or she can do. Generalizations about the problem and global avoidances all entrench the beliefs that the situation is hopeless. Any vague symptoms tend to be taken as proof of the continuation of the problem.

Investigating the Problem. Assessment of fatigue requires a broad perspective. Assuming that there are not underlying diseases requiring medical treatment, the factors that require behavioral assessment and intervention could lie in several areas. There may be sleep disorders. If inquiry reveals problems in this area, assessment and management can follow the program described in chapter 4. The "Checklist for Sleep Problems," pp. 97–98 is useful in alerting the patient to problems in sleep that require alteration. Drug intake is often a problem, so that a careful history and diary of medication, alcohol, and stimulant intake, as well as over-the-counter medications, needs to be obtained. Medication management can be instituted (see chapter 8). Similarly, if other symptom groups are defined, they should be assessed, getting a baseline of illness behavior and coping style.

Self-Evaluation. Self-evaluation is then carried out in order to give the patient a sense of the scope of the problem and alert him or her to his or her participation in the behaviors and thoughts that perpetuate the fatigue. Depending on what factors are present, the self-monitoring will include the most salient features of the fatigue problem (see Figure 2.8). Most likely the patient should do a monitoring of downtime, should be exercise-tested and have the fitness level compared with age and sex norms, and should be given an opportunity to exercise to tolerance on specified exercises, counting the repetitions and minutes as a measure of tolerance. This serves as a base for a multimodal program of setting quotas and increasing tolerance gradually.

Patients who are more psychologically minded might beneficially self-monitor their thoughts and beliefs while engaged in these tasks to gain an appreciation of how their cognitions contribute to the problem, but usually patients with fatigue who come to a psychologist are not initially oriented toward anything but a belief that they are suffering because of the fatigue rather than having fatigue due to their behaviors and beliefs.

Biological Substrates

If the patient suffers from a new problem of fatigue and has not been worked up to a reasonable degree by a physician, this should be done because the complaint of fatigue is a feature of a number of serious disorders, including hypo- or hyperthyroidism, certain vitamin deficiencies, diabetes, rheumatic diseases, toxins, side effects from a variety of medications, anemia, asthma, tumors, heart disease, and major depressive disorder. Mostly, however, the effects of chronic fatigue will be found to be the outcomes of occult chronic anxiety and associated often with other problems such as insomnia or chronic pain.

It is important to recognize that antidepressants are sometimes useful for people who suffer chronic fatigue syndromes, especially when there is a depressive or anxiety disorder present, but antidepressants and other medications more often aggravate rather than alleviate this complaint in the patients who tend to be referred to a psychological practice and in whom other diseases have been ruled out.

Nonspecific Symptoms and Emotional Factors

Because the fatigue complaint is so often associated with different medical and psychological disorders, there is a strong probability that patients will be treated with medications, especially psychotropic drugs. Since the side effects of psychotropic drugs often include fatigue, the treatment can easily be part of the disorder.

Fatigue is a stimulus to inactivity. Inactivity permits deconditioning. Deconditioning predisposes to fatigue. Inactivity also increases the probability of obesity, which then becomes a further cause of fatigue (see chapter 8).

Fatigue promotes discontent in other family members. Poor family morale causes strain to which individuals may respond with depression, and depression causes fatigue. Family members may simply give up on their fatigued member, leading to a lack of stimulation and isolation, which appears as increased fatigue.

When an individual is depressed or anxious, there is an inclination to focus on or be vigilant toward the negative emotional aspects of experience so that nonspecific experiences are emphasized and interpreted negatively, as fatigue for example.

Behavioral contingencies can increase the fatigue problem. If an individual experiences an unpleasant symptom, such as pain, and the response of others is to prescribe rest, there is the possibility that the individual may be receiving operant reinforcement (rest and avoidance of unpleasant situations) in return for pain behavior. The increased invalidism and inactivity is expressed behaviorally as fatigue.

As with many unpleasant experiences, fatigue provokes an apprehension that anticipates future unpleasant experiences; the expectation facilitates an increased attention to fatigue experiences and magnifies them.

Dealing with Avoidance

Most people who are troubled with fatigue worry about their decreasing independence and have an increasing fear of failure. They often avoid this fear by remaining inactive, hoping that something will happen so that they will get better, or hoping to avoid making themselves worse. They usually can recount instances when they have tried to do something, only to find themselves feeling worse later. They begin to see their health and function as a fragile thing, not within their control. By dropping normal daily activities, they no longer have a benchmark to give themselves a sense of personal productivity, and the cognitive aspects of their problem are escalated.

At the same time, a great deal of energy might be invested in maintaining the invalid role in order that significant others might take over. This energy is expended in terms of going to medical appointments and therapy, being involved in family conflict, and worrying. Much of the therapeutic job is to rechannel this energy into goal-directed behavior.

Coping

Treatment of fatigue usually has to be multimodal. The actual choice of modalities depends on the individual patient and the problem list.

Teaching cognitive coping techniques can follow the general education session (illustrated in Information for Patients section, and in chapter 3). Cognitive relabeling involves having the patients learn to identify the fatigue episodes and what they say to themselves at the time of the experience. Have them then engage in a structured supervised activity (such as exercise or occupational therapy). Reinterpret their fatigue as a natural experience that comes from doing a healthy amount of activity again: "The tiredness is natural and a sign that I am doing more. If I keep doing more, I will improve." Implied in this is also education in "reasonable expectations." That is, patients initially hope that participation in the therapy will make fatigue and other symptoms vanish, and at the same time they harbor the fear that participation will make them very much worse. The therapist tells them that neither expectation is correct; participation will bring out a feeling of exertion and effort, which can be tolerated, but which will become progressively less as greater fitness is achieved. Usually, patients with fatigue will not persist in a prescription for activity or exercise unless there are specific time-based quotas, with frequent self-monitoring of progress and plenty of positive reinforcement from the therapist or group.

Another coping strategy is based on the recognition that fatigue patients often have a high occult tension level, even though they may not have insight into the anxiety that lies behind it. Relaxation therapy (see chapter 3) can be taught and applied. The method is to have the patients learn to gradually incorporate short frequent relaxation sessions of 2 to 3 minutes into several activities of every day to build up awareness of the relaxed attitude.

The fitness routine itself builds more than fitness. It alleviates anxiety and increases the sense of self-efficacy. The individual who has withdrawn into invalidism no longer has goals or activity by which to measure his or her productivity or efficacy. The recumbency and invalidism are constant reminders of being ill and disabled. Removal of the recumbency behavior by quota-based activity has the effect of removing the cues that make the patient interpret himself or herself as fatigued.

Communication

People observe their own behavior (verbal and nonverbal) and interpret it. Assertive behavior increases the belief in self-efficacy, whereas fatigued behavior increases the belief in weakness and debility. Even conversation about fatigue is self-defeating. Patients are taught to relabel their fatigue as deconditioning, and their tiredness after prescribed activity as a healthy sign. They are given positive reinforcement from the therapist for discussing their progress in these terms in the weekly (or more frequent) treatment and follow-up sessions.

Feedback

Once medical investigations have not supported the presence of a disease process, the fatigue complaint may not be considered a serious problem by the physician and therefore no comprehensive treatment is initiated. The treatment input may be limited to, "There is nothing medically wrong. Don't worry." The discrepancy between the patient's and the doctor's perception increases the fatigue patient's sense of alarm.

The most frequent advice for fatigued patients is to take it easy for awhile or rest more. While this may be appropriate for certain medical disorders, the chronic fatigue patient may be worsened by inactivity or passivity.

Usually the physician has been struggling unsuccessfully with this fatigue complaint, and would welcome a phone call to discuss how to handle the fatigue complaints in the future. Instead of asking the patient, "How is your fatigue?" the inquiry can be, "How are your goals coming along?" or something similar. Instead of offering another diagnosis, prescription, or lab test if the fatigue complaint reemerges, the effort is directed toward supporting the patient's efforts so far and encouraging consistent follow-through with the behavioral program.

Most importantly, family members will need intervention to teach them to behave in a more constructive way. They can be included in the initial educational session. They can also be invited to an interview to discuss the need for improvement a step at a time by employing goals. Sharing the quotas with the family and having them give selective positive reinforcement (praise and attention) for achievement is also constructive. The analogy is given of how to talk to a disabled (e.g., blind) person—one does not draw attention to what the person cannot do, but discusses what the person does do creatively.

Self-Maintenance

The best guarantees of self-maintenance are keeping the program simple and easy to do at home, training significant others to encourage effort and avoid drawing attention to symptoms, extricating the patient from cues of illness such as unnecessary medication, setting up expectations for activities such as group exercise programs at health clubs where there will be social reinforcement to continue, and making the program dovetail with goals that restore normal role functions for which the natural cues and social reinforcements exist in the environment (e.g., to have as a goal teaching baseball to children by volunteering as a team coach).

FITNESS TRAINING

Types of Exercise

In this section we mainly address formal structured exercise programs. There are, however, four categories of exercise that should be mentioned. One is informal exercise without any particular program of structure, such as going for walks, bicycle riding, hiking, or similar active pursuits. Another is participation in sporting activities, such as tennis, golf, hockey, judo, and so forth, in which the exercise is inherent in the sport. A third is specific conditioning exercises intended to build fitness, on which we will mainly concentrate. The last is therapeutic exercise, intended to remedy some musculoskeletal disorder. Obviously all are important in different ways. For some people, formal fitness training is not a viable alternative because of physical disorders or frailty, but still the general principles of exercising described below are important. We expect that this section be used only as an introduction to the subject. References are included for more detailed study.

The goals of fitness training are in four areas:

1. Fitness training will improve musculoskeletal strength, flexibility, posture, and endurance. By training skilled movements, it will improve efficiency by improving reaction time, speed, and precision.

2. The efficiency of the cardiovascular system in moving oxygen to the muscles during exercise will improve. This cardiovascular fitness improves the sense of well-being and reduces fatigue.

3. There are simultaneous psychological benefits, in increasing the sense of well-being, improving confidence, and enhancing the self-discipline that make for a sense of good health.

4. Exercise is an active therapeutic ingredient in improving sleep, reducing certain painful conditions, promoting tension control, and burning calories to reduce weight.

The training must follow sound conditioning principles, be consistent, and aim toward self-maintenance.

We must take into account the likelihood that many patients have led an inactive life for so long that they are badly deconditioned. For these individuals there is an increased risk of fatigue, discomfort on activity, and possible injury if the training is not appropriately managed. Other illnesses must be taken into account: if there is some concern that patients might be at risk for heart disease, arthritis, or nerve root lesion, for example, they should see their physicians to obtain medical clearance for participation.

A fitness assessment by a physiotherapist or a qualified person at an exercise laboratory can give good parameters for measuring current fitness and recommended starting levels for exercise. Age- and sex-specific norms are published, giving a benchmark for level of current fitness and a guide to fitness goals.

The objective is to establish a well-rounded exercise program, including warm-ups and stretching, which are essential to avoid aggravation of pain or injury. Warm-ups should be followed by a vigorous series of aerobic exercises, followed again by stretching and cool-down exercises to prevent stiffening and to promote relaxation.

For very unfit patients, the exercises may have to begin at a light level of intensity. Some patients may also require a component of passive exercise before beginning unassisted active exercise, in which case a physiotherapist or specialist in exercise should provide some supervision. Exercise quotas of both warm-up and aerobic components are then gradually increased by gradual increments in succeeding days. At first the objective is to establish a regular exercise habit, altering the vicious cycle of inactivity, avoidance, deconditioning, fatigue, and pain.

Problems to Avoid

There are a few risks to be avoided:

1. Initial enthusiasm followed by slumping interest. Initial enthusiasm may lead the patient to attempt things beyond his or her capacity, causing injury or discomfort. The slumping interest may lead to an irregular program in which fitness does not improve, but increased exercise loads cause strain and discomfort. Consistency is promoted by supervision, enhanced by keeping written charts and quotas, and encouraged by exercise in a group.

2. Too much too soon, with attendant aggravation of symptoms or strain, comes from not having realistic goals based on initial measured fitness level, age and sex norms, and instruction in proper techniques.

3. Injury due to technique or equipment. One should be able to have a personal exercise program at home. However, it is a good investment to have some supervision in getting started. Although exercise machines are an attractive idea, not all exercise devices on the market are appropriate, and even for good devices it is important to learn good technique and posture. Without exercise equipment there is less risk, but even without equipment, initial instruction and supervision is to be recommended.

4. Problems due to inappropriate exercise prescription. Some individuals need modifications to the exercise protocol due to particular pathological conditions they suffer or physical vulnerabilities. For example, a person with an arthritic knee may not be able to use an exercise bicycle but may benefit from swimming, walking, and upper body exercise. For a normal individual, fitness assessment and exercise prescription by a trained therapist is a good idea. For someone who has medical problems, fitness assessment and prescription is strongly recommended.

Exercise Testing

Exercise testing is not needed for school-age athletes, for individuals of any age who regularly participate in organized training or competitive sports, or well people younger than age 35. Exercise testing is recommended for unfit people over age 35, well people who have risk factors for heart disease (family history of heart disease at middle age, high blood pressure, hyperlipidemia, or diabetes; are more than 25 lb. overweight or cigarette smokers), and for people with diagnosed heart disease.

Maintaining a State of Well-Being

The goal of exercise is not to become a jock but to improve health and well-being. The exercise is not an end in itself. As fitness increases, the goal is to gradually incorporate more health-inducing activity into the life-style, including tension control, pacing oneself and setting priorities, diversifying one's activity in activities that build a sense of accomplishment, skills, positive social contact, and pleasure. Perhaps sporting activities can be a way to help maintain personal fitness and vigor. Fitness is not a formula, but a component in quality of life.

Specific Suggestions for a Fitness Program

We will discuss an exercise protocol that is applicable to the majority of the population. Modifications may have to be made in individual cases to take into account individual problems. The program consists of warm-ups, aerobics, and cool-downs. An explanation of quotas and scheduling follows. To improve fitness, the exercises must be repeated at least four times weekly, but daily activity is recommended to avoid irregularity.

Warm-Ups. All exercises must be done slowly, completely, and correctly. It is better to do only a few correctly than to do many incorrectly; the numbers and speed will come later. When you are first starting, you will have to determine what your exercise tolerance is. The eventual goal will be 15 repetitions of everything, but you probably will have to start well below that number. Take the exercise to the point of just beginning discomfort, a slow steady stretch, then ease off slowly. This will help stretch your tissues and make you more flexible. Do not force your body through a painful range—improved range of motion will come with repetition, not forcing. Make a chart for your exercises to keep track of number of repetitions and weekly goals (see Table 9.1). The technique for warm-ups is to keep all the warm-ups at the same number of repetitions and increase gradually. (For example, begin at three of everything, in a few days go to four of everything, then five, etc.)

On Your Back

1. Pelvic tilt. Lie on your back with your knees and hips bent, and your fingertips at the hollow between the small of your back and the

TABLE 9.1. Schedule for Five Basic Aerobic Exercises

Level	No. of Repetitions of Each Exercise					No. of Cycles
	1	2[a]	3	4	5	
A	5	5	5	5	5	2
B	10	7	15	7	7	2
C	15	10	20	10	10	2
D	20	13	25	13	13	2
E	25	15	30	15	15	2
F	30	18	35	18	18	2
G	30	20	40	20	20	2
H	30	20	45	20	20	3
I	35	20	50	20	20	3
J	35	20	50	20	25	4
K	40	25	50	20	25	4
L	40	25	50	20	25	5

[a]After becoming comfortable with beginner level push-ups, at 1 to 3 weeks begin to substitute full push-ups until all push-ups are full. The top level of five cycles would be done by a very fit person. Achieving this can take several months.

mat. Tighten your abdominal muscles and flatten your back against the floor so that there is no more space to admit your fingers. Hold it for the count of five and relax.

2. Knee to chest stretch. Lie on your back. Draw one knee up, grasp it with your arms and try to bring it toward your chest. Hold for count of five and relax. Repeat with the other knee.

3. Both knees to chest. Bring both knees to your chest, grasp them and hold for count of five and relax.

4. Hip rotations. Keeping your shoulders flat on the mat, rock your knees to either side, bringing your knees as close to the mat as you can on each side.

5. Leg raises and circles. Straighten your right knee while bending your left knee, bringing your left foot up to your bottom. Now lift your right leg as high as possible with your knee straight. Trace a large circle in the air with your right foot (knee still straight). Trace a small circle in the reverse direction with your right foot. Repeat with the other leg.

On Your Side

6. Side leg raises. Lying on your side, bend your bottom knee for support, keep your upper leg straight, and lift it straight up.

7. Still on your side with the bottom knee bent, raise the top leg, keeping the knee straight, move it as far as possible to the front, then as far as possible to the back, then back to where it started.

8. Stay on your side, straighten the bottom leg, and bend the top knee over it. Now lift your bottom leg as high as you can from the floor. Lie on your other side and repeat steps 6, 7, and 8 with the other leg.

Sitting

9. Lumbar stretches. Sitting on the mat with your legs straight out in front of you and together, lean forward slowly and try to touch your toes. Do not rock or bounce. Count to five and relax.

10. Spread your legs apart as far as they will go, still sitting with your legs straight. Now lean forward to touch your right foot, your left foot, and between, with the five count in each stretch.

Standing

11. Calf muscle stretches. Face the wall, about an arms length away from it. Put the palms of your hands flat against the wall at shoulder level. Keeping your heels flat on the floor, lean slowly toward the wall until you can feel the back of your calf muscles stretching. Hold for a count of five.

12. Trunk lateral stretches. Stand straight up with your hands on your head. Now lean to the left as far as you can, and then lean to the right.

Aerobics. There are five basic exercises. The warm-ups were to prepare your muscles and stretch them so that you could do the faster aerobics. However, you should begin the aerobic exercises slowly and then speed up so that your muscles heat up gradually. Eventually, you will want to generate a training heart rate for these exercises, but at first the goal will be only to do the exercise completely, correctly, and with good body form and some increase in heart rate. Eventually you will be doing a large number of these rapidly, but begin with a small number until you build up your fitness. As you increase the number and speed, do not do so by sacrificing form or completeness. The aerobic exercises are done in sets that are repeated in sequence. With increasing fitness over a period of time, you should increase the number of repetitions of each exercise and increase the number of sets. The aim is to obtain a training heart rate (consult Table 9.2 for approximate recommended heart rates). Likely, it will take a period of time to arrive at a consistent level of exercise at the intensity sufficient to generate a training level of heart rate.

1. Star jumps. Begin in a standing position with your feet together and arms at your sides. Jump, spreading your legs to land with feet 2 feet apart. At the same time, swing your arms fully above your head. Jump and return legs and arms to initial position. This is one count. Do five repetitions of this to start with.

2. Push-ups. Beginner level is from knees. Keeping body straight from knees to neck, face down with palms on floor, push body upward to full arms length and then back to floor. Regular exercise is keeping whole body straight, lifting body from toes. Do five repetitions of this to start with.

3. Abdominal exercise. Lie on your back with your hands behind your neck, lift your right knee while fully extending your left knee, and touch your left elbow to your right knee. Then reverse: left knee to right elbow. This is one count. Do five repetitions of this to start with.

4. Sprinter's exercise. With arms fully extended, facing floor and supporting upper part of your body with your arms (as in a push-up),

Table 9.2. Heart Rate Recommended for Aerobic Exercises

Age (yr)	Exercise Heart Rate
20–30	144–174 beats/min
31–40	132–162 beats/min
41–50	108–138 beats/min

bring your left foot up just behind your hands, with sole flat on floor, while right leg is fully extended. Jump to alternate feet positions. This is one count. Do five repetitions of this to start with.

5. Knee bends. Will arms fully extended in front and heels about 8 inches apart, bend your knees fully to take a squatting position, and return to standing. This is one count. Do five repetitions of this to start with.

All five exercises in sequence is one cycle. The schedule for this program is set out in Table 9.1. Patients should move from level to level as they find they feel more fit. Repetitions must be done quickly. As fitness increases, heart rate will be lower, and repetitions and cycles must be increased (see Table 9.2 for recommended heart rates).

Cool-Downs. Cooling down must be done by walking around slowly to avoid feeling faint. While doing this, stretching can help relax the muscles.

1. Let head nod forward by its own weight (don't force it). Touch your chin now and gently rotate your head to the right side and then to the left to stretch your neck and upper back muscles.
2. Support your right elbow with your left hand at shoulder level, and bring your right arm around your neck as if you were wiping your nose with your right elbow. Then do the same with your left elbow.
3. Swing both arms gently back to stretch the fronts of the shoulder muscles.
4. Put your hands on both hips and lean forward at the waist, and lean to the right, back, left, and forward in a circular motion but with your head always erect. Reverse the direction.

Posture

Part of fitness is attention to healthy posture. Good posture does not mean standing like a soldier on guard duty. Posture must be relaxed and comfortable. It must be balanced when you move, and apprehensiveness should not provoke guardedness of your muscles. Good posture enhances stress control, reduces fatigue, and improves body efficiency.

Stand in front of a full-length mirror and see if you are standing lopsided. Are your shoulders level with each other? Are your facial muscles relaxed? Iron out any frown or tension from your forehead and eye muscles. Let your teeth part slightly, enough to admit just the tip of your tongue, and let your lips be gently closed, so that your facial and jaw muscles relax. Look at the position of your head and neck from the front and then from the side. Your head can make forward and backward movements; move it forward like a bird posture, then back and tuck in your chin like a military guard. Your comfortable neck posture is halfway between these two extremes. Now let your head take a comfortable position on your neck. Practice for a minute so that it takes no tension at all in your neck to balance your head on top of your vertebrae. Take a deep breath, filling your lungs and feeling the breath right down into your belly, then relax, letting the air out, and as you do so relax the whole upper part of your body, letting your arms hang relaxed at your side, and letting your shoulders totally relax so that you are aware of the weight of your shoulders and arms hanging by your side. Do this a couple more times. Take note of your low back. Normally, there is a gentle concavity in the small of your back. Feel to see if it is there. Put both hands on your hips with your thumb tips on the muscles beside your spine. Notice that you can feel those muscles tighten and relax as you change your back posture. Slowly lean back, then slowly lean forward and notice that the back muscles are relaxed and then suddenly contract. Lean back slowly again until you feel the back muscles completely relax. In this posture, your back muscles do not have to do extra work to keep you upright. The center of gravity of your upper body is just above your pelvis and hips so that your back can relax. Feel the back muscles to see that they have relaxed. With your arms hanging in a relaxed way at your sides, shift your weight to your right foot, letting your right knee that bears the weight be fully locked backward and your left knee be slightly bent with the thigh completely relaxed. Now shift the weight to the left leg in the same way and relax the right leg and knee. Do this a few times until you get the feeling that one leg relaxes while the other bears weight, and the weight-bearing leg can relax by having the knee fully extended. Now walk slowly like this, relaxing your legs as you do. Now walk with a little bigger stride, swinging your arms as if they are relaxed weights swinging by themselves from your shoulders. Now that you have become more aware of posture, try relaxing your posture in different positions, such as sitting, checking that your muscles, breathing, and your face relax at the same time. Take a relaxed breath, and as you breathe out slowly say "completely relaxed," quietly and in a relaxed manner. Say it again until you get the feeling that it takes no more effort or pressure than passively breathing out. Listen to the relaxed tone of your voice.

Do this exercise from now on several times a day, spending a moment to check your posture and correct it comfortably. When you pass a mirror, stop for a moment to check that your posture is relaxed and balanced and that your face looks relaxed. Check your breathing several times a day to make sure that you breathe calmly and slowly from your belly.

Chapter 10
Irritable Bowel Syndrome and Related Complaints

DESCRIPTION OF THE PROBLEM

A 24-year-old woman is seen in the emergency department requesting help for severe abdominal pain. She is bent over with her arms crossed tightly over her abdomen, rocking and crying. She claims to have episodes of pain of increasing duration and frequency, beginning gradually over the last year. She gives a list of several clinics and specialists she has seen, and there is an indication that she has visited other emergency departments twice in the last 3 months. Her medication is acetaminophen with 15 mg codeine, six tablets per day; magnesium/aluminum hydroxide tablets, four to six tablets per day; senna tablets and docusate capsules, up to four per day each; chlordiazepoxide and clinidium bromide capsules, four to eight per day; 10 mg diazepam, two to three per day; 1 mg triazolam per night; 50 mg amitriptyline per night; 2 mg loperamide tablets if necessary, up to six per day but sometimes none. The husband who has accompanied her to the emergency room is pacing, angry, and demanding that something be done for his wife, that she be admitted, that she be given something for her pain, and that the chief of service be called rather than an intern or resident. The nurses report that they feel uncomfortable in dealing with him. Opinions of consultants, according to the file, have ranged from endometriosis, possible cholecystitis, leaky capillary syndrome, irritable bowel syndrome, psychogenic pain, and drug addiction. However, there is no evidence that medications are being obtained without prescription.

A 42-year-old man is seen on the ward for chronic abdominal pain. He looks cachectic, sick, and depressed. He is receiving 75 mg meperidine by injection every 3 hours, and usually anticipates his dose with his call button at about 2½ hours day and night. He has additionally been taking oxazepam for sleep for several years at a dose of 60 mg. He moves about little and spends most of his time in bed. His history is that he has been an alcoholic, developed pancreatitis 3 years ago, and has had recurrent bouts

199

of pain ever since. He claims to be on the wagon for the last 3 years. He has been in the hospital for 7 of the last 12 months, in repeated admissions to the anesthesiology, general surgery, internal medicine, and gastroenterology services. No procedures or medicines have helped him. Usually he presents to the emergency department with pain, is admitted with a diagnosis of possible pancreatitis, and is discharged a few weeks later after repeat investigations. He has had three laparotomies, two retrograde endoscopic pancreatograms, and several anesthesiological procedures, including coeliac plexus blocks.

BACKGROUND

A remarkable statement by Rhazes more than a thousand years ago is right in keeping with the viewpoint of this chapter: "If you can help with foods, then do not prescribe medicaments, and if simple ones are effective, then do not prescribe compounded remedies" (Rhazes, 852–932 AD).

There are a host of gastrointestinal (GI) conditions that pose problems in management, with varying components of definable pathophysiology, pain and discomfort, and behavioral problems. These include esophageal motility disorders, reflux esophagitis, peptic ulcers, inflammatory bowel diseases, postmultioperative abdominal pains, postpancreatis pains, chronic constipation, and the irritable bowel syndrome. Although each merits discussion, the disorder that best typifies the problems in assessment and management of GI complaint is the irritable bowel syndrome. It is estimated that up to 50% of referrals to gastroenterologists are for this disorder (Harvey, Salh, & Read, 1983). Because principles relevant to managing irritable bowel are often relevant to other painful GI disorders, our focus will be on this syndrome.

About one person in seven suffers from chronic bowel discomforts, with diarrhea and/or constipation and abnormal bowel awareness, in the absence of structural, infectious, inflammatory, or digestive enzyme abnormalities adequate to explain the problem (Whitehead & Schuster, 1979; Sandler, Nathan, Drossman, & McKee, 1984). However, only about a third of these find their way to doctors for investigation and treatment. This constellation of complaints accounts for a large proportion of patients seen in gastroenterology specialty clinics. Some physicians regard this chronic bowel syndrome as a form of psychosomatic disturbance, while others regard it as a physiological abnormality in which emotion and function play a part.

There are three interrelated syndromes. One is dominated by constipation and includes lower abdominal pain, distention of the abdomen, and perhaps complaints of flatus. Another is dominated by diarrhea and includes complaints of borborygmi, irregular stools, and cramping. The third involves a mixture and alternation between the above two states. The syndromes may be associated with other symptoms including headaches, muscle aches, depression, and insomnia.

Sources of Conceptual Model

A multidimensional model of the irritable bowel syndrome was proposed by Latimer (1981) with an interaction of pathophysiology, behavior, and cognition.

Pathophysiology has been considered by some to be the root of irritable bowel syndrome. The absence of adequate fiber in the diet has been implicated, and this is given at least some support by the relief of irritable bowel symptoms through the addition of extra fiber to the diet. No specific motility problem has been found consistently in this syndrome. Some motility studies suggested that there may be increases in peristalic activity in the irritable bowel syndrome and that such increased activity may be a response to various stimuli: emotional, distention, or neurochemical (Whitehead & Bosmajian, 1982). There appeared to be evidence that sufferers with this condition were more subject to pain elicited by bowel lumen distention. This raised the possibility that these patients may be more pain sensitive, or more prone to complain due to behavioral factors. Irritable bowel syndrome is a common finding in chronic fibromyalgia, which is characterized by decrease in pain thresholds in the soft tissues (Tunks, Crook, Norman, & Kalaher, 1988) and by certain psychological symptoms. This raises the question of whether irritable bowel syndrome may be due to a global reduction in pain thresholds. However, Cook, Van Eeden, and Collins (1987) demonstrated that patients with Crohn's disease and irritable bowel syndrome were both less likely than normals to report a noxious cutaneous stimulus as painful, thereby raising doubt that these patients are more prone to complain about pain or that they are more globally pain sensitive. There are also indications that there is an overlap between this disorder and other common complaints: chronic headache, dysmenorrhea, dyspareunia, frequent micturition, and various nervous symptoms (Latimer & Campbell, 1980). From clinical practice, one finds that a significant proportion of patients who are considered to suffer pains from chronic pancreatitis and multiple abdominal surgeries in fact have the symptoms of irritable bowel syndrome. Latimer studied irritable bowel syndrome patients who were matched to a group of neurotic patients with an equal degree of psychological disturbance, and compared them with normals. A nonsignificant difference was found in colonic activity in the three groups, with the neurotics occupying a midway position in the amount of colonic activity between the normals and irritable bowel symptom patients. Bowel distention produced the same degree of pain in all three groups (Latimer, 1981).

Behavioral factors have a bearing on the presentation of these patients to clinics. Although the symptoms of irritable bowel syndrome are frequent in the community at large, only about one third of these have ever seen a physician about it (Latimer & Campbell, 1980). Those who are seen in specialty clinics for such problems tend to experience a greater loading on psychosocial distress factors (Whitehead, Winget, Fedoravicius, Wooley, & Blackwell, 1982). This parallels the findings of Crook et al. (1986) that chronic pain patients attending a specialty clinic were more likely to show emotional distress and behavioral and functional impairment than chronic pain sufferers who were identified through an epidemiological survey in the community. Irritable bowel syndrome sufferers frequently become dependent on medications that serve to aggravate the symptoms and create abnormalities of bowel rhythm. They may make use of multiple nonprescription agents as laxatives or to quiet the bowel. They may develop idiosyncratic dietary, eating, and toileting habits.

Cognitive factors include misconceptions and fears about bowel function. These ideas may at times take on almost a superstitious nature – fears of toxic influences in the drinking water or in foods. There is a marked preoccupation with bowel regularity; frequency, volume, and character of stools; gas; and reactions to eaten substances or medication. Patients may fear some medications, and cling to others as essential. There may be a lack of admission to psychosocial distress even though such variables are strongly suspected from observation, from other records, and from the patients' own histories. Education programs and the use of stress control and relaxation programs are an essential part of management of this condition (Neff & Blanchard, 1987).

INFORMATION FOR PATIENTS

Irritable bowel syndrome is a surprisingly common problem. One person in seven can be expected to suffer from it at some time. It is important to understand what is is . . . and is not. First of all, it is a real problem, recognized by specialists. It involves an increased suscepti-bility of the intestine to pain caused by certain chemicals and drugs, by stimulation from the material inside the gut, and by stress. You could say that your gut reacts to what you eat and to what is eating you. By understanding yourself and your reactions, it is possible to work with your body, rather than against it, and to improve the health of your digestive system.

The fact is that everyone is susceptible to changes in the gut due to emotion and stress. However, everyone is different in the degree to which he or she reacts to things. The brain has millions of nerve cells that stretch out their connections all over the body. You may not have known that the intestinal system also has a huge network of nerve cells and nerve centers. The nervous systems in your brain and digestive system naturally have to communicate in order to keep organized and to help you adapt to different situations. The gut is equipped with rhythms, warning systems, and built-in ways of responding to various environmental situations or chemicals.

Did you ever notice how you can get accustomed to eating at a certain time, say a midnight snack? Or perhaps you fly to another country and time zone. You suddenly find yourself hungry, with a gurgling stomach, according to yesterday's time zone. Your gut has been keeping track of the time. It can even wake you from sleep and prompt you to raid the refrigerator. These *biological rhythms* are delicate controls that you can disturb if you are not careful, but which you can also change if you learn how to take charge of them. Unfortunately, people often have mistaken ideas about these rhythms, and this leads to problems. For example, many medications that you may take for constipation, nerves, digestion, or diarrhea have a strong effect on the delicate control of gut rhythm. Also, there are incorrect notions, fed by advertising and popular myths. One is that everyone should have his or her daily bowel movement, and that not doing so will lead to some kind of bad consequences, or that having more than one bowel movement a day is bad. It is not unusual to find considerable variation in bowel habits between various people, and any one person is likely to experience a degree of variation in bowel habit from time to time.

Gut movement rhythms are also linked to other body rhythms, such as the sleep–wake cycle, which you should also know about. The overall health of your habits and fitness is very important to having good bowel function. Developing a fairly regular habit of eating and elimination, controlling sleep by good habits, exercise, and avoiding chemicals that affect the gut are some of the secrets to improving bowel function.

You might expect that you gut's *warning system* is pain, but it is not as simple as this. It is true that you might experience pain in some illnesses, such as gallbladder disease or appendicitis. There are other signs by which your body could warn you of problems, such as diarrhea, constipation, nausea, and bloating, but for the most part, these are rather nonspecific and by themselves usually do not mean disease. Pain is the thing that most people worry about because it is also the most unpleasant. You must know that gut pain can be caused by several different factors: by stretching of the inside of the gut, by deficiency in the ability to digest certain foods, and by certain chemicals that your own body produces as part of the regulation of the gut, and it is affected by the way the nervous system itself is behaving. Since one of the stimuli for gut pain is stretching (by gut contents or gas), you have to consider what the threshold is for a given individual that will produce pain. For one person, it may take a lot of stretching, and that person will not usually have pain. For another, less stretching may be enough to cause pain, but in an average day that person will not have enough stretching to have pain. In some people, the threshold is low (the sensitivity is great), so that even small amounts of stretching cause pain. What this means is that pain often is not a warning that something is wrong, or that a laxative or medication is needed. In fact, it might mean that something should not be taken.

Sensitivity to various substances has a lot to do with gut pain. The bowel is often irritated by laxatives, antacids, or other medicines that are given for bowel symptoms, but which unfortunately alter the way the bowel works. Diets may be changed unduly in efforts to make things better, only succeeding in making the problem worse due to changed elimination. Medications such as antidepressants and many drugs for digestion can sometimes help or sometimes interfere with normal gut reactions. Finally, changing the timing of eating and elimination can throw the body off its normal rhythms.

Psychological factors have much to do with satisfactory digestion. This is the reason that kings and rich people would bring in the jesters after their meals. Irritable bowel symptoms are often made worse by being too conscious of the bowel, which causes tension, which in turn leads to a nervous reaction that interferes with the way the bowel works. It is important to know that for the digestive system and gut, people are poor observers, and take the whole thing for granted when things go well, or make too many assumptions when they feel unwell. It is true that significant changes in bowel movements may be one of the many signs of illness, but really there is a great range of normal functioning, and fluctuations in bowel habit should not be surprising. Too rigid fixation on having that daily bowel movement "by hook or by crook or by laxative" is likely to lead to problems. Instead, the focus should be on knowing your bowel, reducing stress and worry, reducing interference by drugs and laxatives, and establishing a routine for bowel movements, but not expecting a "clockwork colon." Being aware of bowel sensations or discomfort should not alarm you while you are working on solving the irritable bowel syndrome. The real goal and proof of improvement is bowel function without artificial interference.

ASSESSMENT AND TREATMENT

The irritable bowel problem is affected by normal and pathophysiological gut function, beliefs and emotional factors, side effects of medications, variations in habits, and coping (Figure 10.1). The rationale for management of irritable bowel syndrome is presented, with an overall description of what will be entailed over several weeks. Self-monitoring is employed to produce self-awareness and activity. Relaxation is taught with the motive to learn to know one's bodily responses and to reduce stress. The emphasis on health is promoted by exercise and avoidance of fad or ill-advised diets, by adopting a balanced diet without superstition, and by elimination of drugs and chemicals that adversely affect the gut.

Evaluations

Beliefs and Interpretations. The above erroneous beliefs about what is normal, the importance of natural rhythms, the relationship of gut

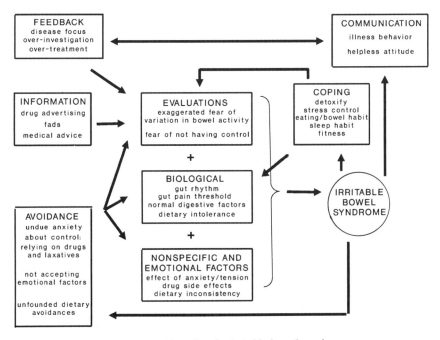

FIGURE 10.1. Algorithm for irritable bowel syndrome.

behavior to psychological factors or tension, the effects of substances on the gut, and the usefulness of promoting sleep, fitness, and good diet are all discussed in didactic sessions. Patients are given a chance to bring in their experiences in successive weeks for discussion.

Investigating the Problem. Before proceeding with behavioral medicine management for irritable bowel syndrome, the therapist must ascertain that there is no other significant systemic illness such as malabsorption syndrome, lactose sensitivity, disease of the gallbladder, parasites, and so forth. For this there should have been a medical workup. Symptoms such as back pain, nighttime diarrhea, weight loss, bloody stool, fever, or a decided change in one's health should all prompt an assessment by a physician. Diarrhea and abdominal complaints can be caused by inability to absorb carbohydrates. An example is lactose, which some people cannot break down into absorbable sugars; it is fermented by bacteria and causes diarrhea and gas. The possibility of the coexistence of irritable bowel syndrome with other gastrointestinal disorders also must be considered.

Much of the behavioral investigation is done by self-monitoring (see chapter 2 and questionnaires at the end of this chapter). In general, the therapist wants to know the following:

1. Use of coffee, tea, colas, caffeine-containing medication or substances.
2. Use of diet sweets.
3. Medications that cause constipation or bowel change (e.g., antihistamines, antidepressants, major tranquilizers, opiate painkillers, etc.). It is good to have a drug reference book to look up all medications taken (United States Pharmacopeial Convention, 1989).
4. Use of laxatives.
5. Use of alcohol and tobacco.
6. Timing of food intake, large or small.
7. Food content (including presence or absence of fiber, excessive junk food, and presence of basic nutrients).
8. Attitudes and fears about the gut.
9. Daily schedule of activity (including sleep habits, relaxation, and exercise).

Self-Evaluation. A simple scale can be adapted to assess the majority of the above factors. Patients are instructed to make a list of all prescription and nonprescription drugs taken and their dosage strengths, and to measure quantities of cigarettes smoked, alcohol, laxatives, coffee, tea, and colas consumed. The quality and quantities of food eaten is monitored: junk food, food with nutritious content, fiber-containing foods. (For information on the fiber content of certain foods, see Table 10.1.) Number of bowel movements with only the notations large or small, and flatus are allowed during the initial monitoring period (Figure 10.2). The recording is then made of daily activity, drugs taken, foods and beverages, physical activity, and actions taken or plans changed directly according to bowel awareness and discomfort. The data is collected frequently to ensure compliance. After a few days, the data can be used as a point of discussion to highlight the variation possible even in one individual. After this, a program is carried out to reduce harmful influences and to learn stress control, choosing a healthful diet based on nutrition and satisfaction rather than on fear of bowel reactions. Monitoring of bowel movements, flatus, and pain is not carried out after the initial monitoring, since focus is on behavior change rather than on symptoms.

Biological Substrates

To establish a good digestive rhythm, there should be regular meals with a balanced diet. Avoidance of eating because the patient fears constipation or diarrhea, for example, only aggravates the intestinal malfunction. The details of a balanced diet are beyond the scope of this

Table 10.1. Symptom Checklist for IBS

Symptom	Check if Present
Specific	
Bloating of abdomen	
Bowel awareness	
Cramp	
Constipation	
Diarrhea	
Intestinal gas	
Flatus	
General	
Loss of appetite	
Malaise	
Nausea	
Headache	
Depression	
Insomnia	
Decreased sex drive	
Urinary retention	
Weakness	
Body aching	
Fluid retention (swelling of feet/hands)	
Increased weight	
Increased appetite	

NAME ___
DATE FROM ___ TO ___

DAY	BOWEL MOVEMENT small large	FLATUS	BORBORYGMI	CRAMP OR PAIN	ACTIVITIES

FIGURE 10.2. Diary for irritable bowel syndrome.

chapter, but the essential thing is that the person should eat regularly rather than skip meals or eat excessively. The food should be nutritious, attractive, and varied, with appropriate amounts of meat, cooked and raw vegetables, cereal, and carbohydrate. Adequately balanced diets as a rule do not need vitamin supplementation. Getting into supplements often is a mark of bad attitudes about eating and lack of confidence in one's own health. Adding an extra cup of bran cereal to each day's diet is a useful source of fiber. In an effort at self-treatment, people with bowel complaints often go to another extreme—the use of excessive fiber. This can cause voluminous stools with intestinal gas.

For irritable bowel syndrome and diarrhea, antidepressants may be helpful but are not a panacea. The problem is that these drugs may cause profound constipation, which is relieved only by stopping the drug. It is important to evaluate whether the drug is doing a service or harm.

A large number of irritable bowel syndrome sufferers have become dependent on laxatives. These people are afraid to be without bowel stimulants but do not realize that laxatives can cause both diarrhea and constipation, with accompanying pain. By making the bowel dependent on irritant laxatives such as senna, phenolphthalein, bisacodyl, castor oil, cascara, or aloes, patients can develop a chronically lazy bowel, often prone to gas and constipation. Saline laxatives such as magnesium hydroxide can cause salt and water metabolism problems after prolonged use. To wean laxatives, the first step is to establish a regular balanced diet and eating habit, including natural sources of fiber, such as bran. Opiates must be eliminated, along with other medication that likely is causing constipation. Laxatives are not given as needed but in fixed doses and gradually weaned over 2 weeks. Stool softeners such as psyllium mucilloid or docusate calcium may be used for a short period of time if the individual was quite dependent on irritating laxatives. A regular breakfast time is chosen. Immediately after breakfast, the patient uses glycerine suppositories as a nonirritating way to stimulate bowel movement. The suppository is used at no other time. If the person remains unable to have a bowel movement for about 4 days, the problem can arise that the bowel becomes too full to have a mechanical advantage enough for elimination. In that case, an enema is used, and the bowel program is continued. Usually with persistence, the bowel will begin to respond naturally and normally.

Nonspecific Symptoms and Emotional Factors

Emotional distress and worried thoughts can increase one's awareness of bowel function, so that a vicious cycle is established of pain-

distress-pain. The worrying may be related to fears abut cancer, anticipating surgery, or having excessive food restrictions. The physiological
disturbance that accompanies anxiety and emotional upset also can add
to the irritability of the bowel.

Bowel awareness and bloating are frequent complaints of irritable
bowel syndrome patients. To some extent, these can come from undue
anxiety about bowel function and from "air-swallowing." But unfortunately the symptoms may also be physiologically based; several kinds of
medication can promote these symptoms. Principal among these are
opiates or other drugs such as antidepressants, which reduce or alter
bowel motility.

Although depression is not formally part of the irritable bowel
syndrome, it is common. It can be aggravated by cognitive factors such
as the sense of loss of control over bowel function, by insomnia, which
may accompany the syndrome, by frustration over failed efforts at
treatment, or by medications prescribed. These medications typically
include benzodiazepine tranquilizers and hypnotics, opiates prescribed
for pain or diarrhea, or antidepressants. (Although antidepressants
often are of great use in major depression, in reactive depressions and
depressions associated with certain physical complaints, the depression
may sometimes be paradoxically aggravated.)

Diarrhea and constipation are frequent complaints in irritable bowel
syndrome. The diarrhea can be precipitated by taking and stopping
medications that have an effect on increasing or decreasing bowel
motility. A partial list includes opiates, laxatives, metoclopramide, and
antidepressants. The patient suffers first a sense of constipation or
bloating, and takes a laxative or alters the diet. When the bowels begin
to move, the patient again alters the diet and takes something for
diarrhea, which causes more cramping and bloating, and so the vicious
circle continues.

Constipation, which is one of the central complaints in irritable bowel
syndrome, can be aggravated by a picky and irregular eating style, and
patients with this problem are also likely to attribute constipation or
diarrhea to themselves after a perceived small change in bowel habit,
which is not out of the normal range of variation. Medications prescribed for the disorder—opiates, tricyclic antidepressants, or clinidium,
for example—often directly aggravate or cause the constipation. In
extreme circumstances, paralytic ileus can occur. This is a condition of
total immobility of the bowel, caused by such medications, and it
represents a medical emergency if withdrawal of the drug does not lead
to resumption of bowel activity. Other things causing constipation
include iron pills, calcium, antihistamines, some tranquilizers, muscle
relaxants, and many other medications. It is useful to refer to a drug

guidebook to check each medication that the patient is taking. One also must be cautious to check with the prescribing physician regarding which medications are necessary for prevention and control of other disorders, so that the nonessential drugs and those prescribed for symptomatic purposes only are eliminated. For example, a patient may be taking an antidepressant for prophyllaxis against a recurrent manic-depressive disorder, in which case the drug would have to be maintained.

Cramp is a central symptom of the disorder. The amount of peristalsis is not likely to be excessive, and the cramp likely has its origins in abnormalities either in the sensitivity of the gut, in the perceptual attributes of the sufferer, or both. Increased worry and attention to the problem bring about increased symptoms. The medications that may be prescribed for the problem could possibly alleviate the cramp, but medications such as metoclopramide and tricyclic antidepressants are also known to cause cramps in some people. A significant minority of the population will suffer from some sort of food intolerance. The best example is lactose intolerance, which means that the individual lacks the necessary enzymes to break down milk sugar in the gut. After ingesting milk, or lactose as an ingredient in some food, the lactose enters the gut where it is not digested and absorbed. Instead, bacteria ferment it, producing gas and bowel discomfort, perhaps with diarrhea. Individuals who have this sort of problem ought to use lactose-reduced milk instead of regular milk, and ought to avoid buying foods that contain significant quantities of lactose. If eating food with lactose cannot be avoided (such as when being invited out for dinner), it is possible to buy lactase enzyme tablets from the pharmacy. These can be taken along with the meal.

People with irritable bowel syndrome are aware of intestinal gas to an increased degree. It can be aggravated by changes in dietary routine in response to the bowel awareness. Intestinal gas comes from several sources. A minority comes from swallowed air, but the proportion of swallowed air can increase if the individual is aware of abdominal distress. The gases produced by fermentation in the large intestine are carbon dioxide, methane, and hydrogen. About 95% of the gases so produced are also reabsorbed, so that only a small proportion becomes flatus. However, in the case of using laxatives or withdrawing from opiates or using caffeine or gut stimulants, the gut motility increases, so that the gas has less time to be absorbed, producing a greater amount of flatus. Other factors may also lead to increased production of intestinal gas and greater abdominal cramp. If the person lacks the necessary enzymes to break down lactose, bacteria in the large intestine may ferment it and produce gas. Another example is use of sorbitol, which is found in sugar-free candy and gum. This too cannot be absorbed, and an excess leads to the same symptoms. Certain vegetables such as legumes, broccoli, or cabbage contain nonabsorbable carbohydrates that are fermented by gut bacteria, forming gas. Thus, a change in diet may lead to a change in gas production. Intestinal gas might be expelled in excess in the presence of a sudden increase in dietary fiber, or in the case of excessive use of fiber-containing laxatives.

Headache is not a standard feature of irritable bowel syndrome, but in practice, a large number of patients suffer this symptom. In some cases, it seems to be in association with the fibrositis syndrome, and in other cases it appears to be a nonspecific stress-mediated symptom resembling tension-migraines. Medication can also be suspected in many cases as contributing to the problem. For example, some irritable bowel syndrome patients may be in receipt of multiple drugs that they take somewhat irregularly dependent on their symptoms. If someone were to take a tricyclic antidepressant irregularly, a headache could be precipitated. Frequent or constant use of opiate derivatives can cause a headache. An occasional side effect of metoclopramide is headache.

Libido is adversely affected by many things including simply feeling ill. Depression and pain on a frequent basis can easily impair sexual feeling and performance. The partner may feel resentment about the chronically ill partner, with resulting withdrawal of sexual interest. Chronic illness behavior leads to a reduction in satisfying social and family roles, diminishing in general the sense of personal worth and damaging the sexual self-image. Libido is further impaired by a variety of drugs, including opiates and benzodiazepine tranquilizers. Tricyclic antidepressants have the potential of causing impotence, even though in some cases they may relieve the depression that caused the loss of libido; the result is continued sexual dysfunction.

The irritable bowel syndrome does not include weakness as one of its features, but the fibrositis syndrome with which it may be associated can produce this symptom. Poor energy can be a characteristic of depression, which may accompany irritable bowel. Feelings of weakness can occasionally be aggravated by a variety of medications, including tricyclic antidepressants, opiate derivatives, clinidium, and benzodiazepine tranquilizers.

Anorexia and malaise can be a nonspecific symptom of the irritable bowel syndrome itself, as well as a side effect of treatment. For example, it has been associated with the prescription drugs loperamide (for diarrhea), codeine (for pain), opiates such as codeine or diphenoxylate for diarrhea, and irritating laxatives such as senna, phenolphthalein, bisacodyl, castor oil, cascara, or aloes.

Although nausea is not a regular feature of irritable bowel syndrome, it is often a result of medications, especially opiate derivatives, and occasionally antidepressants. Urinary retention is also not part of the irritable bowel syndrome, but it can be caused by several drugs that are prescribed; for example, tricyclic antidepressants and clinidium.

Fluid retention is often caused by antidepressants. Since bloating of the abdomen can be part of the irritable bowel syndrome, patients may interpret swelling of feet and hands as further worsening of their disorder, rather than recognizing it as a result of the medication. Water and electrolyte imbalance can be caused, especially in the elderly, by prolonged heavy use of saline laxatives such as magnesium hydroxide.

Appetite and weight increase is a common problem, especially in patients taking tricyclic antidepressants. Paradoxically, these medications (such as doxepin, amitriptyline, imipramine, and others) are sometimes given to alleviate the symptoms and depression that accompany irritable bowel disorder. However, for some patients, the side effects outweigh the benefits.

For all of the above symptoms it is necessary to educate patients regarding the potential for prescribed and over-the-counter medication to aggravate the symptom picture. Rather than interpreting the symptoms as evidence that he or she is getting worse and running to the pharmacy to get more drugs or laxatives, the patient must realize that the treatment itself may in some ways be the problem that must be eliminated.

The pattern of superstitious dieting or irregular eating also must be avoided. If foods are to be avoided, it should be on good grounds, probably on the advice of a physician or dietitian. Regular balanced meals are necessary to permit the gut to develop a good daily rhythm rather than being disturbed and unpredictable.

Dealing with Avoidance

Apart from the kinds of avoidance described above—taking medication or avoiding normal eating to try to avoid symptoms—there are other types of behavioral, emotional, and cognitive avoidance that aggravate the irritable bowel problem.

Some patients get stuck in their problems when they act as if they do not have any part to play in solving their problems. This may manifest as they continue to abuse laxatives, depend on multiple medications, and do not assume control over the diet or eliminate substances that may aggravate the disorder; e.g., excessive coffee. They return to the doctor with the complaint that the last prescription did not work, and with the request that something new should be prescribed. The attitude is reflected in patients looking for the cure outside themselves rather than seeing that they can do something about the problem. They do not look for meaningful relationships between their habits and their symptoms.

Emotional avoidance can be characterized by denial of anxiety and being out of control, alternating with catastrophizing when the symptoms become too persistent to ignore. There can be some resentment toward the doctor who has not solved the problem yet, while others may feel depressed, overwhelmed, and helpless.

Before it can be possible to engage the patient successfully, the avoidance behavior and catastrophizing must be partially overcome. This is done first by educational input with individual or group discussions or reading. The emphasis is to give hope, and to explain how change is possible. The next step involves assignments to monitor behaviors and cognitions about the problem, and a chance to review them with the therapist or group. Then, to take the focus off the whole problem of multiple symptoms, which can seem overwhelming, the problem is addressed through a series of assignments that enable the patient to demonstrate increasing control over the problem.

Coping

The main elements are stress control through a relaxation exercise program (see chapter 3) applied to daily activity, dietary control, bowel regulation, and reinterpretation of the problem in terms of something that patients themselves can control. The general sense of well-being is promoted by eliminating noxious influences and by beginning a program of exercise. For many, sleep disorders will be present; these may require some sessions of sleep control as discussed in the chapter on insomnia (chapter 4).

Communication

Illness behavior in irritable bowel syndrome is most likely to be a problem in the context of doctor–patient relationships in which the patient visits the doctor with the focus on getting better laxatives or medications to control the gut, and in fact, abdicates responsibility for the problem to the doctor. This is addressed in two ways. Patients have to be induced to take a problem-solving active approach to their problem in the irritable bowel syndrome program. Further, it is helpful to have a brochure or letter available to send to the physician who is treating the patient's irritable bowel syndrome as a courtesy to explain the emphasis on the program and the steps in treatment, along with the therapist's name and phone number, so that the patient will not escalate medication treatments during the behavioral program.

Feedback

If the irritable bowel syndrome program is to be carried out in a group, the group is set up in a way to facilitate encouragement between members. This is arranged by the therapist giving the information and cognitive input, and opening the group for discussion of the positive, not the negative, aspects of their experience. For example, after an information session, the therapist can say, "What have you learned about your problem?" Or after a weekend, the group may be asked, "Some of you have probably been finding that the things you have been learning have been helping you. Is there anyone who wants to discuss what he or she has done that has helped the problem recently?" A family session can be scheduled about midway through the program to introduce family members to the concepts of the program, and elicit their support in encouraging change in the patients.

Self-Maintenance

Self-maintenance of change is promoted through building routines that are incompatible with return to previous illness behavior. Exercise regimes, group participation in educative groups, family involvement in the irritable bowel syndrome program, reduced dependency on medical follow-up to reduce the tendency to get prescriptions, well-organized and clear treatment regimes, pleasant and palatable assignments such as improving diet and reducing symptoms, and reduced anxiety or somatic preoccupation via cognitive input and tension control strategies all have the effect of reducing the chance of previous problem behaviors returning. Follow-up on at least two occasions at several week intervals with the group members provides social reinforcement for continued change.

Sample Program

Day 1. In the initial screening, the patients are seen individually to determine their individual problems, to explain to them the expectations of treatment, and to discover their willingness to participate in the program. Inquiry follows the questions described in the Evaluation section. The "Irritable Bowel Questionnaire" at the end of the chapter (pp. 221–222) is given in part to obtain baseline data, but it is also given to sensitize the patient to the types of issues that will be the subject of focus during treatment. Patients are asked to keep a diary (Figure 10.2) for 1 week of the number of bowel movements, marked as big or small only, and number of episodes of flatus, of borborygmi, and of cramp marked as mild or painful. This will be compared at the end of treatment.

Day 2. If the intention is to use groups instead of individual treatment, the next session will be held in group format, beginning with discussion of the value of a group experience. Whether the treatment will be carried out as individual or group treatment, the general format can be more or less as described here.

The flowchart describing irritable bowel syndrome and GI distress is presented. This might be accompanied by patient handouts for reading. Patients are given the choice of carrying on with subsequent sessions, with the understanding that they will commit themselves to try a solution to their problem other than what they have been doing so far. They are told, "This problem has been going on for months or years. You will have to be patient as you learn to be healthy again."

The tension-dysfunction-symptom-tension cycle is explained with regard to irritable bowel syndrome. There is an introduction to relaxation techniques. Using the standard diary (Figure 2.8 or 3.1), patients are asked to monitor depression, anxiety, and stress for a week. They are asked to put an asterisk wherever they think that relaxation would have made them feel or cope better. Patients are also asked to begin a simple daily exercise routine (see chapter 9). A checklist diary is given for the next week. Patients are asked to simply check off all the disturbances that they become aware of during the course of the week (see Table 10.1).

It is a good idea to give a preview of the material that will be covered during the course of treatment, mentioning the need to eliminate constipating drugs, reduce laxative dependency, establish a normal and natural eating pattern, increase dietary fiber, engage in tension control, and deal with associated symptoms, such as fatigue and sleep disturbance, through exercise and sleep control.

Day 3. Discussion regarding results of the checklist should sensitize patients to the possibility of symptoms inadvertently caused by themselves. The material in the Nonspecific Factors section is provided as a lecture and discussion. By now there is a focus on the behaviors that they will have to change. Time should be taken to work on relaxation exercises, and the physical exercise program is reviewed.

Patients are asked to itemize the junk food in one column of their food diary and basic nutrients in another (e.g., raw and fresh greens, meat, bread, fruit, carbohydrate, dairy products, and cereals) and record the amount eaten by number of helpings or cups of food, or times junk food is eaten (see the "Food Diary" at the end of the chapter, pp. 222). The role of fiber in diet should be discussed. Patients are asked to make note of each day's fiber intake, using a handout that lists sources of dietary fiber (see Table 10.2). They are asked to ensure they are getting enough daily fiber by the end of the next week.

Day 4. A lecture is given concerning food habit and eating patterns with regard to the irritable bowel syndrome. Results of the checklist are discussed with respect to changes that patients could make. There is time for relaxation. A talk is given about applied relaxation for specific tension and irritable bowel syndrome situations, and the exercise program is reviewed.

There is a discussion of how routines and remedies may make the irritable bowel syndrome worse. A diary is assigned for monitoring the number of times that something is taken or avoided on account of irritable bowel syndrome symptoms, or fear of causing irritable bowel syndrome flare-up (Figure 10.3).

```
                -----------------taken---------------      -----avoided-----
            drugs    laxatives    smoking   alcohol      food    activities

Monday


Tuesday


Wednesday


Thursday


Friday


Saturday


Sunday
```

FIGURE 10.3. Routines and remedies diary. Use this diary for monitoring the number of times that you take something, or avoid a certain food or activity on account of irritable bowel syndrome symptoms, or for fear of causing irritable bowel syndrome flare-up.

Table 10.2. Fiber Content of Foods

Food	Quantity	Fiber (gm)
Breads		
bran muffin	1 small	2
pumpernickel	1 slice	5
rye	1 slice	2
white	1 slice	0.5
whole wheat	1 slice	2
Cereals		
bran	1 cup	15
puffed wheat	1 cup	2.7
shredded wheat	1 biscuit	2
Vegetables and legumes		
asparagus	1 cup	2
beans (dried cooked)	1 cup	10
broccoli	1 cup	8
Brussels sprouts	1 cup	4
cabbage	1 cup	4
carrot (diced)	1 cup	4
cauliflower	1 cup	2
celery	1 cup	2
chard	1 cup	8
corn (kernel)	1 cup	10
lettuce	1 cup	2
mushroom	1 cup	2
onion	1 cup	2
peas (dried cooked)	1 cup	10
pepper	1 cup	2
potato	1 whole	4
sprouts		
alfalfa	1 cup	2
bean	1 cup	4
string beans	1 cup	4
sweet potato	1 cup	4
tomato (canned)	1 cup	2
turnip	1 cup	4
zucchini	1 cup	2
Fruits		
apple	1 med.	4
apricot	1	1
banana	1 small	4
cantaloupe	1	4
cherries	1 cup	3
grapes	1 cup	2
orange	1 small	2
peach	1 large	1
pear	1 small	2
pineapple	1 slice	1
prune or plum	1	2
raisins	1 cup	15
raspberries	1 cup	8
strawberries	1 cup	4

(continued)

Table 10.2. *(Continued)*

Food	Quantity	Fiber (gm)
Juice		
apple	1 cup	3
orange	1 cup	2
prune	1 cup	4
tomato	1 cup	1

There is no exact prescription for the quantity of fiber, since requirements depend on the state of health, particular medical conditions, and individual differences. In general, a diet should contain 25 to 50 gm of fiber, with about 50% of the diet's energy content coming from fiber-rich starchy foods. The idea is to assess current dietary fiber, and then add natural sources to it if there are problems of constipation or irritable bowel syndrome. At first there may be added production of intestinal gas with large increases of fiber, but gradual increases and consistent fiber input will alleviate this problem.

To increase dietary fiber, use whole wheat breads, unstrained jams, bran and wheat cereals, bran muffins, add fruit or nuts to cereals, replace desserts with fruits, and use whole-wheat flours and vegetables as ingredients when cooking.

Adapted from *Nutritional care manual, 6th edition* (pp. 335-345) by Ontario Dietetic Association, Special Committee, 1989, Don Mills, Ontario: Ontario Hospital Organization. Copyright 1989.

Day 5. Patients are asked to agree to a plan of becoming free of drugs and laxatives, and to focus on building healthy bodies instead. Here individual regimes are most likely necessary, following the guidelines described under the Biological Factors section. In general, opiates and constipating drugs are gradually reduced, while fiber is included in the diet, and laxatives are weaned slowly and steadily. Quotas for change should be set and reviewed weekly, with positive reinforcement from the therapist and group (see chapter 2). Shorter techniques of relaxation are shown and practiced. There is discussion of how the relaxation program is being applied to everyday situations, and the exercise program is reviewed.

Day 6. Progress in dietary change, changing chemical intake, practicing applied relaxation, and getting control over bowel habit is discussed. Time is taken for relaxation techniques. Exercise progress is reviewed. A family day is planned for the next session, discussing the important role of families and communication in irritable bowel syndrome.

Day 7. On family day, the rationale of the program and the gains made so far are discussed. The role of family, especially with respect to reinforcement of health-promoting behavior, is discussed.

Day 8. Sleep problems are discussed (see chapter 4). Assignments may be given. Extra sessions may be added for insomnia problems. During the final week, it is possible to repeat the measures that were used in the initial data gathering. Strategically, it may be advisable not to return to monitoring symptoms, and instead have the patients monitor the changes that they perceive in their behavior. The decision whether or not to monitor symptoms depends on what the motive is of the final follow-up assessment—to gather data for research on biomedical change, to assess symptomatic change, to reinforce altered cognition and coping behavior, to focus attention on subjective improvement, and so forth.

Constipation Program

The problem of constipation was addressed in a section of this chapter. (There is a somewhat related discussion in chapter 3 under Overeating and Obesity.) This section describes a behavioral method for control of constipation. Control must be established over cues. A more regular biological rhythm is needed, and bowel care must be linked to appropriate bowel events. Attitudes that promote more self-control rather than external control must be developed.

Biological Rhythms. Inconsistent bowel habit and irregular eating routines help to perpetuate constipation. These inconsistencies arise often as a reaction to the distress of constipation, but it becomes a vicious cycle. You should establish a regular eating time, eat three times daily, do not skip any meals, and avoid excessive snacks.

Many medications interfere with the gut and can promote constipation. Gradual reduction and discontinuation of these is likely necessary. A partial list includes laxatives, antacids, opiates, and many antihistamines (medications that cause drying of the mouth and slowing of the gut as side effects).

Cues. Overreaction to bowel events may lead to an endless cycle of interferences that disturbs function even more. For example, when feeling constipated, you may take an oral laxative such as senna. When feeling the side effect of cramp, you might take an antacid with magnesium hydroxide, which causes rebound acidity and also some diarrhea. For the diarrhea, you might take something else, or change your usual diet, and so on.

It is also possible to react to bowel non-events. That is, if you are worried too much about constipation, you might be too hasty in taking a laxative when a bit of patience would be better. You might react to gas or a cramp by changing your diet or using a medication, when it is only the bowel trying to adjust itself to normal.

To set up proper cues for the bowel to function, eliminate opiates, antacids, and laxatives. Begin a pattern of regular meals, and add fiber. If the bowel has been dependent on laxatives to function, you should slowly withdraw the laxative and the constipating medications (such as analgesics) over several weeks. If 3 days go by without a bowel movement, add a glycerine suppository every morning after breakfast until a regular morning bowel habit is established. If the glycerine suppository is insufficient, you can temporarily add docusate each evening. Then, slowly withdraw the docusate and lastly withdraw the glycerine suppositories.

IRRITABLE BOWEL QUESTIONNAIRE

1. How much coffee do you drink (times per day, number of cups, size of cups, caffeinated or decaffeinated)?
2. How much tea do you drink (times per day, number of cups, size of cups, caffeinated or decaffeinated)?
3. How much cola do you drink (size of can or glass, number of glasses, caffeinated or decaffeinated)?
4. Do you use any caffeine-containing medications or substances? What is it called? Number of doses per day?
5. Do you eat any diet sweets (gum, soft drinks, ice cream, others)? How much per day?
6. Do you eat bran cereals? How much and how often?
7. Do you use laxatives? Which types, which dose, and how often?
8. Do you use any medications that tend to constipate you (antihistamines, antidepressants, major tranquilizers)? How much and how often?
9. Do you use prescription painkillers containing codeine, meperidine, morphine, oxycodone, hydromorphone, propoxyphene, or other opiate painkillers? In what dose and how often?
10. Do you smoke? How much per day?
11. Do you drink alcohol? How much per day/per week?
12. When do you eat and how much? How often do you snack, how much, and when?
13. What junk food do you eat? How often and how much?
14. Do you eat a balanced diet?
15. Do you have problems with any of the following:

Lower belly pains	Frequent growling in abdomen
Constipation	Headaches
Abdominal swelling	Muscle aching
Excessive abdominal gas	Insomnia
Diarrhea	Depression
Frequent small stools	

16. Do you worry about not having a bowel movement every day? If you do not have a bowel movement every day, do you take a laxative?

17. Do you take laxatives daily to ensure that you have a bowel movement?
18. Do you take some sort of medicine every day because of bowel discomfort?
19. Do you usually have a refreshing sleep?
20. Do you tend to wake up frequently at night?
21. How do you relax?
22. Do you have a regular program of exercise?

FOOD DIARY

For the next week, each time you eat anything, place a checkmark beside the category of food you eat. Regular foods are on the left and junk foods are on the right.

Cooked vegetable	Chips
Raw vegetable	Candy
Potato, rice, or pasta	Ice cream
Bread (white)	Chocolate
Bread (whole grain)	Cakes or pies
Cereal	Soda
Meats	Alcoholic beverage (each drink)
Eggs	Doughnuts
Milk or cheese	Coffee or tea
Fruit	Other
Nuts	

Chapter 11

Post-traumatic Stress Syndrome

DESCRIPTION OF THE PROBLEM

Mrs. B., a 38-year-old medical secretary, was involved in a motor vehicle accident. Since then, a variety of physical and psychological problems emerged. Some of the difficulties she dates directly from the accident. These include pain and spasms in the neck. Within 2 or 3 months she began to complain of bouts of depression, insomnia, and vivid recollections of the accident, brought out by conversations about her problem and occurring during dreams, and she had extreme fears of being in an automobile. She cannot drive, a necessary activity in order to continue her work and to take care of her family. She presents with a moderate amount of dysphoria and bouts of crying. She has received a diagnosis of fibrositis. She reports that the motor vehicle accident occurred the same week that her mother died of terminal cancer.

BACKGROUND

It is well accepted that trauma can produce physical disorders, but it is increasingly recognized that the meaning of the trauma experienced can also produce psychological disorders. Furthermore, the interaction between the physical and the psychological factors can produce a unique symptom picture, traceable to the injury. The concept of post-traumatic disorders has been in the literature since the early writings of Sigmund Freud in 1895 (Freud, 1940) and the writings of Kraepelin (1896). Initially the syndrome was considered to be within the context of war (war neurosis), identified otherwise as reactive depression or adjustment disorder. By the 1980s, the syndrome became part of a revised nosological system under the label of post-traumatic stress disorder. It is considered along with the anxiety disorders, and is taken to mean the symptoms following any traumatic event usually outside the range of human experience. The fundamental features as outlined by DSM-III-R (1987) consist of the following:

1. The experience of an event that is not part of the usual human experience and that intrinsically acts as an intense stressor.
2. This experience leads to distressing intrusions such as dreams, imagery or flashback episodes, and the activation of distress when confronted with real or symbolic reminders of the trauma.
3. The development of avoidance behavior, which leads to restricted functioning.
4. Increased autonomic arousal with its concomitant cognitive and behavioral events.
5. Chronicity of the distressing experiences or symptomatology.

Although this syndrome continues to be associated with military activities throughout the world, in Western culture the clinical manifestation is generally seen as a result of other traumatic events. Individuals present for clinical help because of physical and psychological reactions following traumatic events such as accidents (motor vehicle crashes, exposure to toxic substances, airplane crashes), serious crimes (rapes, assaults), and natural disasters (flooding, fire). In addition, it has been suggested that patients may experience a post-traumatic stress syndrome if they are chronically exposed to toxic substances, stimulants, and ongoing stress.

To a great extent, the literature on post-concussional syndrome describes a similar symptom and prognostic picture, and likely there are more similarities than dissimilarities. In some cases, there are indications that subtle neuropsychological deficits may underlie vague memory and concentration difficulties in these patients. In short, the post-traumatic stress disorder is a clinical phenomenon that may emerge as a consequence of exposure to a variety of intense physically and psychologically noxious experiences or the accumulation of stress. The degree of impairment and severity of symptoms is not generally proportional to the degree of objectively demonstrable injury. Indeed, it may occur in individuals who initially appeared to escape unscathed and may be absent in some individuals with severe injuries. This syndrome leads to various degrees of chronicity and disability.

Persistent pain is often a feature in patients with this condition, and is often the chief complaint, so that these patients are often sent to pain clinics or headache clinics. Usually there is headache, with features that resemble cervicogenic, mixed, or psychogenic headaches. Dizziness (meaning a feeling of unsteadiness) is a frequent accompaniment. At times patients are encountered who have marked exacerbations, similar to cluster headaches. Pain may also be a complaint in neck or back or other parts of the body that were injured, with a given diagnosis of chronic soft tissue pain. Disability in these patients usually can be explained only partly by the pain, since they also show traits of anxiety, depression, poor concentration, and low stress tolerance. The pain problems are often complicated by dependence on too many analgesics and sedatives, which in turn might be aggravating the biological aspects of the problem. Often, the depression and pain are both resistant to any medical mangement, and in these cases the best strategy is to deal with these people as one would with a chronic pain patient, by cognitive–behavioral and activation techniques.

Some experts have raised questions as to whether this syndrome is really a specific disorder. Lishman (1978) and Trimble (1985) have noted that there is some evidence that people with the disorder are not clearly distinguishable from certain other people with neurotic anxiety and depression but without histories of injury. Furthermore, there is some evidence that people with this syndrome may be subject to similar episodes at other times during their life, but without history of injury. This suggests that a predisposition to affective disorder may be a factor in some cases.

The most conservative definition of the disorder still restricts it to cases where there has been a dramatic accident, stress, or exposure to a noxious agent. Yet, the observation that it may take several months for the syndrome to emerge leads to the likely conclusion that the meaning of the injury to the individual is an important variable in whether there is psychotrauma. That is, the same objective injury may be interpreted in a way that is psychotraumatic to one person, more than it is to another. It follows from this that car accidents and work injuries may also be the causes of the post-traumatic syndrome, providing that the individual was somehow psychologically vulnerable to the perceived threat in the injury. Factors in the vulnerability include personality, previous history of illness or injury, beliefs about that particular injury, anxiety experienced during the injury, beliefs acquired after the injury, and psychosocial events temporally associated with the injury. It is not our purpose to argue for one position or another, but rather to suggest a treatment approach so that, for practical purposes, we will take the syndrome to be one that apparently arises after a trauma and involves the clinical symptoms described above and illustrated in the case study.

INFORMATION FOR PATIENTS

Our bodies have tremendous capacity to react to stress and injury. After exerting our muscles, the muscles become tougher and stronger. If we use our hands, our skin grows callouses. If we cut ourselves, the wound is healed with tougher scar tissue. If we face hard experiences, our minds become more accustomed to handle stress the next time. All of these are examples of natural processes that the body uses to react to injury or stress. Normally, during the period when we are becoming accustomed to a new situation or healing from a wound, there are symptoms, which then get better again. There are some examples, however, where normal processes happen in abnormal ways. A simple example might be a skin wound that overheals, leaving a scar that is too thick and too stiff. The body is still trying to do a normal job of healing, but conditions have not been just right for it. Another example might be the development of fears. If we get burned we become anxious about touching a hot object the second time. That would be normal. However, if we became afraid of touching any object in the kitchen, we would have to say that the development of a fear is a normal process aimed at protecting us, but in this case the conditions somehow made the learning process happen in an abnormal way.

How then can normal things happen in an abnormal way? If we go back to the example of burning ourselves, normal learning might happen if we burn ourselves without otherwise being upset. The burn is an unpleasant surprise, we withdraw from the hot object, assess the injury, and then go about our tasks while avoiding getting burned again. But suppose that we were already anxious because of someone else getting seriously burned there, and suppose the hot thing was an appliance that normally is not hot, and that the burn happened along with an electric shock. The combination of anxiety-provoking things can have the effect of adding two elements to the learning. The body might learn an intense reaction to the situation, such as trembling, sweating, fast heart and breathing rates, and mental excitement when we approach the kitchen again. The other is that the fear learned can be generalized so that anything in the kitchen, or maybe any appliance anywhere, might cause fear. This example can help us understand the post-traumatic syndrome. Injuries can happen when we are more or less prepared for them and not upset, or they can happen during times of greater emotional arousal.

1. The greater arousal can happen because the thing that caused the injury is frightening, as in a plane crash.
2. The arousal can come from how we understand the injury, such as in finding out that the thing that injured us is radioactive or a toxic chemical that has hurt other people.
3. The high arousal might come as part of a perception of being deliberately hurt, as for example when the injury happens during an assault or rape, or in a battle zone.

The circumstances make us learn, but the learning includes strong unpleasant body reactions and the anxiety is attached to too many things. This helps us understand why different people who have experienced different trauma end up with such similar symptoms: nightmares and flashbacks to the injury, insomnia, fears of experiencing the injury again, startling easily (being jumpy), feeling depressed and crying easily, having poor memory and concentration, having tension pains like headaches or neck pains, or withdrawing emotionally. The symptoms are rooted in this learning experience and involve learning of physical reactions that keep repeating themselves, and generalizing the learning so that the upset reactions happen in many situations and not just in the place where the injury originally occurred. If we are frightened and if we then avoid something, we learn to keep avoiding it because this makes us feel safer, but it does not help us get over the fear. If our body learns to tighten up physically, the tension can cause pain; we can avoid the pain by avoiding activity; this leads to getting out of shape, so that we become more painful on activity, leading to more fear and tension. If we are anxious, our minds are on the anxiety so that we have less energy for concentrating and remembering, but this distraction makes us afraid that we are losing our ability to think and remember, which leads to more anxiety. In this way, what we have learned leads to vicious cycles that keep themselves going.

How do we get out of this cycle? We can stop worrying about losing our minds, because we now understand that learning itself is normal. Although we learned in a way that caused a problem, we can now learn in a way that makes us more healthy. We can do things that will let us learn to feel safe in safe places. We can teach our bodies to react more normally.

ASSESSMENT AND TREATMENT

Horowitz (1986) has summarized the treatment of post-traumatic stress syndrome as depending on five main therapeutic objectives. These are (a) the teaching of cognitive control of symptoms and distress, (b) learning to decrease stress, (c) improving the quality of interpersonal interaction, (d) coming to a more healthy and less threatening meaning of the traumatic event, and (e) improving the self-image. The role of self-evaluation procedures in this is to address the above aspects of self-awareness, while drawing attention to a more positive focus for well-being, one that is within the patient's grasp of goalsetting and striving. Clinical assessment of the post-traumatic stress syndrome requires an investigation of the interrelationships between injury, emotional and cognitive function, interpretations and beliefs regarding the injury, iatrogenic or self-induced problems, illness behavior, behavioral reinforcement, and coping factors (see Figure 11.1).

Evaluations

Beliefs and Interpretations. Typically people who suffer from the post-traumatic syndrome display one or more of the following patterns of belief.

1. There may be great preoccupation about mental experiences, in which patients fear they are losing their minds, losing their memory, becoming demented, having a brain disease, or other similar fear. These fears are sometimes not admitted to directly, but are rather alluded to until the therapist labels them directly.

2. Post-traumatic patients may interpret their problem as due to the accident, and deny in effect any participation of their own. This passive victim mentality focuses angrily on those to blame, and patients do not accept that they indulge in illness behavior, or that they could participate meaningfully in overcoming the disability.

3. The focus is often on physical symptoms, such as pain, dizziness, or fatigue. Although there may be admission of psychological distress,

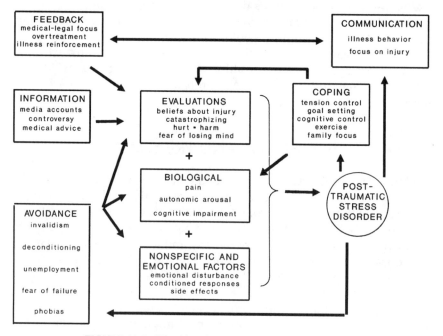

FIGURE 11.1. Algorithm for post-traumatic stress disorder.

patients hasten to explain that this is due only to these other pains and symptoms. The belief is that unless the doctor takes away the symptoms, patients will not be able to have a normal life. However, it is impossible, patients believe, to take away the symptoms, because they are due to the injury, which cannot be erased.

The doctor's focus in most of these cases typically involves one or more of the following three beliefs:

1. The patient is believed to be malingering, perhaps for the purpose of financial gain or avoiding responsibility.
2. The patient's symptoms are considered only in part, with attention to things such as pain or dizziness, giving them medical explanation only, and restricting investigation and treatment to physical intervention.
3. The problem is viewed as being psychiatric only, and the doctor refuses to deal with it. The patient is referred elsewhere.

Investigating the Problem. Because of the large number of variables affecting this disorder, the clinician must be prepared to assess most or all of the following: events that trigger reactions, level of function, avoidance behavior, neuropsychological parameters, iatrogenic factors, and influence of family transactions. Psychological tests have utility, but problems differ considerably between patients, and most of the understanding depends on clinical interviews and observations.

Trigger reactions. In the post-traumatic stress syndrome, some symptoms are persistent, whereas others are evoked or triggered by stimuli. Those that are evoked may be triggered by daily happenings, symbolic events, or situational contexts.

Everyday events may trigger specific symptomatic and behavioral reactions due to a high level of perturbability, a great deal of generalization of cues that are conditioned to produce symptomatic responses, or a high level of avoidance so that there is no safe ground for the patient. Avoided everyday events are usually those that involve some sort of productive or out-of-home activity (work, driving, homemaking), or involve being in certain places. There may be some generalization; for example, a person who had been trapped in an automobile at an accident may now be afraid of being in an enclosed space such as an elevator.

Some events produce problems because of their *symbolic significance.* For example, a person who was struck from behind in a car accident and who has interpreted this as a personal assault may afterward become afraid of being attacked when people approach from behind. To take another example, in an accident or assault, the individual may have lost consciousness. Now symptoms may recur on becoming sedated with alcohol, on relaxing, on starting to fall asleep, or on being drowsy.

Certain psychological (internal) states can evoke emotional distress and symptoms. Perhaps due to the mechanism of state-dependent learning, or due to the letting down of one's defenses at certain times, relaxing, drinking alcohol, falling asleep, or having drowsiness and low arousal can signal danger and provoke symptoms for some individuals. They may cry, become anxious, or have flashbacks or panic attacks. They may be afraid of suffocating or dying. States of high arousal can also provoke a reaction: excitement, surprise, anger, and other arousal states can reawaken the associations associated with the original trauma.

Level of function. Inquiry is directed to the activities of a typical day to determine function, with specific examples. Some activities can be quantified in terms of hours. This gives important information about baselines of activity that will be needed when goal-setting tasks begin.

Avoidance behavior. Depending on the amount of generalization and withdrawal, the avoidance will be more or less extensive. Some people with post-traumatic syndrome have relatively little avoidance or phobic behavior, and some have relatively more. A useful question giving an estimate of disability due to avoidance is the number of hours of rest or recumbency during the day.

Neuropsychological parameters. There is increasing circumstantial evidence that some of the cognitive and behavioral problems experienced by accident victims may be due to diffuse brain injury that does not show on conventional laboratory or neurological testing (Ommaya, 1982). These brain changes may occur in individuals who have not had a verifiable loss of consciousness or post-traumatic amnesia. It may occur in people who have had whiplash or minor concussions. It is important to realize, however, that emotional disturbance (depression and anxiety) can also cause cognitive changes. One way to sort out the cognitive elements of the problem is to conduct neuropsychological assessment. Obviously this is something that would be reserved for cases where it is necessary to document the extent and origins of the cognitive changes or in cases when the therapy has been apparently successful for the illness behavior but the cognitive problems remain.

Iatrogenic factors. There is a very real risk of iatrogenic disorder in patients with post-traumatic syndrome. Given that these patients already may have problems with their cognition, medications that further interfere with thinking will add to the dysfunction and to the patient's alarm about what is happening to the memory, mood, and thinking (see chapter 8). The point here is to be aware that patients who are alarmed about their inability to function adequately will be more alarmed if they experience side effects. Although some people who suffer from post-traumatic syndromes also suffer from anxiety disorders and depressions that might respond to psychotropic drugs, the responders are in the minority and the responses when present are usually only partial. Many patients show the characteristics of having exacerbation of symptoms when their psychological state is chemically altered. For all of these reasons, medical and medication intervention and its effects, or lack of effects, must be assessed.

Influence of family transactions. Serious behavioral symptoms should be assessed whenever possible within the family context when dealing with post-traumatic syndrome (or any other serious psychological disorder). A good beginning is to conduct the initial assessment with the closest family member present: spouse, parent, even a roommate. Interactions that maintain the illness behavior can be observed. This is discussed below.

Self-Evaluation. The purposes of self-evaluation are to a degree for assessment purposes in order to obtain a self-reported baseline of the problem. In addition, there is the hidden purpose of focusing the attention away from the subjective symptoms and patterns of attribution, and having the patient attend to a focus that is more useful in therapy. The self-evaluation process is a success when the patient has a flash of insight that he or she is doing something that is maladaptive, or not doing something that is normal for good health, and realizes that there is personal agency involved and not just bad luck.

In keeping with this, one strategy is to choose a health-related variable, but one in which the patient does not have preconceived attributions. For example, the patient may fear pain and fatigue, which he or she attributes to the accident and believes is irreversible. The therapist then tells the patient that the true measure of bodily fitness is heart rate at a given exercise intensity—not fatigue or pain. The patient is then asked to make a chart in which only heart rate and intensity of exercise and time are recorded. Quotas are agreed on for gradually increasing the exercise. The results are shown to the patient and interpreted in terms of norms for fitness (which will likely show up as initially low for the patient), and rate of improvement, which the patient may now see as evidence that he or she truly is able to make a difference in his or her health.

In another example, if the behavior is one in which the patient believes he or she has no control, the patient can be asked to monitor a specific aspect of the symptom, with the object of gaining a sense of personal agency. Take for example a patient who has developed the problem of emotional lability and frequently breaks into tears at little provocation. This person may be fearful of making a scene, and therefore may avoid social contact, or always present tearfully. The patient feels that he or she has no control, and is likely to abdicate control to the therapist. The therapist takes control by saying, "If I am to help you, you have to do everything I ask you to do, and if you think it seems a bit strange, do it anyway." The patient is given two instructions. The first is to make no effort whatsoever to stop crying. If the feeling of tearfulness begins, the instruction is to immediately look at his or her watch and note the beginning and ending time of the tearful episode. The patient is asked to use the diary (Figure 2.8) to document exactly the number of tearful sessions, and duration in minutes and seconds, over a 1-week period. The following week, the daily average of tearful episodes and average duration is then calculated with the patient present. The therapist then throws out the question, "Do you believe that it is possible that in a week's time you might cry this number of times in a day, and cry for this long?" (The patient has to agree, because this is his or her own record.) The next question is, "If this happened last week, could it happen next week?" When the patient agrees that this is reasonable, the instructions are to change the diary process slightly. The patient is to set a fixed time every day in which to cry, exactly this number of times and exactly this duration, and to check off these episodes on the diary to ensure that they are carried out. A practice dry run is suggested with the therapist present in order to avoid any misunderstanding. Any other tearful episodes are freely permitted, and no effort should be made to stop them, only marking their times. The following week, the progress is reviewed. Almost certainly the patient will have great difficulty in crying on cue. Even though he or she will rationalize it as "You can't just cry on cue!", there will be another attribution born of the difficulty in doing the exercise, which is "But I can't cry!" Usually there will be a great drop in tearful episodes, with the patient resisting to do any more of the exercise, but the therapist holds the patient to the agreement. When the patient complains of the inability to produce tearful episodes, the therapist tells the patient to try harder next week, and to really concentrate on crying for the correct duration of time, and to ensure that this is done daily. In a few weeks, the therapist says, "In the beginning you believed that you could not avoid crying. Now it seems you do not cry easily. In a sad event, in a sentimental moment, anyone will cry, and that is natural. But the crying you were doing is not the problem it was. Every once in awhile, I suggest you do this exercise again, and try to cry. If you still can't, then leave it for now." As a variation to the above, sometimes the patient will be able to cry on cue the second week. In this case, the instructions are, "So, you see you can cry this number of times for this duration when you put your mind to it. Next week, can you cry one extra time each day, and mark it in the diary?" The following week the question is, "Can you now cry one fewer time each day, and mark it in the diary?" The result is the same, with the patient getting the feeling that he or she is actually in control of the crying.

In these examples, the initial baseline self-monitoring and self-assessment gets turned into a procedure for symptom and behavioral control through setting a different criterion for control.

Biological Substrates

The biological factors that are important to various degrees in cases of post-traumatic syndrome include conditioning effects, subtle brain injuries, and alterations in autonomic reactiveness. The individual's cognitive and behavioral repertoire interacts with the biological factors to create the clinical symptoms. Under conditions of high stress and arousal, conditioning of certain autonomic responses may be particularly rapid and powerful. The conditioned responses generally have an element of strong arousal and fear that is reawakened when the individual is reexposed to a situation that resembles in some way the original traumatic event. There is also the possibility of generalization of stimuli that can reevoke the fear response.

Although in general the period of post-traumatic amnesia and the episode of unconsciousness are guidelines for estimating the seriousness of concussion and the possibility of neuropsychological sequelae, there is evidence that brain injury may occur in cases where the head injury was relatively slight (Oppenheimer, 1968). The possibility of this occurring has been further suggested from laboratory research in monkeys (Ommaya, 1982). Even whiplash injuries in some cases can produce small areas of brain damage. The important question is whether in any case this damage is extensive enough or located in such a way that clinical neuropsychological effects might result. The evidence for mild head injury causing persistent symptoms has been reviewed elsewhere (Binder, 1986).

A related line of clinical evidence has come from industrial medicine research in patients who have been exposed to certain industrial toxins, particularly solvents. It is known that excessive exposure to chlorinated hydrocarbons that are used as solvents and degreasers can cause a variety of clinical disorders, including injury to liver, kidney, nervous system, and heart (Husman & Karli, 1980). In clinical work with workers who have complained after such exposures, it often has been found that there are important psychological effects, such as anxiety and depression, and possibly other risk factors such as alcohol abuse, along with suspicious neuropsychological defects that might indeed be due to chemical exposures. Here again, the possibility of a biological substrate to some of the symptoms cannot be ruled out.

The role of the sympathetic nervous system after injury is the shadowy component of pathophysiology that is now beginning to attract attention. There are some indications that sympathetic overactivity is a factor in conditions such as myofascial pain, certain limb pains after traumatic injury, and perhaps in anxiety syndromes that link the psychology of the injured individual to the pathophysiology of the associated medical complaints. It is possible that sympathetic overactivity might be conditioned by psychologically stressful events, and thus set in motion a psychobiological illness, which is recognized as the post-traumatic syndrome.

It is interesting to note that many people who suffer post-traumatic syndromes show a clinical picture that is hard to distinguish from an affective disorder with features of anxiety and depression. These individuals sometimes have a history of similar episodes at other times in their lives, unassociated with trauma (Lishman, 1978). In all of this, the illness cannot be understood in biological terms alone, but rather as an interaction of physical symptoms combined with psychological symptoms.

Nonspecific Symptoms and Emotional Factors

Of all the emotions, anxiety has a particularly disruptive effect on cognition. The anxious person, furthermore, is often inclined to be overly vigilant about his thinking, with a tendency to interpret concentration problems as evidence of brain disease or some other catastrophic problem. Depressed people likewise may have a reduced efficiency of thinking. The emotional distress associated with the post-traumatic syndrome usually involves a vicious circle between the individual's emotional state and cognitions about that state and perceived impairment in thinking. In addition, the individual's expectations regarding other symptoms (like pain, weakness, or dizziness, for example) likewise affect the severity and expression of these symptoms.

Often, there are medico-legal aspects to the problem. Although it would be hasty to assume that a patient's symptoms are usually due simply to the possibility of secondary gain, the unsettled legal matters, the required visits to many doctors, the uncertainty of the compensation issue, and the imposed adversarial atmosphere, all serve to emphasize to the patient an awareness of symptoms and may be a stimulus to overinterpret symptoms as being more serious than they should be.

Not to be ignored are the side effects of medication and iatrogenic illness caused by multiple treatments, by the individual's confusion that arises from too many medical opinions, and by the effects of inactivity and deconditioning that result from too much of a laissez-faire approach of the doctor.

Dealing with Avoidance

The neurovegetative aspects of restricted biological drive (poor libido and reduced energy) are likely to interact with the lack of mental stimulation or lack of positive feedback due to being unemployed and inactive, so that avoidance becomes a way of life and self-perpetuating. Additionally, the specific fears associated with memories of the injury may be inhibitory to adaptive activity, especially if the fears are generalized. For example, if someone is injured in a traffic accident, the acquired fears may attach themselves to any form of travel, preventing return to work, socializing, or even self-sufficiency. Dealing with this must involve a series of stepwise goals: perhaps learning a technique of muscle relaxation, using systematic desensitization to the idea of travel, setting realistic and progressive goals and doing self-monitoring as important tasks are taken on such as driving a car in different conditions, being a passenger, and doing shopping or other things that depend on having to be mobile. In a nonspecific way, the loss of confidence in self can be partly overcome by learning again to have a sense of mastery over one's own body through exercise programs; in this way the focus is taken off symptoms and put instead on health indicators.

Coping

The intervention for post-traumatic stress disorder may involve several specific foci for treatment. In the first session, adversarialness is reduced by defining the task as enhancing health rather than as testing the individual's credibility. Since the patient likely has anxieties regarding the effect that the injury is having on his or her mind and function, and may be fearful that anything he or she does will fail, the subject of motivated action might be addressed something like this: "You sometimes fear that your situation is nearly hopeless and that very little can be done. If you are not hopeless, and you do something to help yourself, you will improve. If you are almost hopeless, but you do something to help yourself, you still may improve somewhat. If you are not hopeless, but you do nothing, you will lose your chance to improve. If you are hopeless, and you do nothing, you will remain unchanged. You have much to gain, and nothing to lose by trying, regardless of how hopeless you have felt. If you do nothing, you will always fail." A rationale is given that after injury, the individual rests initially to help healing, and then it is necessary to become active to facilitate improvement in strength and in practice. Not doing so causes weakness, inefficiency, depression, and anxiety. The simple cure is gradually resuming things that make one healthy.

Goals are set for increasing daily activity in a few areas, including social roles, health enhancement, stress control, productivity, and fitness. Baselines are set for these, and quotas are established, with self-monitoring and weekly or daily reviews (depending on the setting and program intensity). Getting fit uses the same self-monitoring, and can use the fitness program described in chapter 9.

Stress control involves defining the situations in which the person feels stressed, and then devising a stepwise approach to reinvolvement in those activities. This is done hand-in-hand with teaching a self-control or relaxation technique. Cognitive preparation or desensitization techniques may also be used (see chapter 3).

At the same time, supportive psychotherapy is useful to help the patient deal with the meaning of the injury and the anxieties about progress. This becomes especially important at a point when the program is nearing completion, when the patient is worried about getting back to work or returning to family and normal role functions.

The treatment program is phased into goals for restoring social roles, beginning with symbolic changes such as group participation, then outings, then increasing social and family contacts, so that isolation is gradually overcome.

Communication

Patients are taught that communications occur both verbally and nonverbally, by what is done and by what is not done, and that communications affect both the patient and those around. "You have to decide how you want people to react to you—to feel sorry for you and ask you all kinds of questions about how you feel every time they see you—or to treat you as normal. If you want to be treated normally, you have to let people know how you want them to view you—as an invalid or as a normal person."

Feedback

The person with post-traumatic syndrome is not alone in his dilemma. The family is likewise often enmeshed in the pattern of illness. To deal with this, one must first defuse family anger that is directed against both the patient (who may be viewed as not trying or as making too much of the problem) and others, who may be viewed as having caused the problem or added to the burden by not doing what they could. Then, the focus has to be taken off the injury and off who is to blame, and must be redirected onto restoring normal role expectations. This can be done by having the family a party to the goal-setting, while teaching them to give support and reinforce function rather than engaging in talk about symptoms or rehashing the annoyances of the past.

Self-Maintenance

There are three practical suggestions to assist self-maintenance and bridge the gap from treatment to discharge. Challenges for new activity must be introduced gradually. It is wise to help the patient set a tentative schedule for resuming various normal activities so that there is progress, but not too much too soon. The therapist and significant others should join in actively reinforcing efforts at change without exposing the patient to high risk. For example, an individual injured in a vehicle accident having poor concentration should be urged to take up traveling again, gradually increasing distances and independence, rather than rushing to have the patient try to immediately return to a job as a driver, where the risk of failure or the fear of accident is initially greater. Vocational assistance is often valuable in cases where a job is not readily available, or where there are cognitive or physical problems that interfere with the return to work. The vocational agency needs to be involved before the behavioral medicine program is completed, in order to make a smooth transition.

Chapter 12

The Worried Well

DESCRIPTION OF THE PROBLEM

After years of medical investigations, a 45-year-old woman presents with a number of physical concerns that have persisted for a year. She has had lower abdominal pains since being a teenager. For the last 20 years she has reported leg pains. From time to time she has complained of headaches, "sharp, shooting" groin pain, problems with her eyes, and skin irritations. A long list of consultations accompany her chart. Over the years she has consulted general practitioners, orthopedists, ophthalmologists, gynecologists, gastroenterologists, and other specialists, all with negative findings. Over the years, she has been described as an individual who "is rather more reactive to anxieties and tension than the average person." Various diagnoses had been considered, including irritable bowel syndrome, possible multiple sclerosis, and a variety of functional descriptions.

BACKGROUND

Some patients present themselves to medical settings over and over with physical complaints for which doctors find no adequate physical illness, despite thorough and repeated examinations. Some of these individuals have long, complex medical histories and multiple surgeries. In the psychiatric literature, they have been considered hypochondriacal, or as suffering conversion reaction or hysteria. Recently, the broader term somatoform disorders has been preferred. (For a discussion of the relationship between disease and illness, acute and chronic, and illness behavior, see chapter 1.)

A recent review by Kellner (1986) indicates that functional somatic symptoms are common in the general population. There are estimates that from 20% to 80% of people who visit their physicians have no detectable organic cause for their symptoms (Kellner, 1986; Lowy, 1975); even the most conservative estimate is that the "worried well" is a ubiquitous problem.

It is with the patients that present as the worried well that the interrelationships among biological, biochemical, behavioral, and psychosocial cannot be ignored. These patients haunt the halls of medical and surgical clinics, and retreat from psychological interpretations. Yet, psychosocial dimensions are more important than medical illness in initiation, exacerbation, and maintenance of their disorder (Lowy, 1985; Tunks et al., 1990). To deal with this, we must make a shift in focus, such that the treatment tends to highlight how behavior and belief influence physiology and symptomatology, rather than taking the traditional biomedical route in emphasizing how physiology creates symptomatology, thus influencing behavior and belief.

The group of worried well is not homogeneous. It represents some who would be diagnosed as somatoform disorders, some whose anxieties have been exacerbated by an excess of adversities, others who are alert to the possibility of illness because of negative and positive economic considerations, some who have major depressions or anxiety disorders, and some who have iatrogenic problems caused by excessive medical intervention or inadequate medical explanation.

Somatoform Disorder

Patients with somatoform disorder have symptoms suggesting physical disease for which there are no demonstrable organic findings or known physiological mechanisms and for which there is positive evidence or strong presumption that the symptoms are linked to psychological factors or conflict (DSM-III-R, 1987, 255). There are several subcategories in this group of disorders.

1. Body dysmorphic disorder: The patient becomes preoccupied with the idea that there is a serious defect in physical appearance.

2. Conversion disorder: There is an alteration or loss of physical functioning that implies a physical disorder. However, socio-psychological factors are judged to create the situation.

3. Hypochondriasis: There is a fixed preoccupation about having various diseases, not supported by actual physical signs, and not reassured by reasonable investigation and explanations.

4. Somatization disorder: There is a long history of nonorganic symptoms referred to multiple organ systems.

5. Somatoform pain disorder: The primary focus of complaint is pain. Pain complaints and disability cannot be adequately explained on the basis of physical disorder.

Characterological traits of somatization that fall short of frank somatization disorder are frequently found in the population. These people are not necessarily disabled or patients most of the time, but their threshold for becomining symptomatic is low at times of stress, ambiguity, or minor illness.

Somatic Concern Provoked by Circumstances

People can sometimes become preoccupied about somatic symptoms because of their specific circumstances. A mother who is in the midst of family stress may be more likely to consult a doctor when she is not ill (Eisenberg & Kleinman, 1981, p. 14). An individual with a family to support and heavy financial burden may react to a personal injury or illness with anxiety since that illness may signify possible loss of security if the illness is not quickly eliminated. If there is more than one breadwinner, and both are injured or ill, the significance of a lesser illness may be catastrophic from a psychological point of view. A person who becomes ill after an injury may be thrust into an adversarial or litigation posture, putting the patient on the defensive about his or her injury and symptoms, and thus perpetuating awareness of the symptoms. Some individuals become sensitized about illness because of preoccupations generated in communications from others; friends or relatives may have experienced serious consequences, or may have had serious illness misdiagnosed until it was too late. The patient may have had bad experiences with medical professionals during previous illnesses, and may be afraid that the current symptoms will be ignored. Grieving individuals may be more prone to somatic symptoms in the absence of obvious lesions. Sometimes there is a hidden fear, such as exposure to acquired immunodeficiency syndrome (AIDS), which has not been discussed as yet. The main point is that the particular psychosocial circumstances and the meaning of that illness to that patient need to be identified and discussed. More ample discussion of the above differential diagnosis can be found in other references (Walker, Brown, & Gallis, 1987).

Somatic Concern as a Symptom of Affective Disorder

Both anxiety and depressive disorders are characterized by an increase in somatic complaint. In the presence of anxiety or depression, what may be a minor stimulus to another person may be intensified and perceived as a distress experience signifying serious or impending illness. Sometimes delusional states may be marked by hypochondriacal beliefs. The important thing here is that a serious major affective disorder, which might benefit from pharmacological treatment, should not be overlooked or put down to hypochondriasis alone.

Iatrogenic Causes of Somatic Preoccupation

Inadequate explanations to patients, contradictory explanations and diagnoses from various health-care professionals, and excessive treatment and investigations of chronic patients all serve to reinforce the illness preoccupation of the patient. As long as physical treatments and investigations are repeated, the patient's belief is that there must be an elusive physical illness responsible. The essence of not creating iatrogenic illness is for one clinician to manage the investigations and physical treatment, and for that person to clearly communicate with the patient about what is or is not known about the condition and to indicate when further treatment and investigation of that kind is no longer appropriate.

Early Stage of Disease Not Yet Diagnosable

Some physical conditions, like hyperthyroidism or hypothyroidism, can precipitate at first vague physical symptoms and altered autonomic states, which can be confused with hypochondriacal and nonorganic disorders. Slater (1965) found that a sizable proportion of patients who initially were diagnosed as having symptoms without lesions ("hysterical disorders" was the term used in the study) were on later follow-up found to suffer from serious psychiatric or physical diseases. This is not to say that the worried well should continue to be investigated and treated for their feared physical ailments, nor should they be told that there is absolutely nothing wrong with them, but rather the focus should be on the attitude. "It is not fruitful, and it may be even harmful right now, to continue to search high and low and take cures that are not helping. Everyone is entitled to a reasonable amount of medical supervision and occasional check-ups if there are distinct changes in health, but otherwise the safest course is to accept that we should be concentrating on improving health, rather than repeating ourselves in things that do not help."

In the following sections we will deal with the relationship of health worries to beliefs and illness behavior. Our main purpose here is to help clinicians keep in mind three related issues:

1. Altered internal states, feelings, and symptom presentations may reflect the patient's experience of a psychological state, and not just information about a physical illness.

2. There is a need to explore links between the presenting physical illness picture and the patient's emotional need, motive, or secondary pain.

3. The patient then needs assistance to make links between psychological and interpersonal factors and the experience of physical distress.

Illness Beliefs

Estimates indicate that 80% of physically healthy individuals may experience somatic symptoms in a week's time. Three out of four individuals may experience physical discomfort sufficient to alter their behavior in any one month period. If healthy people keep careful diaries of all the symptoms they experience, the typical individual records one possible symptom of illness one day out of four, and has about 80 such events per year. Only about 15% do not report symptoms over a 2-week period (Dunnell & Cartwright, 1972; Hanney, 1979). Yet, most of these people do not become patients. Evidently, the majority of the population experience symptoms of some kind on a relatively frequent basis. We can regard these symptoms as ambiguous events. Most people do not evaluate these symptoms as illness. They attach little weight to them and promptly forget them, so that they do not initiate a health worry. Some people, for personal or situational reasons, or because of cognitive style, evaluate ambiguous events differently, as signifying disease. Further health-related events, such as having medical tests, taking pills, seeing specialists, hearing medical opinions, being the object of concern by family, being off work, or getting indemnities, can all promote the evaluations that the ambiguous symptoms are due to diseases. Thus, the illness belief promotes behaviors and consequences that cause entrenchment of the illness beliefs. All further ambiguous symptoms, or even the verdict that there were negative findings on a test, serve to convince the patient that there really is some hidden pathology.

Illness Behavior

As was discussed in more detail in the introduction (see chapter 1), the concept of illness behavior recognizes the following:

1. Patients differ in how they perceive and interpret their bodily experiences, and in whether they report to clinicians about them.

2. The individual's background, culture, immediate context, and social learning history all influence the propensity to express illness behavior in a certain way.

3. The clinician needs to understand the complaint in context of sick-role performance by the patient and sick-role expectations by the health-care system.

4. The patient cannot be regarded as being a passive recipient of care or as being the passive sufferer of disease, but rather the patient has to be helped to understand his or her illness, the expectations appropriately directed to the patient for his or her participation in recovery, and the knowledge of the treatment process so that treatment will be a cooperative event.

This concept is particularly relevant when problems in coping are presented to the clinician in terms of physical symptoms.

INFORMATION FOR PATIENTS

It is suggested that the clinician develop a dialogue with the patient, using questions that elicit his or her beliefs about the illness (Kleinman, Eisenberg, & Good, 1978). Then a rationale for a new way of looking at things can be presented.

What do you think has caused your problem? The clinician should receive the patient's answers in a nonjudgmental fashion, not attempting at this point to argue or correct the patient's misconceptions. However, the patient's own doubts about his beliefs might be elicited by asking follow-up questions like, "Have you ever thought that there might be another explanation for this?"

What is your greatest concern about your illness? Here, one might elicit hidden fears about dying, becoming paralyzed or destitute, being misunderstood, or having suffering that cannot be relieved. If these fears are suspected, it may be necessary for the clinician to express the question quite directly, since patients may be afraid to admit to these fears.

Why do you think it started when it did? Attributions involving blame or resentment may lie hidden unless there is probing about the circumstances surrounding the (perceived) onset. Follow-up questions may be directed to discovering what other life events coincided with the period when the illness began. These other events may be emotionally charged and explain much of the current emotional problem.

What do you think your illness does to you? Follow-up questions may be necessary since some patients give vague answers about suffering and distress to this question. To help focus the answers, questions can be asked about downtime (recumbency due to symptoms during the day), tolerance of common tasks such as reading at a table, sitting in a car, walking in a supermarket, cutting grass, and so forth. One can also get an idea about impairment of various role-functions.

What are the main problems that your illness has caused? To follow up the previous question, the patient's perception of the effect of his or her illness on the environment and life-style is explored. This may include financial problems, legal tangles, dependency on pensions, loss of friends or status, alienation of family, conflicts, and so forth.

How severe do you think your illness is? At first, most patients will respond about subjective experiences such as pain, and inability to sleep or work. There are other aspects to this, including the amount of impairment of self-care, social, family, sexual, and occupational functions. The patient's own ideas about the likely prognosis are important, both to assess depression and also to determine hopefulness or positive expectation and motivation. One can ask, "Do you think that people with your problem ever improve? How? What would have to change?"

What kind of treatment do you think you need? The most important answers have to do with whether the patient sees the treatment as something he or she will receive passively, or participate in actively, and whether or not he or she believes that the treatment is available or possible. Follow-up questions are things like, "What decisions do you think you would have in this treatment?"

If you receive this treatment, what do you think the results would be? Inquiry is to determine the patient's expectations and priorities for change in attitude and function.

How do you feel about coming here? Patients may harbor potential adversarial attitudes, feelings of hopelessness, hidden agendas that have to do with wanting to see you for medico-legal reasons, skepticism, or idealizations of the clinician.

Theories and notions held by the patient are not just erroneous beliefs, but are expressions of anxiety and emotional conflict. To fall into the trap of arguing with the patient about them fails to be convincing because it addresses only the cognitive element and not the emotional energy that lies behind it. Rather, a less threatening explanation can be offered without discrediting the patient's experiences, but undermining the beliefs that cause anxiety and casting doubt on the patient's catastrophic fears. A possible rationale of this type is offered in the script below.

"The body is complex, with literally millions of reactions going on in it every day and in every part. It is all movement and response, inside and out. The whole thing is connected by a complicated nervous system, with the brain like a central switchboard, monitoring everything. Many reactions are controlled by the body's and the brain's internal controls, without the reactions even becoming conscious. For example, we do not have to think in order to breathe, although if we do think about it, we can change the way we breathe for awhile. It is very hard to control the heart rate by thinking about it, and movements of the gut are completely without our control, even though sometimes we are aware of something going on in the bowels. The brain must make decisions about what it will pay attention to, and it makes decisions about whether all is well or if there is some problem. In general, the kinds of sensations that the brain monitors are external to the body, as in sight or sound, at the body surface as in touch, or internal, as with being aware of breathing or gut reactions.

"It is interesting to know that some people suffer from a disease in which the sense of pain is absent. For a moment, this might seem like a nice thing, never to suffer pain, but in fact it is a very great problem, because these people can have severe illnesses or injuries, and never be aware of it until they have incurred great damage. This would be a case of not having enough sensitivity to body events.

"The opposite occurs, too. There are other people who are very sensitive to things that affect the body. By itself, the ability to be sensitive is a good thing, but if it is sensitivity to the wrong things, it can present problems. Do you remember the story of the princess and the pea? A princess dressed as a commoner was in the home of someone who wanted to know if she were a true princess. In the story, they conducted a test. They made her sleep on a bed in which 20 mattresses were piled, and under the bottom one they put a pea. They reasoned that if she were used to luxury and fine beds like a princess, she would still sense the pea. When she couldn't sleep because she could sense something rough in the bed, they knew she was a true princess. Some patients are like that. They are aware of things going on in their bodies that most normal people can't or don't sense. These sensations attract their attention, and they might worry about them and look for explanations. The explanations are usually worries that something serious might be wrong (like with the princess in the story). These experiences are real, but the events that give rise to them are ones that the brain should usually ignore. But listen—the goal is not to become less sensitive, but to make better use of this sensitivity by learning to become more aware of perceptions that improve your control over your health."

With your therapist, a partnership will be set up, not to discover the pea, but to begin to notice things that promote and maintain health, by tension control, attention control, and exercises that improve well-being.

ASSESSMENT AND TREATMENT

Clinical assessment entails evaluation of (a) the patient's cognitive and emotional factors, (b) the pattern of health-care utilization, and (c) patterns of reinforcement of the illness by other individuals in the patient's environment. Important elements in the problem may include ambiguous physical stimuli that provoke alarm in the patient, side effects and iatrogenic symptoms, latent or incipient psychiatric disorders, and the effects of psychosocial stresses (Figure 12.1).

Evaluations

Beliefs and Interpretations. Patients' beliefs about their health, and their interpretations of their experiences, are the most important elements in treatment of the worried well. It is this set of beliefs and the fact that they are not amenable to reassurance, reasoning, or medical authority that defines the problem. The important thing is how to handle these beliefs.

One must avoid the pitfall of getting caught up in the patient's system of somatization by appeals to more laboratory tests or many medical

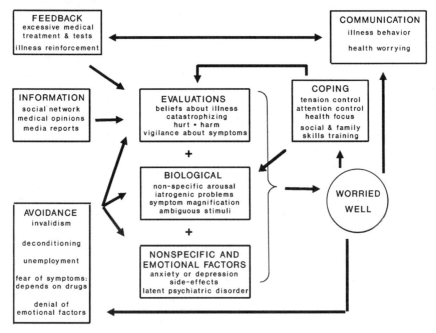

FIGURE 12.1. Algorithm for worried well.

opinions. Negative investigations or logical arguments based on somatic considerations only serve to indicate to the patient that the "disease" is still escaping detection, that the doctor is not trying, or that the patient is not being believed. Another way of looking at it is that the continued focus on laboratory tests and "disease talk" reinforces the cognitions that focus on somatic concern. By analogy, you cannot deal with a hungry person by reasoning that he or she should not be hungry, since even talking about it increases the attention paid to it.

Another cognitive position taken by some of these patients is a kind of stoicism in which the patient views him- or herself as coping courageously with an irresistible disease. The patient presents him- or herself as a model patient and rejects any notion that his or her coping could be improved or that there are any relevant psychological factors. The patient may also quote other medical experts in taking issue with your opinion, unless you agree not to confront the patient. In a word, this is denial of affective issues.

Somatizing patients are often in an adversarial role with professionals by whom they feel misunderstood. Arguing and pulling rank will not be successful. Instead, defuse the situation. First suspend judgment about the cause of the morbidity by accepting that there is real suffering. Then ask the patient to consider with you the probable outcome of several possible courses of action:

> "If you continue to look for causes, when all other investigations to date have ended in frustration, how much would you be willing to bet that these investigations will be any more fruitful?"

> "If you continue to concentrate on your symptoms, rather than on what you can do to improve health, what will be the effect on quality of life and relationships, and on peace of mind?"

> "If a new strategy is chosen to enhance wellness by using techniques that simply build good health, what is there to lose? But there is much to gain."

An alternative framework is proposed to replace the notion that symptoms mean disease. In doing so, the belief system that underlies somatization is not directly confronted, but instead it is proposed to the patient that "the majority of people recover from the majority of illnesses by growing healthy again, rather than taking specific cures for their symptoms. If this were not so, the whole population would be spending whole lifetimes in doctors' offices." The strategy proposed is to take the latter course of health promotion, rather than looking for diseases (trying to find the pea).

Investigating the Problem. Part of the problem in the case of the worried well, is that the somatic preoccupation has been maintained by investigations that have been based on a somatic focus. Usually, diagnoses have been made by exclusion: hysteria, nonorganic symptoms, hysteromalingering, and so forth. To obtain a therapeutic focus, more positive data is needed. To do this, the therapist can begin by using a standard self-monitoring chart (Figure 2.3 or 2.8) to collect systematic data about the frequency, intensity, and duration of symptoms. The symptom(s) in question are rated on a five-point scale along the timeline on the left side of the chart. At the same time, the patient is asked to record specific events over the course of the day. The events chosen for recording depend a great deal on the therapist's experience and understanding of the problem and hunches drawn from the clinical interview with the patient. However, there are a few specific factors that very likely will be relevant. These have to do with verbal and nonverbal behavior of family members and others in response to, or in initiation of, the patient's somatization. Therefore, it is likely fruitful to have the patient record (a) who is present at the time he or she notices the symptom, (b) what that person is doing or saying, (c) what the patient recalls that that person has been doing or saying in the minutes before the symptom was noticed, and (d) what happens next. Recording should not be made of too many factors at one time or there will be poor compliance with everything. After the first assignment, there can be more assignments to record other factors. For example, have the patient record the environmental factors (location, stress, tasks, and social setting) that are associated with the symptoms or that precede or follow the symptom patterns.

A third area to be assessed is the particular interactions with the health-care system, since illness behavior may be reinforced by behavior of health-care providers. It is easier to investigate this through interview with the patient, family informants, and through discussing the case with professionals who are having contact with the patient. This need not appear to be threatening or confrontational. There is apt to be good cooperation with the referring source. Sending a copy of the consultation note, with the patient's permission, to certain other professionals who are seeing the patient establishes a professional atmosphere with them also: the consultation letter can mention the intent to discuss the case with the patient's doctors. The stated purpose of the follow-up call to the doctor is to get the doctor's point of view on the nature of the problem, on what difficulties the doctor has had in his or her attempts to treat the patient, and what the doctor has tried in the way of advice, explanations, or treatments in order to get around the problem. The call ends with an offer to keep in contact and invitation for the doctor to feel free to call if he or she has further questions or concerns in the future.

Self-Evaluation. The self-evaluation that is begun during the assessment phase is already part of the treatment, in sensitizing the patient to the fact that external variables might have something to do with having or noticing symptoms. During the intervention itself, further self-evaluation is carried out, usually to make the patient aware of behavioral responses that aid coping. For example, the patient can be asked to write down each time he or she uses a particular low-arousal or imagery procedure, and the effects it produces. During the maintenance phase, where the emphasis is on the consolidation of gains and on making the patient autonomous, monitoring can be done of goal achievements. (Here, goals chosen are those that are contradictory to somatizing concerns; e.g., increasing activity, increasing exercise, decreasing medication or treatment use, improved participation in home life, hours worked, etc.) The principle is that during treatment, the focus is not on symptoms, but on monitoring and drawing attention to positive behaviors that improve health or reduce illness behavior.

Biological Substrates

As discussed above, the essential concept is that the worried well individual responds to ambiguous sensations, situations, and cues by interpretations that attribute these things to diseases. Because of increased anxiety, the experiences are sensed even more keenly, and minute changes are perceived as serious complications. The ambiguous internal stimuli are frequently the nonspecific physiological features of anxiety, which can include rapid heart beat, the effects of sighing or hyperventilation, muscle tension, gastrointestinal motility changes, or in more extreme cases, panic symptoms. These can be perceived as heart attacks, strokes, paralysis, or other illnesses that the patient will not always directly admit to, but may secretly fear (such as AIDS). Considering this, a main focus for treatment is arousal-reduction therapy; relaxation or biofeedback-assisted relaxation, especially when combined with breathing control techniques, can significantly reduce the ambiguous biological stimuli. This does not eliminate the possibility of hypochondriacal beliefs, but it reduces the cues that support and trigger them.

Try this experiment for yourself. Sit very still for 2 minutes, and as you do survey each part of your body to make yourself aware of what you are feeling in your hands, your legs, your head, your abdomen, your neck, and so on. Count how many different sensations you can feel. How many of them might be classed in some way as a bit uncomfortable? The worried well might respond to any of these symptoms by interpreting them as signs of illness. They may also respond to verifiable but mild organic symptoms, such as colds, aches, stiffness, cramps, or tiredness, for example, interpreting these as much less innocuous events. Because the pattern of physical sensations can be so varied, it is easy to see how such patients can eventually present with multiple, vague, and confusing symptomatologies.

Nonspecific Symptoms and Emotional Factors

In chapter 8 there was discussion of the adverse effects of medications. Because there is the tendency for doctors to respond to the worried well by prescribing active drugs of some sort, and frequently those that alter mood and subjective state, these patients are at risk for iatrogenic disorders, which become incorporated into the web of somatic concern. In addition, the very act of receiving a drug alters the individual's attributions. The medication-taker tends to interpret his or her problem as inflicted and outside his or her own control. Improvement in symptoms is apt to be attributed to the effects of the drug, and if the drug is absent, the symptoms will be expected to return. Instead of adopting active coping strategies, the medication-taker tends to be passive and focused only on symptom persistence or relief.

Emotional disorder can be a cause and an outcome in the case of the worried well. Depression may result from analgesics and sedatives that are prescribed for these patients. Anxiety may result from the abuse of analgesics with caffeine, from irregular use of benzodiazepines and alcohol (producing an intermittent withdrawal effect), and from the use of antidepressants in some persons. High fatigue and low stamina result from the inactivity, depression, and combined use of psychoactive medications. Anger and resentment are the expressions of bad coping when the focus of both patient and doctor is on a somatic cause only, because in this case the doctor is either treating in vain or denying the existence of a problem, whereas the patient is demanding a physical explanation and cure.

The worried well present under a variety of possible complaints: gastrointestinal distress, headache, neck or back pain, insomnia, and other common problems. Specifically addressing these complaints through a cognitive–behavioral program may be necessary. For this, see the other chapters in this book.

Dealing with Avoidance

There are basically three kinds of avoidance in people who are worried well. There is avoidance of activity, where the patient may fear that the activity will lead to further symptoms, or where inactivity is sought as a means to self-nurse (which is self-reinforcing). There may be attempted avoidance of symptoms by taking medication or treatment. This medication may have some, little, or no pharmacological effect in reducing symptoms, but will be taken because of beliefs about it or because of a reinforcing effect. There may be avoidance of unplesant affect, in which the patient clings to somatic concerns in order to avoid the more unpleasant feelings that are symbolized in the somatization or that may go with accepting the responsibility in maintenance of the problem.

The patient's initial focus will be to have a cure. This must be replaced with specific short-term goals that take the focus off the somatic symptoms and use a new definition of getting well, such as enhanced fitness, stress control, and healthy living.

We can conceptualize the avoidance behavior as consisting of a sequence of perceptions, cognitions, and behaviors, leading to more perceptions and cognitions. Intervention can be made at the level of cues that signal the problem, at the reinforcement that is paired with the stimulus or with the behavior, or at the revised responses that encourage adaptive behavior.

For example, the cues may be internal stimuli that are interpreted as symptoms of disease; bowel activity, discomfort, cardiac rate, or activity. This would cue the individual to interpret this as an attack of some kind. The response may be to cease work or other activity. The reinforcement may be reduction of anxiety that has become conditioned to the activity, thus perpetuating the avoidance behavior. The alternative is to have the individual gradually increase activity in a controlled fashion, using short-term goals, until he or she is less anxious (desensitized), and give encouragement and verbal feedback for each small gain. In another example, the cue may be an oversolicitous spouse. The patient's interpretation may be that the illness must be obvious, and the reinforcement comes in the way of sympathy and exemption from expectations when the patient responds with illness behavior. The alternative is to teach the family members to respond only when there is a specific, active, adaptive behavior shown, such as setting a performance goal, doing part of a task, or participating socially.

In general, internal cues are events that can be interpreted as symptoms. These are dealt with by carrying out a contradictory behavior that allows for desensitization so that the cue no longer provokes alarm.

Reinforcement for internal events often is exemplified in avoidance of a feared situation; this leads to reduction of anxiety, but strengthening of avoidance behavior. In therapy, alternative reinforcement is arranged by setting quotas for increased activity, promoting desensitization. External reinforcement often is related to the behavior of solicitous people (often verbal reinforcement) in response to signs of illness behavior. The therapeutic aim is to provide alternative reinforcement by training people in the patient's environment to give attention for behavior that is nonavoidant.

Short-term goals are aimed at fostering beliefs, adaptive behaviors, and coping techniques that encourage adaptive behavior. The behavior is gradually shaped toward increased and more versatile performance.

Coping

Patients with excessive somatic concern attend excessively to internal events, being vigilant about any sign of disease. A first step in promoting coping is attention control, in which a rationale is given for attending to other factors. The therapeutic exercise is to have the patient self-monitor some health-related activity that is to be improved upon, such as exercise, participation with family, reduction in medication, or tension control. The focus is kept on the health-related parameter through short-term goal-setting, and there is reinforcement (encouragement) by the therapist.

Tension control is taught through some sort of formal relaxation technique. The patient is then taught to apply this technique in a variety of situations. For example, rather than just do 30 minutes a day of relaxation, the patient is given assignments to catalog events in which relaxation might have been useful, to come up with strategies to apply the relaxation in a variety of circumstances, and the patient is shown methods for rapid 3-minute relaxations that can be done with eyes open or in various body attitudes. For people who relax poorly, biofeedback-assisted relaxation may be particularly helpful as a way to shift the patient's inward bodily focus from symptom preoccupation to a more coping-oriented awareness, such as muscle relaxation, calm breathing, and relaxed posture (see chapter 3). Formal exercise promotes self-confidence, reduces anxiety about activity, and provides a structured experience for self-monitoring of progress toward health (see chapter 9).

Many of the worried well focus on somatic concerns and avoid affective issues that underlie their problems because they lack a facility to deal with emotional conflict. This may be due to a combination of factors, including acquired loss of confidence, personality traits, lack of learned coping skills during their growth and development, emotional problems for which they have not been able to see the solution, and replacement of normal role behavior during a long illness. Along with the more structured relaxation training and exercise, social skills training is important to coping. It needs to be carried out not only with the patient but usually with the spouse and possibly family, since illness behavior involves illness transactions in the family setting. Particular social coping skills may be taught by role-playing, rehearsal of problem-solving techniques, and assertiveness training.

In dealing with the worried well, one possible pitfall would be to transfer the patient from one clinic to another while not affecting the illness behavior. Some patients cling to the illness and patient role, and become in a way addicted to therapy. Therefore, it is strategically necessary to diversify the program so that the more formal elements such as exercise, relaxation, or role-playing are balanced with activities that increase integration into real living. Short-term goals need to be set and continually refined to encourage family participation and engagement in productive activity such as study, work or volunteering, and recreation. The aim is that the individual must gradually shed the identity of patient and integrate health-promoting activities into daily life. As was discussed in chapter 2, self-monitoring charts can be set up to monitor and set quotas for a variety of key activities, aiming toward normalization.

Communication

Thoughts lead to behavior, but behavior also leads to thoughts. When the illness behavior and communications about somatic preoccupation are allowed to continue, the patient reinforces his or her beliefs and increases the strength of the somatic anxiety. Verbal and nonverbal illness behaviors also create behavioral conditions that may be reinforced by others. Since it will not work to confront or negate the abnormal illness beliefs, the effort is directed at providing an acceptable rationale to change the illness communications. This can be done by presenting the idea that sometimes it is inappropriate to draw attention to someone's handicap. An example of how to explain this to the worried well patient is given here.

"It may be considered a sign of good manners and compassion to visit someone in the hospital after an operation and inquire about the patient's health. Yet when people suffer from a chronic problem with which they are trying to cope, calling attention to it may be an unwelcome intrusion.

Consider a blind person; how does one show appropriate interest? It is not by asking, 'How is your blindness today? You must be very sad to be blind all the time!' The blind person would consider this the peak of insensitivity, and it would not at all convey compassion. The best way to show compassion would be to inquire about quality-of-life issues, 'How has your week gone? Who have you met lately? Do you have plans for the evening?' and so on. In the same way, you are trying to cope as a normal person despite your problem, and you and everyone else should agree to keep the topics on a positive focus."

The general rule is given that positive topics focus on future goals, coping, and improving health. Role-playing can be done to show how to field questions from oversolicitous or nosey people. Bodily postures that convey the idea of sickness should also be identified through feedback from others (as in a therapeutic group), looking in a mirror, making a video or audiotape, and then practicing healthier ways of presenting oneself.

Feedback

It is the actions of others with whom we interact that provide important stimuli and consequences that affect our behavior. Family members must be instructed to increase their awareness of how their actions provide the patient with signals and consequences for the symptomatic behavior. This explanation should not be limited to the excessive concern expressed by the family member or the escalation process in conflictual communications, but should also include the everyday habitual interactions that maintain the focus on illness. At the same time that the illness communications of the patient are challenged, a similar rationale is given to the main family members, with opportunities to discuss the problems that have been observed at home and to practice different ways of responding. It is best if the discussion with family members takes place with the patient present to avoid a conspiracy feeling. Family members are given specific target behaviors that need either to be rewarded in order to strengthen them or extinguished by not reinforcing them. Instructions should be explicit, with illustrations, since many families cannot grasp the theoretical notions behind the reinforcement, and because some families would use the change in reinforcement in a punitive way, which would be self-defeating. Advice to the attending physician and other therapists involved with the patient must be provided in much the same way. Doctors often feel guilty when patients complain and ask for a prescription. They need to know how to confront these problems tactfully but firmly. (See the discussion of illness transactions in chapter 2.)

Self-Maintenance

It would be simplistic to view the condition of the worried well only with respect to an operant learning model, even though there are cases in which it is more or less applicable. On the other hand, the most important factor in reducing the illness behavior and maintaining a healthier adjustment is social reinforcement. Initially this comes from the therapist and/or therapy group. During the postdischarge period, maintenance of gains comes from the patient's personal support systems: family, friends, and workmates. For this reason, therapy is focused on the patient and family both. Part of the key to successful long-term outcome is acquisition of a pattern of social activities in which reinforcement is built in. Patients are taught to balance priorities and times for work, family, pleasure, and health promotion. The advice to the patient is to carry out at least some activities in groups, rather than alone, in order to make the best use of social reinforcement. Learning social skills and assertiveness is important, therefore, in preparing the patient for this increased social involvement.

A second important factor in maintenance of treatment gains is to recognize and act on behaviors and habits that put the patient at risk for illness. Examples of this are reduction of smoking, control of alcohol, and use of appropriate diet. Other references in the other chapters and the Reference and Selected Reading section of this book can be consulted for more information on programs for health and life-style management.

References

American Psychiatric Association. (1987). *Diagnostic and statistical manual of mental disorders* (3rd ed., rev.). Washington, DC: Author.

Andrasik F., & Holroyd, K. A. (1980). A test of specific and nonspecific effects in the biofeedback treatment of tension headache. *Journal of Consulting and Clinical Psychology, 48*, 575–586.

Association of Sleep Disorders Centers. (1979). Diagnostic classification of sleep and arousal disorders. *Sleep, 2*, 1–137.

Bakal, D. A. (1982). *The psychobiology of chronic headache.* New York: Springer.

Bandura, A. (1977). Self-efficacy: Toward a unifying theory of behavioral change. *Psychological Review, 2*, 191–215.

Barlow, D. H. (1988). *Anxiety and its disorder: The nature and treatment of anxiety and panic.* New York: Guilford.

Beck, A. T. (1976). *Cognitive therapy and the emotional disorders.* New York: International University Press.

Beecher, H. K. (1956). Relationship of significance of wound to pain experienced. *Journal of the American Medical Association, 161*, 1609–1613.

Bellissimo, A., & Tunks, E. (1984). *Chronic pain: The psychotherapeutic spectrum.* New York: Praeger.

Benson, H. (1975). *The relaxation response.* New York: William Morrow.

Binder, L. M. (1986). Persisting symptoms after mild head injury: A review of the postconcussive syndrome. *Journal of Clinical and Experimental Neuropsychology, 8*, 323–346.

Bradley, L. A. (1988). Assessing the psychological profile of the chronic pain patient. In R. Dubner, G. F. Gebhart, & M. R. Bond (Eds.), *Proceedings of the 5th World Congress on Pain* (pp. 251–262). Amsterdam: Elsevier.

Buck, R. (1985). Prime theory: An integrated view of motivation and emotion. *Psychological Review, 92*, 389–413.

Budzynski, T. H., Stoyva, J. M., Adler, C. S., & Mullaney, D. J. (1973). EMG biofeedback and tension headache: A controlled outcome study. *Psychosomatic Medicine, 35*, 484–496.

Buss, A. H. (1962). Critique and notes: Two anxiety factors in psychiatric patients. *Journal of Social Psychology, 65*, 426–427.

Carver, C. S., & Scheier, M. F. (1982). Control theory: A useful conceptual framework for personality, social, clinical and health psychology. *Psychological Bulletin, 92*, 111–135.

Cleghorn, J. M., Kaplan, R. D., Bellissimo, A., & Szatmari, P. (1983). Insomnia: 1.

Classification, assessment, and pharmaceutical treatment. *Canadian Journal of Psychiatry,* *28,* 336–346.

Cook, I. J., Van Eeden, A., & Collins, S. M. (1987). Patients with irritable bowel syndrome have greater pain tolerance than normal subjects. *Gastroenterology, 93,* 727–733.

Crook, J., Rideout, E., & Browne, G. (1984). The prevalence of pain complaints in a general population. *Pain, 18,* 299–314.

Crook, J., Tunks, E., Kalaher, S., & Roberts, J. (1988). Coping with persistent pain; a comparison of persistent pain sufferers in a specialty pain clinic and in a family practice clinic. *Pain, 34,* 175–184.

Crook, J., Tunks, E., Rideout, E., & Browne, G. (1986). Epidemiologic comparison of persistent pain sufferers in a specialty pain clinic and in the community. *Archives of Physical Medicine and Rehabilitation, 67,* 451–455.

Dement, W. C. (1985). Disordered sleep—Why? *Diagnosis, (March),* 34–43.

Dunbar, J. (1980). Adhering to medical advice: A review. *International Journal of Mental Health, 9,* 70–87.

Dunnell, K., & Cartwright, A. (1972). *Medicine takers, prescribers, and hoarders.* London: Routledge and Kegan.

D'Zurilla, T. J. (1986). *Problem-solving therapy: A social competence approach to clinical intervention.* New York: Springer.

Eisenberg, L., & Kleinman, A. (1981). *The relevance of social science for medicine.* Boston: D. Reidel.

Erikson, E. H. (1950). *Childhood and society.* New York: W W Norton.

Flor, H., & Turk, D. C. (1984). Etiological theories and treatments for chronic back pain. 1. Somatic models and interventions. *Pain, 19,* 105–121.

Fordyce, W. E. (1976). *Behavioral methods for chronic pain and illness.* St. Louis: C V Mosby.

Fordyce, W. E., Brockway, J. A., Bergman, J. A., & Spengler, D. (1986). Acute back pain: A control-group comparison of behavioral vs. traditional management methods. *Journal of Behavioral Medicine, 9,* 127–140.

Fordyce, W. E., Fowler, R. S., Lehmann, J. F., DeLateur, B. J., Sand, P. L., & Trieschmann, R. B. (1973). Operant conditioning in the treatment of chronic pain. *Archives of Physical Medicine and Rehabilitation, 54,* 399–408.

Frank, J. D., Hoehn-Saric, R., Imber, S. D., Liberman, B. L., & Stone, A. R. (1978). *Effective ingredients of successful psychotherapy.* New York: Brunner/Mazel.

Freud, S. (1940). The justification for detaching from neurasthenia a particular syndrome: the anxiety-neurosis. In *Collected papers (Vol. 1).* New York: Basic Books.

Goldfried, M. R. (1971). Systematic desensitization as training in self-control. *Journal of Consulting and Clinical Psychology, 37,* 228–234.

Goldfried, M. R., & Davison, G. (1976). *Clinical behavior therapy.* New York: Holt, Rinehart, & Winston.

Graff-Radford, S. B., Reeves, J. L., & Jaeger, B. (1987). Management of chronic head and neck pain: Effectiveness of altering factors perpetuating myofascial pain. *Headache, 27,* 186–190.

Hall, R. C. (Ed.) (1980). *Anxiety in psychiatric presentation of medical illness: Somatopsychic disorders.* New York: S.P. Medical and Scientific Books.

Hanney, D. R. (1979). *The symptom iceberg: A study of community health.* London: Routledge and Kegan.

Harvey, R. F., Salh, S. Y., & Read, A. E. (1983). Organic and functional disorders in 2000 gastroenterology outpatients. *Lancet, 1,* 632–633.

Hohl, M. (1974). Soft-tissue injuries of the neck in automobile accidents. *Journal of Bone and Joint Surgery, 56-A,* 1675–1682.

Horowitz, M. J. (1986). *Stress response syndromes (2nd ed.).* Northvale, NJ: Aronson.

Husman, K., & Karli, P. (1980). Clinical neurological findings among car painters exposed to a mixture of organic solvents. *Scandinavian Journal of Work and Environmental Health, 6,* 33–39.

Jacobson, E. (1938). *Progressive relaxation.* Chicago: University of Chicago Press.

Jessup, B. A., Neufeld, R. W. J., & Merskey, H. (1979). Biofeedback therapy for headache and other pains; an evaluative review. *Pain, 7,* 225–270.

Jouvet, M. (1969). Biogenic amines and the state of sleep. *Science, 163,* 32–41.

Kanfer, F. H., & Goldstein, A. P. (1980). *Helping people change: A textbook of methods (2nd ed.).* Elmsford, NY: Pergamon Press.

Kanfer, F. H., & Saslow, G. (1965). Behavioral analysis: An alternative to diagnostic classification. *Archives of General Psychiatry, 12,* 529–538.

Keefe, F. J. (1982). Behavioral assessment and treatment of chronic pain: Current status and future directions. *Journal of Consulting and Clinical Psychology, 50,* 896–911.

Kellner, R. (1986). *Somatization and hypochondriasis.* New York: Praeger.

Kleinknecht, R. A., Mahoney, E. R., & Alexander, L. D. (1987). Psychosocial and demographic correlates of temporomandibular disorders and related symptoms: An assessment of community and clinical finding. *Pain, 29,* 313–324.

Kleinman, A., Eisenberg, L., & Good, B. (1978). Culture, illness and care: Clinical lessons from anthropologic and cross-cultural research. *Annals of Internal Medicine, 88,* 251–258.

Kraepelin, E. (1896). *Psychiatrie (Vol. 5).* Leipzig: Barth.

Kudrow, L. (1982). Paradoxical effects of frequent analgesic use. In M. Critchley, A. P. Friedman, S. Gorini, & F. Sicuteri (Eds.), *Advances in neurology, Vol. 33 — Headache: Physiopathological and clinical concepts* (pp. 335–342). New York: Raven Press.

Last, C. G., & Hersen, M. (1988). *Handbook of anxiety disorders.* Elmsford, NY: Pergamon Press.

Latimer, P. R. (1981). Irritable bowel syndrome: A behavioral model. *Behavioral Research and Therapy, 19,* 475–483.

Latimer, P., & Campbell, D. (1980). Behavioral medicine and the functional bowel disorder. *International Journal of Mental Health, 9,* 111–128.

Lichstein, K. L., & Fischer, S. M. (1985). Insomnia. In M. Hersen, & A. S. Bellak (Eds.), *Handbook of clinical behavior therapy with adults* (pp. 319–352). New York: Plenum Press.

Linton, S. J., Bradley, L. A., Jensen, I., Spangfort, E., & Sundell, L. (1989). The secondary prevention of low back pain: A controlled study with follow-up. *Pain, 36,* 197–207.

Linton, S. J., & Melin, L. (1982). The accuracy of remembering chronic pain. *Pain, 13,* 281–285.

Lishman, W. A. (1978). *Organic psychiatry.* Oxford: Blackwell.

Lowy, F. H. (1975). Management of the persistent somatizer. *International Journal of Psychiatry and Medicine, 6,* 227–238.

Magora, A. (1973). Investigation of the relation between low back pain and occupation: 5. Psychological aspects. *Scandinavian Journal of Rehabilitation Medicine, 5,* 191–196.

Marks, I. (1969). *Fears and phobias.* New York: Academic Press.

Marks, I. (1987). *Fears, phobias, and rituals: Panic, anxiety, and their disorders.* New York: Oxford University Press.

Mechanic, D., & Volkart, E. H. (1961). Stress, illness behavior, and the sick role. *American Sociological Review, 26,* 51–58.

Meichenbaum, D., & Turk, D. C. (1987). *Facilitating treatment adherence: A practitioner's guidebook.* New York: Plenum Press.

Moskowitz, M. A., Saito, K., Sakas, D. E., & Markowitz, S. (1988). The trigeminovascular system and pain mechanisms from cephalic blood vessels. In R. Dubner, G. F. Gebhart, & M. R. Bond (Eds.), *Proceedings of the 5th World Congress on Pain* (pp. 177–185). Amsterdam: Elsevier.

Myers, J. K., Weissman, M. M., Tischler, G. L., Holzer, C. E., Leaf, P. J., Orvaschel, H.,

Anthony, J. C., Boyd, J. N., Burke, J. D., Kramer, M., & Stoitzman, R. (1984). Six-month prevalence of psychiatric disorders in three communities. *Archives of General Psychiatry, 41,* 959-967.

Neff, D. F., & Blanchard, E. B. (1987). A multi-component treatment for irritable bowel syndrome. *Behavior Therapy, 18,* 70-83.

Nelson, R. O., & Barlow, D. H. (1981). Behavioral assessment: Basic strategies and initial procedures. In D. H. Barlow (Ed.), *Behavioral assessment of adult disorders* (pp. 13-43). New York: Guilford Press.

Nisbett, R. E. (1968). Determinants of food intake in human obesity. *Science, 159,* 1254-1255.

Noyes, R., Jr., Garvey, M. J., Cook, B. L., & Perry, P. J. (1988). Benzodiazepine withdrawal: A review of the evidence. *Journal of Clinical Psychiatry, 49,* 382-389.

Ommaya, A. K. (1982). Mechanisms of cerebral concussion, contusions, and other effects of head injury. In J. R. Youmans (Ed.), *Neurological surgery* (pp. 1877-1895). Philadelphia: W B Saunders.

Oppenheimer, D. R. (1968). Microscopic lesions in the brain following head injury. *Journal of Neurology, Neurosurgery, and Psychiatry, 31,* 299-306.

Parsons, T. (1951). *The social system.* New York: Free Press.

Pearce, J. W., Lebow, M., & Orchard, J. (1981). Role of spouse involvement in the behavioral treatment of overweight women. *Journal of Consulting and Clinical Psychology, 49,* 236-244.

Pilowsky, I. (1969). Abnormal illness behavior. *British Journal of Medical Psychology, 42,* 347-351.

Robins, L. N., Helzer, J. E., Weissmann, M. M., Orvaschel, H., Gruenberg, E., Burke, J. D., & Regier, D. A. (1984). Lifetime prevalence of specific psychiatric disorders in three cities. *Archives of General Psychiatry, 141,* 949-958.

Roy, R. (1988). Impact of chronic pain on marital partners: Systems perspective. In R. Dubner, G. F. Gebhart, & M. R. Bond (Eds.), *Proceedings of the 5th World Congress on Pain* (pp. 286-297). Amsterdam: Elsevier.

Royal College of Physicians and British Nutrition Foundation. (1984). Food intolerance and food aversion. *Journal of the Royal College of Physicians of London, 18,* 83-124.

Rubenstein, J. S., Bellissimo, A., & Watters, W. W. (1983). *Teaching psychotherapy: Therapeutic stance.* Paper presented at the Hincks Memorial Lectures, McMaster University, Hamilton, Canada.

Sahakian, B. I. (1982). The interaction of psychological and metabolic factors in the control of eating and obesity. *Applied Nutrition, 36-A,* 262-271.

Sandler, R. S., Nathan, H. P., Drossman, D. A., & McKee, D. C. (1984). Symptom complaints and health care seeking behavior in subjects with bowel dysfunction. *Gastroenterology, 87,* 314.

Sargent, J. D., Green, E. E., & Walters, E. D. (1972). The use of autogenic feedback training in a pilot study of migraine and tension headaches. *Headache, 12,* 120-125.

Schachter, S., Goldman, R., & Gordon, A. (1968). Effects of fear, food deprivation, and obesity on eating. *Journal of Personality and Social Psychology, 10,* 91-97.

Schachter, S., & Singer, J. E. (1962). Cognitive, social, and physiological determinants of emotional state. *Psychological Review, 69,* 379-399.

Seligman, M. (1975). *Helplessness.* San Francisco: W H Freeman.

Selye, H. (1936). A syndrome produced by diverse noxious agents. *Nature, 33,* 32.

Sicuteri, F. (1979). Headache as the most common disease of the antinociceptive system: analogies with morphine abstinence. In J. J. Bonica, J. C. Liebeskind, & D. Albe-Fessard (Eds.), *Advances in pain research and therapy (Vol. 3)* (pp. 359-365). New York: Raven Press.

Slater, E. (1965). Diagnosis of hysteria. *British Medical Journal, 1,* 1395-1399.

Spitzer, W. O. (1986). *Rapport du groupe de travail Québecois sur les aspects cliniques des affections vertebrales chez les travailleurs.* Montréal: L'Institut de Recherce en Santé et en Securité du Québec.

Sternbach, R. A. (1974). Varieties of pain games. In J. J. Bonica (Ed.), *Advances in neurology Vol. 4: Pain* (pp. 423–430). New York: Raven Press.

Sternbach, R. A. (1986). Survey of pain in the United States: The Nuprin Pain Report. *The Clinical Journal of Pain, 1,* 49–53.

Stunkard, A., & Koch, C. (1964). The interpretation of gastric motility: I. Apparent bias in the reports of hunger by obese persons. *Archives of General Psychiatry, 11,* 74–82.

Tan, S-Y. (1982). Cognitive and cognitive-behavioral methods for pain control: A selective review. *Pain, 12,* 201–228.

Trimble, M. (1985). Post-traumatic stress disorder: History of a concept. In C. R. Figley (Ed.), *Trauma and its wake: The study and treatment of post-traumatic stress disorder* (pp. 5–14). New York: Brunner/Mazel.

Tunks, E., & Bellissimo, A. (1988). Coping with the coping concept: A brief comment. *Pain, 34,* 171–174.

Tunks, E., Bellissimo, A., & Roy, R. (Eds.), (1990). *Chronic pain: Psychosocial factors in rehabilitation.* Melbourne, FL: Krieger.

Tunks, E., Crook, J., Norman, G., & Kalaher, S. (1988). Tender points in fibromyalgia. *Pain, 34,* 11–19.

Turk, D. C., & Flor, H. (1984). Etiological theories and treatments for chronic back pain. II. Psychological models and interventions. *Pain, 19,* 209–233.

Turk, D. C., Flor, H., & Rudy, T. E. (1987). Pain and families. I. Etiology, maintenance, and psychosocial impact. *Pain, 30,* 3–27.

Turner, S. M., & Beidel, D. C. (1988). *Treating obsessive-compulsive disorder.* Elmsford, NY: Pergamon Press.

United States Pharmacopeial Convention. (1986). *About your medicines.* Kingsport, TN: Kingsport Press.

Walker, J. I., Brown, J. T., & Gallis, H. A. (Eds.), (1987). *The complicated medical patient.* New York: Human Sciences Press.

Weissman, M. M. (1988). The epidemiology of panic disorders. In A. J. Fraser & R. E. Hales (Eds.), *Review of psychiatry, Vol. 7.,* (pp. 54–66). Washington, DC: American Psychiatric Press.

White, R. (1963). Ego and reality in psychoanalytic theory. *Psychological Issues, Monograph 11.*

Whitehead, W. E., & Bosmajian, L. S. (1982). Behavioral medicine approaches to gastrointestinal disorders. *Journal of Consulting and Clinical Psychology, 50,* 972–983.

Whitehead, W. E., & Schuster, M. M. (1979). Psychological management of the irritable bowel syndrome. *Practical Gastroenterology, 3,* 32–43.

Whitehead, W. E., Winget, C., Fedoravicius, A. S., Wooley, S., & Blackwell, B. (1982). Learned illness behavior in patients with irritable bowel syndrome and peptic ulcer. *Digestive Diseases and Sciences, 27,* 202–208.

Wolff, H. G. (1948). *Headache and other head pains.* New York: Oxford University Press.

Selected Readings

CHAPTER 3: CLINICAL PROCEDURES: RELAXATION, BIOFEEDBACK, AND COGNITIVE COPING

Bellissimo, A. (1981). Biofeedback in medicine. *Modern Medicine of Canada, 36,* 630–633.
This is a brief description of the basic concepts and methods in biofeedback procedures and a summary of its clinical applications.

Bellissimo, A., & Tunks, E. (1984). *Chronic pain: The psychotherapeutic spectrum.* New York: Praeger.
Chapters 7 and 8 discuss the use of imagery and hypnosis, with special application to the treatment of chronic pain.

McMullin, R. E. (1986). *Handbook of cognitive therapy techniques.* New York: W W Norton.
A comprehensive collection on "how to" help patients apply cognitive coping techniques.

Meichenbaum, D. (1985). *Stress inoculation training.* Elmsford, NY: Pergamon Press.
This practitioner's guidebook gives theory and detailed description of cognitive strategies for coping with stress and anxiety.

Poppen, R. (1988). *Behavioral relaxation: Training and assessment.* Elmsford, NY: Pergamon Press.
This book deals with both assessment and training techniques. Special populations are considered.

Schwartz, M. S. (1987). *Biofeedback: A practitioner's guide.* New York: Guilford Press.
This is a comprehensive guide to the extensive clinical applications of biofeedback.

CHAPTER 4: INSOMNIA

American Medical Association. (1984). *Guide to better sleep.* New York: Random House.
This is a nontechnical review of the literature on sleep and sleep disorders. It is intended for the general public.

Association of Sleep Disorders Centers. (1979). Diagnostic classification of sleep and arousal disorders. *Sleep, 2,* 1–137.

This classification incorporates clinical descriptions of sleep disorders and physiological data.

Borbely, A. (1986). *Secrets of sleep*. New York: Basic Books.

This is a book useful for self-help and information for patients.

Coates, T. J., & Thoresen, C. E. (1977). *How to sleep better: A drug-free program for overcoming insomnia*. Englewood Cliffs, NJ: Prentice-Hall.

This is a book useful for self-help and information for patients.

Coleman, R. M. (1986). *Wide awake at 3:00 A.M.: By choice or by chance?* New York: W H Freeman.

This book explores biological rhythms, jet lag, and shift work schedules.

Dement, W. C. (1985, March). Disordered sleep—Why? *Diagnosis*, pp. 34–43.

This article offers practical guidelines for information and assessment and diagnosis of sleeping disorders.

Lacks, P. (1987). *Behavioral treatment for persistent insomnia*. Elmsford, NY: Pergamon Press.

This book is an excellently written and comprehensive review of the behavioral treatment of insomnia, using group treatment.

Long, M. E., & Psihoyos, L. (1987, December). What is this thing called sleep. *National Geographic*, pp. 787–821.

This is a well-illustrated article useful for general interest and background information about sleep processes.

CHAPTER 5: ANXIETY, FEARS, AND PHOBIAS

Barlow, D. H. (1988). *Anxiety and its disorders: The nature and treatment of anxiety and panic*. New York: Guilford Press.

This is a comprehensive and scholarly book on anxiety. Its best feature is the integration of current knowledge.

Goldstein, A., & Stainback, B. (1987). *Overcoming agoraphobia: Conquering fear of the outside world*. New York: Viking Press.

Written for the general public, it is a step-by-step program in coping with anxiety. Lists U.S. clinics for the treatment of fears and anxiety.

Last, C. G., & Hersen, M. (1988). *Handbook of anxiety disorders*. Elmsford, NY: Pergamon Press.

We recommend this book for the discussion of combined psychological and pharmacological treatment of anxiety disorders.

Marks, I. M. (1987). *Fears, phobias, and rituals: Panic, anxiety, and their disorders*. New York: Oxford University Press.

This is a well-integrated basic knowledge text, with an interdisciplinary perspective linking behavioral sciences and clinical investigations.

Mathews, A. M., Gelder, M. G., & Johnston, D. W. (1981). *Agoraphobia: Nature and treatment*. New York: Guilford Press.

This book includes a programmed practical manual for exposure treatment with directions for both therapist and patient.

CHAPTER 6: CHRONIC BACK AND NECK PAIN

Bellissimo, A., & Tunks, E. (1984). *Chronic pain: The psychotherapeutic spectrum*. New York: Praeger.

This book examines the psychological therapies and psychotherapies in treatment of chronic pain patients.

Catalano, E. M. (1987). *The chronic pain control workbook*. Oakland, CA: New Harbinger Publications.

This is a self-help book that presents an educational package, relaxation and exercise activities, and self-monitoring techniques. It includes specific chapters devoted to varities of head pain, back and neck pain, and other topics.

Corey, D. T., & Solomon, S. (1988). *Pain: Learning to live without it*. Toronto: Macmillan.

This book can be recommended for patients to read for information about chronic pain as well as for a step-by-step program improving coping skills.

Hall, H. (1980). *The back doctor*. Toronto: Macmillan.

This is a self-help book that answers questions about causes, treatments, and self-management of back pain.

Loeser, J. D., & Egan, K. J. (Eds.) (1989). *Managing the chronic pain patient: Theory and practice at the University of Washington Multidisciplinary Pain Center*. New York: Raven Press.

This multiauthored volume is recommended as information about multidisciplinary treatment of chronic pain.

Melzack, R., & Wall, P. D. (1988). *The challenge of pain* (3rd ed.). London: Penguin Books.

This is recommended primarily as an introductory book, suitable for laypeople and students.

Sternbach, R. A. (1987). *Mastering pain*. New York: Putnam.

This self-help book concentrates on attitudes and relationships as they relate to the chronic pain problem.

Tunks, E., Bellissimo, A., & Roy, R. (Eds.) (1990). *Chronic pain: Psychosocial factors in rehabilitation*. Melbourne, FL: R E Krieger.

This is a clinician's or student's sourcebook. It deals with psychological, medicolegal, and social factors in chronic pain, major psychological treatments, and how these dimensions interact.

CHAPTER 7: CHRONIC HEADACHE

Bakal, D. A. (1982). *The psychobiology of chronic headache*. New York: Springer.

This presents a review of etiological concepts, and a critical survey of available medical and psychological treatment methods, with suggestions as to how these can be coherently integrated.

Blanchard, E. B., & Andrasik, F. (1985). *Management of chronic headaches: A psychological approach*. Elmsford, NY: Pergamon Press.

This practitioner's guidebook offers a detailed account of assessment, and comprehensive psychological treatment procedures for chronic headaches.

Catalano, E. M. (1987). *The chronic pain control workbook*. Oakland, CA: New Harbinger Publications.

This is a self-help book that presents an educational package, relaxation and exercise activities, and self-monitoring techniques, with specific chapters devoted to varieties of head pain, back and neck pain, medication problems, arthritis, irritable bowel syndrome, and neuralgias.

Corey, D. T., & Solomon, S. (1988). *Pain: Learning to live without it*. Toronto: Macmillan.

This book can be recommended for patients to read for information about chronic pain as well as for a step-by-step program improving coping skills.

Diamond, S., & Dalessio, D. J. (1982). *The practical physician's approach to headache* (3rd ed.). Baltimore: Williams & Wilkins.

This book describes the perspective and practice of a headache specialty clinic.

Graff-Radford, S. B., Reeves, J. L., & Jaeger, B. (1987). Management of chronic head and neck pain: Effectiveness of altering factors perpetuating myofascial pain. *Headache, 27,* 186–190.

Integrating the specific management of myofascial trigger points with more general patient education, mobilization and exercise, posture correction, and dealing with general health factors produces the best results in management of myofascial pains involving the head and neck.

Saper, J. R. (1987). *Help for headaches.* New York: Warner Books.

This is an authoritative reference book for laypeople.

Sternbach, R. A. (1987). *Mastering pain.* New York: Putnam.

This self-help book concentrates on attitudes and relationships as they relate to the chronic pain problem.

Turk, D. C., Meichenbaum, D., & Genest, M. (1983). *Pain and behavioral medicine: A cognitive-behavioral perspective.* New York: Guilford Press.

This book presents a comprehensive discussion on the use of cognitive-behavioral techniques for management of pain and associated behavioral problems.

CHAPTER 8: ADDICTIONS (DRUGS, FOOD, AND TOBACCO)

Agras, W. S. (1987). *Eating disorders: Management of obesity, bulimia, and anorexia nervosa.* Elmsford, NY: Pergamon Press.

This psychology practitioner's manual presents detailed information about assessment and treatment of this complex of affiliated disorders.

Catalano, E. M. (1987). *The chronic pain control workbook.* Oakland, CA: New Harbinger Publications.

This is a self-help book that presents an educational package, relaxation and exercise activities, and self-monitoring techniques.

Long, J. (1985). *The essential guide to prescription drugs.* New York: Harper & Row.

This general information book is well written and comprehensive.

Mondanaro, J. (1989). *Chemically dependent women: Assessment and treatment.* Lexington, KY: D.C. Heath.

This book dealing with chemical dependency in women includes a chapter on benzodiazepine dependency and detoxification.

Russell, M. L. (1986). Weight control. In *Behavioral counseling in medicine: Strategies for modifying at-risk behavior* (pp. 166–199). New York: Oxford University Press.

This chapter provides a step-by-step behavioral counseling program for achieving weight loss.

United States Pharmacopeial Convention. (1989). *About your medicines.* Rockville, MD: U.S.P.C. Inc.

A complete layperson's guide to medications. It gives practical advice including main effects, side effects, cautions, and risks. It classifies and explains the groupings of drugs.

CHAPTER 9: FATIGUE

American College of Sports Medicine. (1980). *Guidelines for graded exercise testing and exercise prescription.* Philadelphia: Lea & Febiger.

This book provides useful information about assessment and implementation in the therapeutic use of exercise and fitness training.

Bartley, S. H. (1965). *Fatigue*. Springfield: Charles C Thomas.
The problem is considered from different conceptual approaches.

Basmajian, J. V. (1984). *Therapeutic exercise* (4th ed.). Baltimore: Williams & Wilkins.
Although not dealing with fitness training per se, this text deals with the physiology of exercise and discusses exercise prescriptions in various types of illness and disability. It is a valuable reference on therapeutic exercise.

Berris, B., & Rachlis, A. (1977). Investigation of fatigue. *Canadian Family Physician, 23*, 465–466.
This summary is appropriate especially for the primary care practitioner, and suggests a workup that covers the major conditions that present to a doctor as fatigue.

Burns, D. (1980). *Feeling good*. New York: New American Library.
This is recommended for patients who want to know how the cognitive aspects may contribute to their fatigue problems.

Dobkin, B. H. (1989, July 16). Ill, or just the blahs? *The New York Times Magazine*, section 6, pp. 36–37.
This is recommended to patients as a clear and concise discussion of the many causes of fatigue.

Podell, R. N. (1987). *Doctor, why am I so tired?* New York: Pharos Books.
This book can be recommended to patients to help them become aware of the various aspects of the problem of fatigue.

Russell, M. L. (1986). Physical activities. In *Behavioral counseling in medicine: Strategies for modifying at-risk behavior* (pp. 215–247). New York: Oxford University Press.
This chapter describes in detail how to initiate a physical fitness exercise program. It uses behavioral counseling rationale and strategies to carry out the fitness program in a step-by-step approach that makes the subject clear even to an inexperienced clinician.

CHAPTER 10: IRRITABLE BOWEL SYNDROME AND RELATED COMPLAINTS

Almy, T. P., & Rothstein, R. I. (1987). Irritable bowel syndrome: Classification and pathogenesis. *Annual Review of Medicine, 38*, 257–265.
This is a brief overview of the phenomenology, etiology, psychopathology and pathophysiology of irritable bowel syndrome.

Catalano, E. M. (1987). *The chronic pain control workbook*. Oakland, CA: New Harbinger Publications.
This is a self-help book that presents an educational package, relaxation and exercise activities, and self-monitoring techniques. Specific problems, including irritable bowel syndrome, are discussed.

Latimer, P. R. (1983). *Functional gastrointestinal disorders: A behavioral medicine approach*. New York: Springer.
This book deals with the psychological treatment of functional gastrointestinal disorders, and with review of treatment outcome data. Treatment approaches described are education, symptom management, stress management, and contingency management.

Royal College of Physicians and British Nutrition Foundation. (1984). Food intolerance and food aversion. *Journal of the Royal College of Physicians of London, 18*, 83–124.
Food intolerance complicates the irritable bowel syndrome picture. This report attempts to present a balanced account of food intolerance.

CHAPTER 11: POST-TRAUMATIC STRESS SYNDROME

Figley, C. R. (Ed.) (1985). *Trauma and its wake: The study and treatment of post-traumatic stress disorder.* New York: Brunner/Mazel.

This comprehensive overview of posttraumatic stress disorder addresses theoretical concepts regarding the disorder, research findings, and some of the treatment options.

Horowitz, M. J. (1986). *Stress response syndromes* (2nd ed.). Northvale, NJ: Jason Aronson.

This book deals with theory and clinical practice, using detailed case examples.

Scrignar, C. B. (1988). *Post-traumatic stress disorder* (2nd ed.). New Orleans: Bruno.

The book begins with the clinical issues around the concepts of posttraumatic stress disorder, the diagnosis and the treatment, and concludes with medicolegal issues.

Van der Kolk, B. A. (1987). *Psychological trauma.* Washington, DC: American Psychiatric Press.

This is recommended reading in studying the complex of biological and psychological effects of trauma.

CHAPTER 12: THE WORRIED WELL

Calnan, M. (1987). *Health and illness: The lay perspective.* London: Tavistock.

The focus of this book is a discussion of the common views of health and illness, how we evaluate ourselves, and our health care.

Kellner, R. (1986). *Somatization and hypochondriasis.* New York: Praeger.

This book reviews the current state of knowledge about various aspects of functional disorders and hypochondriasis.

Rice, P. L. (1987). *Stress and health: Principles and practice for coping and wellness.* Pacific Grove, CA: Brooks/Cole.

The focus is on the relationship between stress and health, and the strategies for maintaining well being.

White, N. F. (1990). A socio-ecological model of pain. In E. Tunks, A. Bellissimo, & R. Roy (Eds.), *Chronic pain: Psychosocial factors in rehabilitation* (pp. 74–103). Melbourne, FL: Krieger.

Using chronic pain as a focus, this chapter presents a discussion of the concepts of disease, illness, and morbidity, and a strategy for treatment that is consistent with a behavioral medicine model.

Author Index

Subject Index

About the Authors

Eldon Tunks is Professor of Psychiatry in the Health Sciences Faculty at McMaster University, Hamilton, Ontario. He obtained his M.D. from the University of Toronto in 1969, and completed his residency in Psychiatry at McMaster University in 1974. Since 1974, his clinical work has been particularly devoted to the management of chronic pain. His publications, chapters, and books deal mainly with psychological aspects of pain and its management. The Chedoke-McMaster Pain Clinic that he directs is a multidisciplinary rehabilitation unit, affiliated with Chedoke Rehabilitation Center and McMaster University.

Anthony Bellissimo is Associate Professor of Psychiatry in the Health Sciences Faculty at McMaster University, Hamilton, Ontario. He received his BA from the University of Toronto in 1964 and his MASc and PhD from the University of Waterloo in 1968 and 1974, respectively. He has published in the areas of chronic pain, schizophrenia, psychotherapy, anxiety, stress, and coping. His teaching appointments have included the coordination of training programs in psychotherapy, postgraduate psychiatry, and the teaching of cognitive-behavioral procedures.

Psychology Practitioner Guidebooks

Editors
Arnold P. Goldstein, Syracuse University
Leonard Krasner, Stanford University & SUNY at Stony Brook
Sol L. Garfield, Washington University in St. Louis

J. Kevin Thompson—BODY IMAGE DISTURBANCE: Assessment and Treatment

William J. Fremouw, Maria de Perczel & Thomas E. Ellis—SUICIDE RISK: Assessment and Response Guidelines

Arthur M. Horne & Thomas V. Sayger—TREATING CONDUCT AND OPPOSITIONAL DEFIANT DISORDERS IN CHILDREN

Richard A. Dershimer—COUNSELING THE BEREAVED

Eldon Tunks & Anthony Bellissimo—BEHAVIORAL MEDICINE: Concepts and Procedures

Alan Poling, Kenneth D. Gadow & James Cleary—DRUG THERAPY FOR BEHAVIOR DISORDERS: An Introduction

Ira Daniel Turkat— THE PERSONALITY DISORDERS: A Psychological Approach to Clinical Management